MANY WERE
HELD BY THE SEA

Lt. Samuel E. Levy, the young commander of American troops aboard HMS Otranto. *Courtesy of Nathalie Goodrich, Milledgeville, Georgia.*

MANY WERE HELD BY THE SEA

THE TRAGIC SINKING OF HMS *OTRANTO*

R. Neil Scott

Foreword by Rt. Hon. Lord George Islay MacNeill Robertson

ROWMAN & LITTLEFIELD PUBLISHERS, INC.
Lanham • Boulder • New York • Toronto • Plymouth, UK

Published by Rowman & Littlefield Publishers, Inc.
A wholly owned subsidiary of The Rowman & Littlefield Publishing Group, Inc.
4501 Forbes Boulevard, Suite 200, Lanham, Maryland 20706
www.rowman.com

10 Thornbury Road, Plymouth PL6 7PP, United Kingdom

British Library Cataloguing in Publication Information Available

Library of Congress Cataloging-in-Publication Data
Scott, R. Neil.
  Many were held by the sea : the tragic sinking of HMS Otranto / R. Neil
Scott.
    p. cm.
  Includes bibliographical references and index.
  ISBN 978-1-4422-1342-5 (cloth : alk. paper) — ISBN 978-1-4422-1344-9
(electronic)
  1. World War, 1914-1918—Naval operations, British. 2. Otranto (Troopship)
3. Kashmir (Troopship) 4. Marine accidents—Great Britain—History—20th
century. 5. Transports—Great Britain—History—20th century. 6. World
War, 1914-1918—Transportation—Great Britain. 7. World War, 1914-1918—
Casualties—Great Britain. 8. Shipwrecks—Scotland—Islay. I. Title. II. Title:
Tragic sinking of HMS Otranto.
  D772.O77S33 2012
  940.4'5941—dc23

                                                                    2012003033

♾™ The paper used in this publication meets the minimum requirements of
American National Standard for Information Sciences—Permanence of Paper
for Printed Library Materials, ANSI/NISO Z39.48-1992.

Printed in the United States of America

Dedicated to the memory of
Lt. Cdr. Francis W. Craven, RN,
of Dalton-on-Furness, England,

commanding officer of the destroyer HMS *Mounsey*, whose efforts on the cold, stormy morning of October 6, 1918, saved 301 American soldiers, 266 Royal Naval personnel, and 30 French fishermen from certain death,

and

Police Sergeant Malcolm MacNeill; David McTaggart; Donald McLachlan; Donald Ferguson; Donald, John, Margaret, and Maggie McPhee and their parents; Andrew Stevenson; Peter Ferguson; Duncan McRae; Katie McLellan; Archie Torrie; Donald McIndeor; Isabella McIntyre; Elizabeth Grant; Sam and Andrew Clark and their parents; Rev. Donald Grant; Lt. Col. C. Heaton-Ellis; and the multitude of other residents of Islay, Scotland, who attended to the living, dying, and dead soldiers and sailors who washed ashore from the HMS *Otranto*,

and

my good friend Mark Newell, PhD.

CONTENTS

ACKNOWLEDGMENTS

Just as the waters of a mighty river often originate in a small creek somewhere hundreds of miles away, the words of this book had their origins in a conversation I had with my father, Johnny T. Scott Jr., while walking through the Eastside Cemetery in Statesboro, Georgia, more than a dozen years ago. It was one of those hot, humid, and sticky Southern summer days when you feel as though your skin is going to melt right off if you don't find some shade, cold water, and just sit back and relax. But we were persistent as we ambled around the cemetery, stopping here and there to look at grave markers, talk about what was going on in our lives, and catch up on family gossip.

At the time, my father was living in Jacksonville, Florida, while I lived in the small town of Milledgeville, Georgia, just a few hours west, where I was on the faculty of Georgia College & State University. My dad had always wanted to show me the area in and around Statesboro where he had grown up, and it was as part of that tour that we ended up at the cemetery.

Reflecting back, I am glad that I took the time to dutifully jot down notes regarding the names and birth and death dates of various cousins and great-uncles, as well as portions of our conversations. At the time I was thinking that such information might come in handy if and when I ever had the opportunity to write a family history for my three children.

More than anything, however, the trip was an opportunity for my father and me to get together and visit and for me to hear his stories of growing up as the son of a sharecropper in and around Statesboro; of joining his cousin, Harold G. Cowart, in the Marine Corps at sixteen and being wounded the following year on Iwo Jima; and of his friendship with and the death of my first-name namesake—buried there in the Eastside Cemetery—Rupert Dorse Riggs Jr., who was killed in action on Okinawa in 1945. Then, he told me about how after World War II, he came home and—after a year competing with other just-home soldiers for civilian jobs—joined the US Army at age twenty, for two years, just for the opportunity to jump out of airplanes with the 82nd Airborne Division. Later, inspired by the exploits of his cousins in the US Air Force, Gen. Robert Lee Scott Jr. (author of *God Is My Co-pilot*) and Col. Roland Scott, he transferred into the US Air Force, where he spent the rest of his twenty-year military career—first in search-and-rescue units in the American West, then, as he got older, in a variety of other assignments stateside and in Morocco, Germany, and England. Needless to say, my father always had a good story to tell.

Such was the context of the story he told that afternoon that set this book in motion. We were walking amid the headstones and moss-covered oak trees when I came upon the grave of a great-uncle, Horace M. Cleary. The stone reflected the glare of the hot Georgia sun as I looked at the marker and read the inscription aloud: "Horace M. Cleary, Georgia, Pvt 5 Co 56 Artillery, World War I, July 25, 1890–March 5, 1966." My father came to stand next to me and began talking. I am thankful that I took notes on the sweat-stained yellow legal pad I was carrying:

> Horace was on board that ship that was torpedoed and sank in World War I. He survived, but your other great uncle, Frank, didn't. You see, Horace, in this grave, was Frank's best friend. They grew up together. Horace said Frank had influenza and he couldn't get Frank to come up from the infirmary to one of the top decks. Frank told him that he was just too weak to stand up. Horace told me once that—by the time everyone on board realized how bad things were—it was too late to do anything about Frank. He went down with the ship. After the war, Horace came home and courted and married Frank's sister, your great-aunt Caddie. So, he married into the family and became your great-uncle, too.

Later that afternoon, after my father had left to return home, I stopped and visited the Statesboro Regional Library on Main Street, mostly to use the air-conditioning to revive myself from the heat but also to see if they had any local history resources worth photocopying and adding to my file.

There I happened to strike up a conversation with a man who introduced himself as Smith Banks. Mr. Banks turned out to be a local history buff, and when I mentioned my curiosity about the headstone and my father's reference to the *Otranto* being torpedoed, he said, "Oh no, I don't think so. I believe she was rammed by another ship." He then scanned the shelves and pulled a few volumes of local history. Skimming the index of each, he finally poked his finger on one entry, turned to the appropriate page, and began reading aloud. He was right. The *Otranto* had been rammed by another ship—the HMS *Kashmir*—off the coast of Scotland. Hundreds of the men aboard were killed, many of them from the Statesboro area and other small towns throughout central Georgia.

I read the entry, and we chatted about the disaster as I photocopied what he had found. Mr. Banks commented that he found it odd that there was no monument to the men. Then—with time passing—I thanked him for his help and walked to my car for the drive home. Somewhere during that drive between Statesboro and Milledgeville, I made up my mind to find out more about this obscure event. Thus, I suppose it could be said that I began writing this book that day, mostly in my head at first, but then more and more on paper as I pursued the facts of the story more earnestly. This quest led me to archives in Washington, DC, England, and Scotland to follow up on references, verify facts, and seek the assistance of scores of individuals along the way.

Among the many who helped is my friend and colleague Dr. Mark Newell, who earned his PhD in underwater archaeology at the University of Saint Andrews in Scotland and currently serves as director of the Georgia Archaeological Institute. His expert assistance in helping me interview the last survivor of the *Otranto* disaster, Pvt. Donald Cooper, in Augusta, Georgia, and his companionship and support during our research visit to Islay, Scotland, inspired and motivated me to write the best book possible.

The numerous individuals who patiently read and commented on portions of the manuscript include my dear friends Marie F. Harper of the Los Alamos National Laboratory in New Mexico and Dr. Irwin Streight of the Royal Military College of Canada.

Several faculty colleagues in the James E. Walker Library at Middle Tennessee State University read portions as well, including Dr. Alan

Boehm, Christy Groves, Suann Alexander, Dr. Rachel Kirk, Suzanne Mangrum, Kristen West, Ginny Vesper, and John Hitchcock. I am fortunate to have such congenial and helpful colleagues.

For research assistance, I am particularly indebted to Mitchell Yockelson in the Modern Military Records Unit of the US National Archives in College Park, Maryland, for guiding me to archival resources related to the disaster. His knowledge was impressive and helpful. I also thank Joanna Buddle, Kiri Ross Jones, Liza Verity, Hellen Pethers, and Andrew Davis at the National Maritime Museum in Greenwich, England, for their assistance during my visit. P&O historian and archivist Stephen Rabson in Greenwich, England, helped clarify a variety of technical issues regarding the *Otranto*'s role and schedules during her prewar P&O years. Cori Convertito-Farrar, assistant archivist in the P&O Heritage Collection at DP World, assisted in locating photographs of the *Otranto*. And Allison E. Duffield at the Imperial War Museum in London provided cordial and helpful research assistance during my visit there.

Thanks also to Dr. Margot Perrons, Irene Miller, Louise Airlie, Mary McGregor, and Malcolm Ogilvie of the Museum of Islay Life, in Islay, Scotland, for their guidance and help in using their extraordinary collection regarding the disaster donated by Rt. Hon. Lord George Robertson (former British defense secretary and secretary general of NATO) of Port Ellen, Scotland. Lord Robertson's willingness to take time to write the foreword and his generous donation to the Museum of Islay Life of a collection of research materials and memorabilia that belonged to his grandfather, Sgt. Malcolm MacNeill, MBE, were most helpful in supporting my efforts to write the *Otranto*'s story.

Others I wish to thank include Carl Reavey, editor of the *Ileach* newspaper, and Ray Husthwaite and Becky Williamson, all of Islay, Scotland, for their encouragement regarding the project, help in locating photographs related to the *Otranto* disaster and funerals of the victims, and review of and suggestions for portions of the manuscript. They certainly went the extra mile, and I am grateful for their efforts. Also, I wish to extend a special thank-you to Timothy Epps, who owns the salvage rights to the *Otranto*, and to John James MacLellan, Scott Urquhart, Shirley Cogan, and Rhona and Hamish Scott, as well as to the many other residents of Islay who each demonstrated such warm hospitality during my research visit to the island.

Joseph J. Hovish, librarian at the National Headquarters of the American Legion in Indianapolis, Indiana, helped identify, and sent photocopies of relevant articles from, the "Then and Now" section of *American Legion Monthly* and *American Legion Weekly*.

Julie Sikes of the Zach S. Henderson Library at Georgia Southern University assisted with locating materials in the "American Legion Auxiliary Dexter Allen Unit No. 90 Collection." The staff of the Georgia Historical Society in Savannah, Georgia, assisted in locating material related to the history of Tybee Island's Fort Screven. Ann Hassinger, of the United States Naval Institute in Annapolis, Maryland, identified and supplied photocopies of articles from the 1918 issue of the *Naval Institute Proceedings*.

To the numerous individuals who responded to telephone calls, "letters to the editor," requests for assistance, and other shout-outs asking for help, I extend my hand in thanks: Hugh Harrington of Milledgeville, Georgia, and Forrest Anderson of Edinburgh, Scotland, for their assistance in tapping various military history listservs for helpful, relevant information; Joseph E. Hewell Jr. for sharing a handwritten journal that his father had left him regarding his experience aboard the *Otranto* during the disaster; Georgia historian Todd Womack of Douglas, Georgia, whose book *Georgia and the Great War* (2002) was particularly helpful for background regarding Ernest M. Viquesney's statue *Spirit of the American Doughboy*; Julie Pendergrass, for responding to an article on my research in Galesburg, Illinois's *Zephyr* and providing information related to her grandfather (Loyd William Harmison of Oneida, Illinois), who was aboard the *Otranto* at the time of the tragedy; Neil McCart, in acknowledgment of his excellent chapter on the *Otranto* in *Passenger Ships of the Orient Line* (1987).

For their assistance in identifying descendants in the Sylvania, Georgia, area of World War I–era American soldiers who had been aboard the *Otranto*, I thank Will Davis (publisher) and Doris Boyer (former news editor) of the *Sylvania Telephone*. I am indebted to Judy Mays of the Screven-Jenkins Regional Library in Statesboro, Georgia, for help in contacting family members of the last-known living survivor, Donald Cooper, and to Scott Schoner for his help in identifying Donald Cooper's military unit and records. Also, thanks to Alex Lee, Grace Weeks, and Emma Oglesby Osteen of Sylvania, Georgia, and Eugene Marsh and Grace Burke of Tybee Island, Georgia, for their cordial and helpful assistance in identifying descendants of World War I–era soldiers from the coastal Georgia area. In the Nashville, Georgia, area, I appreciate the efforts and hospitality of Judge John P. Webb and Judge Susan W. Griner of the Probate Court of Berrien County for providing information regarding Shellie L. Webb. Webb was one of twenty-eight local men lost on the *Otranto* whose names are inscribed on a tablet on the base of their World War I memorial sculpted by Ernest Moore Viquesney, titled *Spirit of the American Doughboy.*

Orient Line postcard collectors Daslav Petricio of Santiago, Chile, and Gregg Nicholls of Australia were generous with their time in helping me discern differences between the *Otranto I* and the *Otranto II* in photographs. And Janet and Jean-Louis Boglio of Maritime Books in Queensland, Australia, were most helpful as I acquired specific books related to P&O Line ships.

Though Lt. Samuel Levy died on December 26, 1968, I was fortunate to locate and interview his daughter, Nathalie Goodrich, of Milledgeville, Georgia, and his grandson, Charles "Chuck" Freedman, of Atlanta. I sincerely appreciate their assistance in providing helpful details regarding Lieutenant Levy's life, personality, and role as commanding officer of the American soldiers aboard the *Otranto.*

I owe yet another debt to my retired friend George Toth, formerly Slavic cataloger at the Library of Congress, for his translation of articles, including one by Marcel Choyer, "Le double naufrage des marins du *Croisine* en 1918," that provided background information regarding the *Otranto*'s collision with the fishing schooner *Croisine* off the coast of Newfoundland.

I thank Lynda Duke, Mandi Pitt, and Kisha Ledlow in the James E. Walker Library Digital Media Studio at Middle Tennessee State University for their assistance in evaluating and scanning photographs for inclusion in the text.

For administrative and financial support, I am indebted to Bill Richards, director, and Nancy Davis Bray, associate director for special collections at the Ina D. Russell Library of Georgia College & State University, as well as to Dean Don Craig, Access Services Team Leader Mayo Taylor, Coordinator of User Services Christy Groves, and Reference and Instruction Team Leader Sharon Parente at the James E. Walker Library of Middle Tennessee State University. In addition, I thank my colleagues who served on the Faculty Research and Wier grant committees at Georgia College & State University and on the Faculty

Research and Creative Project Award Committee at Middle Tennessee State University. The research for this book could never have been accomplished without the administrative support and funding I received for this project.

I am truly grateful to Niels Aaboe, executive editor at Rowman & Littlefield Publishers, for selecting my manuscript from among the hundreds of proposals they receive each year. I also appreciate the efforts of Carrie Broadwell-Tkach, associate editor for American history; Alden Perkins, senior production editor; Jen Kelland, copyeditor; and the rest of the Rowman & Littlefield production staff. Their patience, expertise, and support for this project were superb. As I said from the beginning, "While I've written other books, this is the one I always *wanted* to write!" I do not believe I could have picked a better publishing team to work with.

Most of all, however, I acknowledge my wife, Sheila, our son, David Winston Scott, and our daughters Stephanie Gravely and Sherry Shrewsbury, for their continued love and support while I roamed all over Georgia, South Carolina, Washington, DC, England, and Scotland following this story.

FOREWORD

Rt. Hon. Lord George Islay MacNeill Robertson of Port Ellen, KT, GCMG, HonFRSE, PC

No one who has visited the beautiful island of Islay, Scotland, needs to be told about the power of the sea. Although sailors in other parts of the world may talk of ten- or fifteen-foot waves, some North Atlantic storms bring to Islay's wind-swept, western coastline thirty-, forty-, and fifty-foot monsters. These waves must be seen to be believed, and over the years they have played a pivotal role in the drama of man against the waves and weather on Islay.

My childhood home of Islay (pronounced "Eye-la") is located fifteen miles off the western coast of Scotland and twenty-three miles north of Northern Ireland. It has a population of about thirty-five hundred residents and is blessed with fertile land with vast peat fields and farmland. Local farmers raise beef cattle and sheep and support these endeavors through the growing of grass (stored as silage) and feed barley. Islay is the southernmost island of the Inner Hebrides, and while its waters are warmed by the Gulf Stream, its weather varies greatly from one day to the next. However, Islay's climate is milder, with more sunshine, than that of the Scottish mainland and draws many visitors.

With its beautiful windswept and cliff-lined coastline, rolling moors, and wide-open farmland, coupled with the simple, stark lines of village houses with spectacular views of the ocean, more than fifty-five thousand tourists visit Islay every summer. Though the island is only nineteen miles across and twenty-five miles long, visitors come from near and far to rest and relax, enjoy bird watching, and fish or scuba dive among the variety of wrecks just offshore. Others come from all over the world to tour the island's distilleries and sample our unique and award-winning malt whisky. And those interested in history and archaeology, because we can trace our history back to Neolithic times, enjoy hiking to see our castle ruins, early Christian stone crosses, grave slabs, and other such archaeological sites.

Although I could easily write at length about Islay's history, natural beauty, and friendly people, I am writing here, instead, to introduce readers to a sad and heartbreaking time during the island's long history. I am referring to the second of two maritime disasters that occurred near Islay during World War I, the sinking of HMS *Otranto* just off the island's rocky western shore.

I was born in the police station in Port Ellen in 1946—nearly thirty years after these disasters—but I am well aware of this and other shipwrecks that have shaped Islay. My maternal grandfather, an island policeman, played an active role in the aftermath of both of the maritime disasters that befell us during World War I: the first was the torpedoing of SS *Tuscania* by the German submarine U-77 in February 1918; the second—the focus of this book—was the loss of HMS *Otranto* in October of the same year after she collided with HMS *Kashmir* just offshore. Both had been luxury liners during the prewar years and contributed to the war effort through service as troopships.

These disasters took the lives of hundreds of American soldiers and British sailors. My grandfather's correspondence with the grieving families—which sat unread in an uncle's cupboard for many years—provides fascinating primary source material that reflects the horror and sense of duty the islanders felt during this sad time. Even though almost one hundred years have now passed since those dark days, the stories related to these disasters and our forefathers' response to them are still very moving. I was reminded of this again just a couple years ago when I returned home to Islay to help with a BBC Radio documentary about the events.

The first disaster was that of the SS *Tuscania*, an Anchor liner of 14,348 tons built by Alexander Stephens and Sons at the Linthouse Shipyard in Clyde, Scotland, in 1914. After a prewar career of sailing between New York and British ports, she was serving as a troopship, ferrying troops across the North Atlantic when—on February 5, 1918— she was torpedoed and sank in the North Channel, seven miles off Islay's Mull of Oa. Of the estimated four hundred men lost, more than two hundred of their bodies drifted ashore and were dashed against

Islay's rocks. Then, eight months later, on October 6—just weeks before the armistice that would end the war—HMS *Otranto* collided in horrendous, stormy weather with HMS *Kashmir* and sank in Machir Bay, off the west coast of the island.

These two disasters rocked Islay to its core. Every family was affected, and scores of volunteers, young and old, helped to recover the dead and assist survivors. The sorrows of the World War had already reached Islay, of course, as the island's men, like those from every community in Scotland, had volunteered or been drafted into the armed forces in great numbers. Sadly, by war's end, more than one hundred from the community of Port Ellen alone had already died in the fighting. Thus, those left behind to farm the land or fish were typically boys and older men. It was to these that, on the stormy night of February 5, 1918, the challenge and responsibility fell for the rescue of *Tuscania*'s survivors and—eight months later—the *Otranto*'s as well. When the news of the *Tuscania*'s sinking reached the United States, it had a dramatic and shocking effect as this was the first wartime tragedy since the Civil War in which America had incurred such a number of casualties on a single day. The emotional toll was further compounded when news of the loss of HMS *Otranto* and its casualties spread across the front pages of US newspapers. Americans were, again, horrified and hit hard emotionally.

My grandfather, Malcolm MacNeill, was the police sergeant in Bowmore, who—long before the availability of patrol cars—used his bicycle to travel about the island. It fell to him, after each of these disasters, to report what had happened and then undertake the distressing job of examining each body and its identity disc to compile a list of the names and serial numbers of the deceased. For those whose discs had been torn loose, he made careful note of tattoos and other distinguishing marks that might later help identify them.

The notebooks he used to record this information, which I have since donated to the Museum of Islay Life, make for powerful reading. In meticulous, handwritten detail, his entries describe the bodies that washed ashore. Most sorrowful are those entries for the unidentified bodies, as many of these had been savagely battered by the rocks and ship's debris. For these, my grandfather could only describe their tattoos, scars, or the contents of their pockets. For example, an entry for one such soldier simply reads, "25-year-old male. Tattoo of 'Mum' on right arm. No other identifying marks."

So many dead bodies washed ashore that his descriptions fill eighty-one pages of a notebook. And after all the bodies had been buried, it also fell to him to respond to families in the United States and England, desperate for news of their loved ones. While most of the letters were postmarked from Georgia, others came in from the Midwest and northern states; each mentioned a birthmark, tattoo, scar, or other such detail that might help identify a husband, brother, or son among the unidentified dead. My grandfather was obviously an extraordinarily dedicated and compassionate public servant, as he patiently replied to each letter, providing what information he could based on his previous efforts to identify the dead for these grieving families. His kindhearted and diligent efforts during those difficult and terrible nights were recognized by the American Red Cross, and he received the honor of being made a Member of the Order of the British Empire (MBE).

Professor R. Neil Scott has written a detailed, scholarly account of this disaster and its impact on my small island. Readers will enjoy how he traces the *Otranto*'s story, from its launch in March 1909 from the Workman, Clark & Co. shipyard in Belfast, to its service as a P&O liner traveling as a Royal Mail Ship (RMS) carrying passengers between England and Australia, its being drafted into the war effort by the British Royal Navy and subsequent conversion into a His Majesty's Ship (HMS) auxiliary cruiser assigned to Adm. Christopher Cradock's South Atlantic Squadron, and its role in the Battle of Coronel, as well as the reasons why it was one of only two British ships to survive that engagement. He then follows a contingent of American soldiers assigned to Lt. Sam Levy as the men—mostly recently drafted farm boys from Georgia—depart from Fort Screven, Georgia, and travel by train to Camp Merritt, New Jersey, and on to New York City. There, after being joined by a rough group of soldiers assigned to two "casual companies," they board the *Otranto* for their journey to England.

Bringing the reader aboard, Scott then gives us a good look at what it was like for both the British crew and the American passengers as we follow the *Otranto* across the stormy, submarine-plagued North Atlantic. Most of the soldiers are seasick and more than one hundred are suffering from the Spanish Flu when they collide with a fishing boat in the mid–North Atlantic. Both craft were sailing that night with their lights out when the *Otranto* ripped through the fishing schooner *Croisine*. It could have been worse, as she was just one of a fleet of twenty-two fishing boats that crossed paths with the HX-50 convoy that night as they sailed home to France after a season of fishing for cod off Newfoundland.

With no choice but to stop and bring the *Croisine*'s captain and crew aboard, the *Otranto* then has to make up for lost time by speeding to catch up with the rest of the convoy. As they race ahead, however, the crew members find their situation going from bad to worse as they encounter an ever-increasing North Atlantic storm. With the men now even more miserable from seasickness and the Spanish Flu as they battle hurricane-force winds and waves, the convoy becomes scattered. Prevented by the weather in those pre-radar days from determining their position, the ships' navigators are uncertain of their location as the convoy approaches the entrance to the North Channel between Northern Ireland and western Scotland. This uncertainty will cause the action that will result in the disastrous collision between the *Kashmir* and *Otranto* off Islay.

It is just before dawn on October 6, 1918, as the HX-50 convoy enters the North Channel. The promised British destroyers, whose mission is to guide them and protect them from enemy submarines, are nowhere to be found. Having retreated the night before to a safe harbor from the storm, they have left that safety—only hours beforehand—to come out and meet them. Then, amid heavy rain squalls and Force 10 winds, the storm's haze lifts just long enough for ships' officers to see a high, rocky coast in the distance ahead and to the right. At last, they have sighted land, but what coast is it? Are they looking at the coast of Northern Ireland or that of western Scotland?

Most of the vessels—including HMS *Kashmir*—correctly decide that it is Scotland and turn southward. Unfortunately, the *Otranto* turns northward, leaving its side directly exposed to the fast-overtaking *Kashmir*. Although they see each other and blow their whistles, then try mightily to maneuver away from one another, their efforts are for naught. The *Kashmir* rides a massive fifty- to sixty-foot wave and knifes into the *Otranto* with tremendous force. The action thrusts her bow deep into the side of the *Otranto*. Crew and passengers alike on both vessels are jarred by the impact and frightened by the hollow roar of tearing metal. Many of the crew in the *Otranto*'s engine rooms and soldiers standing topside—at the point of impact—are killed instantly. All aboard both ships believe they have been torpedoed. Then, just as suddenly, a trough in the waves pulls the *Kashmir* up and away, and—with her engines in reverse—the next wave twirls her around; first she is on one side of the wave going in one direction, and the next moment she is traveling in the opposite direction. The captain of the *Kashmir* has no choice but to follow wartime regulations and leave the *Otranto*—still seaworthy but with a large, jagged hole in her bow—behind, dead in the water.

Scott's description of the heroic rescue of nearly six hundred men aboard the *Otranto* by Lt. Francis W. Craven, RN, of the British destroyer HMS *Mounsey*, makes for truly exciting reading. Risking both his ship and the lives of his seventy-nine-man crew, Craven slams his 896-ton vessel, time and again, against the side of the much larger twelve-thousand-ton *Otranto* in order to give its crew and passengers a chance to save themselves. It is a dizzying jump as the men leap from one heaving ship to the other. For some it is only an eight or nine foot distance; for others, it is forty feet or more as the decks heave up and down in the forty- to fifty-foot waves. Many, never having learned to swim, refuse to jump and stand back from the ship's railing. Others, seeing dozens of their comrades smashed between the two ships or washed off the *Mounsey* by the massive waves, decide to take their chances; they also stand back and remain aboard.

Craven takes aboard as many as he can and then guides his vessel away. With men crammed shoulder to shoulder below her decks in every compartment, and with a badly damaged vessel, he limps back to port in Belfast. For his efforts, Craven is awarded the Distinguished Service Medal and the Navy Cross by President Woodrow Wilson and the highly coveted Distinguished Service Order (DSO) by the British.

Meanwhile, the hundreds of men left aboard the *Otranto* find themselves in truly dire straits. The mountainous swells have moved the ship even closer to shore, and all aboard can now see massive fifty- to sixty-foot waves smashing against thirty- to forty-foot sheer cliff walls along Islay's rocky shoreline. As the men cling in terror to pieces of the ship that are still intact, they soon have no choice: at about ten o'clock that morning, the *Otranto* is forced across a reef, ripping out her bottom, and the breaking waves then tear the rest of her to pieces. The last souls clinging to her are then flung into the water to swim amid massive, debris-strewn waves. It is only a mile or so to shore, but it is an unfair battle. Of the nearly five hundred men left aboard the *Otranto*, only twenty-one survive the swim. Of these, two later die of their injuries.

After the *Otranto* went down on Islay's west coast, an American newspaper carried the following account by a survivor, Dave Roberts, who described how he was saved:

> The waves carried me away from the ship, then one about as high as a house came over me and whirled me around like paper in a whirlwind. I went under. [I then made it to shore, where] a Scotch lad got hold of a sailor and me and took us to a cottage. All I had left on was my underwear, pants and shirt and one sock. When we got to the shore, they put us to bed. It sure was fine, two pair of woolen blankets. The people there could not have treated us any better.

For the residents of Islay, the tragedy was almost overwhelming. Despite the storm, they rushed from all over the island to try to save the hundreds of young soldiers and sailors swimming to shore. Here is an excerpt from one of my grandfather's reports to superiors that describes, in his words, the event:

> Sir, the following people took an active part in the rescue of survivors from the water, and afterwards materially assisted them in recovering from the effects of their long and terrible exposure. The first persons on the scene so far as I am able to ascertain were David McTaggart, farmer Kilearan, who had previously to this dispatched horse and van for life saving apparatus, and Donald McLachan, ploughman. These two men brought three survivors out of the water with the aid of a long broom handle. One girl, Kate McLellan, Coulerach, in my opinion deserves special mention. She happened to be on the rocks when the McPhee boys rescued the first three survivors, one of whom was scantily clad. The girl at once in the midst of hail and sleet stripped off her own overcoat and wrapped it round the rescued soldier.

In another report he filed on the wreck, my grandfather made a point of commending the ordinary folk of Islay who—though they themselves had so little to give—gave so generously to help the men cast upon their shore. He praises the many elderly women who provided soup and other food to the survivors despite the ongoing food shortages caused by the war effort.

To continue the story, Scott then describes how the aftermath was physically and emotionally draining, as—for three miles along the coast—debris and wreckage were piled amid the rocks more than fifteen feet high. The searchers frantically looked for survivors but instead found only hundreds of mercilessly battered bodies buried amid the rubble. One contemporary reporter commented that the storm was so intense that he saw where debris had been carried by the huge waves over the cliffs that lined the shoreline and then pushed a quarter of a mile inland by the hurricane-force winds. Even parts of the *Otranto*'s engine had rolled along the ocean bottom and been pushed up and onto the rocky shore. The work of gathering and identifying the bodies went on for weeks.

After my uncle Dr. Hector MacNeill (Sergeant MacNeill's eldest son) died, I discovered my grandfather's letters, notebooks, and correspondence with the families of those who had been lost. After reading them, I realized their importance and donated them to the Museum of Islay Life in Port Charlotte. There, they now reside among mementos of the *Tuscania* disaster—including the salvaged ship's bell—and HMS *Otranto* memorabilia.

In addition to my grandfather's log book and correspondence, living memories of these maritime disasters survive as well. For example, Port Ellen fisherman Jim MacFarlane told me about hearing stories of how groups of women were seen standing in the streets of Port Ellen, weeping as the bodies of young soldiers and sailors were carried through town to a temporary mortuary set up in what is now the town's cybercafe. Another reporter at the time, describing the emotional impact on residents, wrote,

> The wreck of the troopship *Otranto* with the loss of life involved, has cast a gloom over the whole of Islay. Distress and sorrow in Port Ellen over the calamity are witnessed on every hand, and there [is no] meeting of individuals without an expression of grief over the sacrifice of so much valuable life on an exposed coast in a tempestuous sea, when human aid was impossible.
>
> Pulpit utterances [continue to] voice the sympathy and condolences of the community with the bereaved relatives of the brave American soldiers and British seaman lost on this lamentable occasion.

Duncan McPhee, who lives at the coastguard residence at Kilchoman with his mother, is the grandson of one of the two McPhee brothers who waded into the surf in Machir Bay to rescue survivors of the *Otranto*. Thanks to the bravery of these boys—who used a walking stick to reach out to the men in the water—three lived who otherwise would surely have drowned. I stood in their living room and examined memorabilia about that night, which had been passed down through their family. These included newspaper clippings and a small photograph album produced and sold by a local photographer soon after the *Otranto*'s sinking. Looking through these now-faded images, I found it hard to believe that these disasters had occurred more than ninety years ago.

There is, of course, physical evidence of the wrecks as well, as divers routinely go down and bring up shell casings, bullets, and other dark mementos from the Great War. As for the cemetery at Kilchoman, once filled with the graves of the *Otranto*'s American soldiers and British sailors, the American government ordered in 1920 that the soldiers' bodies be exhumed and either brought home or sent to the American military cemetery at Brookwood, Surrey, England, for reburial. Thus, most of the bodies left there now are those of British sailors who drowned alongside the Americans that day. Notably, in the same year that the bodies were removed, the American Red Cross erected—in honor of the Americans who died in these two maritime disasters—an impressive stone tower at Islay's Mull of Oa that can be seen from far out at sea.

The sad story of the sinking of these two ships is not the only connection between Islay and the United States. There are many ties, including, most notably, Revolutionary War leader Alexander McDougall. Born on Islay in 1732, he immigrated with his family to New York in 1738. There, after prospering as a master of cargo ships, he used his savings to purchase boats of his own. By 1769, he had become active in politics as an outspoken street leader of the New York Sons of Liberty and member of the Continental Congress. Imprisoned for writing revolutionary pamphlets that brought him fame throughout the colonies, after his release he was appointed colonel of the First New York Infantry Regiment. George Washington found him an excellent field commander, and he eventually rose to the rank of major general and commander of forces along the Hudson River at West Point. As a member of Congress, he was appointed first secretary of the Marine of the United States, but he chose instead to recommend John Paul Jones, a fellow former Scotsman, to head American naval forces. After the war—until his death at fifty-three in 1786—McDougall served in the New York State Senate and as president of the Bank of New York.

My own career has cemented many ties to America as well. Born in 1946 on Islay in the Port Ellen police station, I have had the privilege and good fortune to serve my country as a member of the British parliament for six terms (1978–1999), as defense secretary under Tony Blair (1997–1999), and as secretary general of the North Atlantic Treaty Organization (1999 to 2003). Among my many memories is a conversation I once had with Colin Powell, then serving as US secretary of state, wherein I recounted the story of the *Otranto* disaster and told him about the body of a sailor—whose memorial stone simply reads, "Unknown Negro/Known Unto God"—that lies still buried in the rich soil of the Kilchoman Military Cemetery and how that sailor had died alongside his American comrades.

It always strikes me how wars draw human beings from one part of the world to another and inspire genuine acts of heroism amid the most unexpected occurrences. I know this from my own experience, just as I have learned that it takes a very long time for memories of war to fade. That said, I also know how war can bring out the incredible resourcefulness of men and true kindness from ordinary people.

Having given a great deal of thought to this episode in Islay's history during my participation in a BBC Scotland broadcast a few years ago, I am pleased that Professor Scott has dedicated himself to write about these extraordinary events regarding the sinking of HMS *Otranto* and the many Islay folk who sprang into action to help those in need. His recounting of the stories of heroism displayed by Cpt. Ernest Davidson and others aboard HMS *Otranto*, Lt. Frances W. Craven and his crew aboard HMS *Mounsey*, and the fathers, mothers, and grandfathers of my fellow islanders, who came to their aid, makes for a truly exciting read. I remain convinced that the events of this story and the efforts of all involved will be remembered as belonging to one of the finest episodes in the history of the British navy and the island of Islay.

Rt. Hon. Lord (George Islay MacNeill) Robertson, KT, GCMG,
   HonFRSE, PC
Port Ellen, Islay, Scotland[1]

IN MEMORY OF THE *OTRANTO* DISASTER OFF ISLAY, OCTOBER 6, 1918

Twas the latest month of Autumn,
The sixth day as I recall,
When we hailed the ship *Otranto*
With full freight and heroes all;
They left home to fight for justice,
Liberty had heard the call,
And the Stripes were now unfurling
On the war-torn fields of Gaul.

Little thought they when they parted
From their friends beyond the main,
That upon the shores of Islay
Soon that Death would make his claim;
Though they fought not in the battle,
Nor did the strife descend,
Far from dear ones, home and kindred,
Still they met a hero's end.

On the peaceful sward full daisied,
Where the winds of ocean blow,
Shrouded in their own loved banner

Tenderly we laid them low;
And the few that Death had spared us,
To the utmost love can know;
They were tended well and bravely,
As our Gaels were wont to show.

Many are the loving mothers
That now mourn the sons they bore,
Many are the winsome maidens
Lost their loved ones on yon shore.
Never more with hearty greetings
Will they meet them on the Strand,
For alas! They now lie sleeping,
'Neath the flowers in a distant land.

Till the last dread trump be sounded,
Never will Columbus' Land
Cease to think with pride, but sadly,
Of green Islay's distant strand.
There the brave ones in their hundreds
Sleep beneath its grassy sod,
Till they waken on yon morning
In the skies to meet their God.

Translated from the Gaelic poem
by Charles McNiven (Kilchoman, Islay, Scotland)

MANY WERE
HELD BY THE SEA

1

PRIDE OF THE P&O LINE

BIRTH OF A LUXURY LINER

The *Otranto* was scheduled for launch in the Workman, Clark & Co. shipyards of Belfast, Ireland, on March 23, 1909, but on that day, because frost had hardened the lubricated tallow along the ramp, she refused to conform to expectations and slid only twenty feet down the launch way, then stopped.[1] She was a stubborn piece of work. Laborers tried using hydraulic jacks to move the six-thousand-ton hull, but she was stuck and refused to move.[2] Shipyard engineers then tried a variety of other strategies, but in the end, left with no other choice, they had to rebuild portions of the launch way so that laborers could use jacks to manually push and pull the recalcitrant ship the rest of the way down. It took the shipyard laborers, "putting their backs to the task over and again," four days to get the *Otranto* into the water.[3]

She was a beauty, though, and took her romantic-sounding name from the Otranto Straits that separate Italy and Albania.[4] Built for the Peninsular & Oriental (P&O) Steam Navigation Company to help them fulfill the terms of a twelve-year contract with the Australian government, she and her sister ships—the *Ophir, Orsova, Otway, Osterley, Orvieto,* and *Orama*—were all designed to carry mail and passengers back and forth between England and Australia.[5, 6]

Capable of carrying 235 first-class, 186 second-class, and 696 third-class passengers, the sleek, twin-screw, twelve-thousand-ton *Otranto* was 535 feet long, 64 feet wide, and 38.5 feet deep.[7] She was a coal burner with permanent bunker space to load 1,600 tons and a reserve of 680 tons. Part of her cargo area was insulated, and she had five holds with hatches. Her deck gear included two cranes and twelve derricks.[8] In short, she was state of the art.

After her launch on March 27, the *Otranto* spent three months being fitted for sea trials. Then, on June 29, 1909, she headed out from Belfast to be inspected. First, ship's officers checked her speed: 18.975 knots; then, her coal consumption: 127 tons while traveling 409 miles at seventeen knots. Item by item, they went down their checklists, testing her equipment and vital systems.[9] She performed impressively. Powered by two sets of quadruple-expansion engines with eight cylinders, each with a stroke of sixty inches driving two three-bladed propellers, her boiler pressure of 215 pounds per square inch produced 1,947 horsepower, enough to push her through the water at a cruising speed of eighteen knots.[10]

After acknowledging that her test results met all required standards and specifications, the P&O Steam Navigation Company agreed to complete the purchase. They accepted the *Otranto* for delivery in July 1909.

Their newest addition was a luxurious and beautiful ship. She had a black hull; her upper decks and works were painted white, and she had two yellow funnels.[11] Higher and wider than some of her counterparts leaving Glasgow's Clyde River shipyards, her schooner rig gave her a yacht-like appearance, and all considered her a handsome addition to the P&O fleet.[12]

The *Otranto* was immediately pressed into service. She spent the rest of the summer of 1909, along with her sister ship—the *Ophir*—sailing back and forth between England and the fjords of Norway, stopping here and there among the northern capitals of Europe along the way.[13]

Her first-class passengers were assigned cabins amidships on three decks.[14] The first-class dining salon—decorated in the style of Louis XVI with oak-paneled walls bleached to a silvery grey—seated 156 passengers. And to give these wealthy passengers an even greater sense of luxury, the walls of the dining area were lined with reproductions of some of the finest paintings of the eighteenth century.[15]

Cabins for second-class passengers, many of whom shared two-berth rooms, were situated on the upper and shelter decks. A promenade, very similar to the one provided for those in first class, was available to these middle-class passengers on the shelter deck. The second-class dining area seated 150 passengers at a time and extended the full width

The music room of SS Otranto. *Postcard from the author's personal collection.*

The second-class dining room of SS Otranto. *Postcard from the author's personal collection.*

The smoking room of SS Otranto. *Postcard from the author's personal collection.*

of the ship. It was situated just aft of the first-class dining salon. These passengers also had use of a smoking parlor, "paneled and furnished in oak and leather, with a sofa running around the room."[16] Such high-end accommodations for second-class passengers were unusual; indeed, as one passenger remarked, "The style and finish of the berths and cabins . . . is [so] similar to first class . . . [that it] induces the query as to whether it is *worth* going first class when such accommodation is provided in the second."[17]

Third-class cabins were located on *Otranto*'s lower, main, and upper decks. These passengers also had access to a promenade on the aft boat deck and a ladies' lounge and a men's smoking room on the upper deck. Their dining room seated two hundred passengers at a time and was located on the lower deck. While not as plush as those for first- and second-class passengers, accommodations for third-class passengers were still far superior to those offered for passengers in the same class on other P&O Line ships.[18]

Just forward of the decks for passengers was the flying bridge, with a chart room and accommodations for the captain and officers on duty.[19]

THE *OTRANTO* IS PLACED IN SERVICE

On October 1, 1909, only six months after her launch, the *Otranto* was assigned to the route for which she was purchased—carrying passengers back and forth between England and Australia.[20] Throughout that fall and into early January 1910, she sailed to and from Brisbane, first completing two round-trips. Then, after a seventeen-night cruise from London to various ports in the Mediterranean, she spent the rest of the year and the early part of 1911 completing three more round-trips to Australia.[21]

The *Otranto* was a popular ship. Then, with the award of a contract to carry British mail and her designation as a Royal Mail Ship (RMS), she became even more sought after. One of her officers, A. B. Campbell, remembered that "she made a fine sight with her gleaming paintwork in the tropical sun" and that the small, white Royal Mail flag she flew, signifying that she was a "mail steamer," entitled her to certain benefits.[22] This preferential treatment stemmed from a contract between

RMS Otranto. *Postcard from the author's personal collection.*

the British government and Suez Canal authorities ensuring that British mail steamers were taken through the canal as quickly as possible. Indeed, one clause of the agreement stipulated that the British government would receive £1,000 for every twenty-four hours that such ships were late getting through. The express trip through the canal took days off the long journey to and from Australia.[23]

Then, in mid-summer 1911, RMS *Otranto* made the twenty-day voyage to North America where she participated in the Coronation Naval Review held in honor of King George V. Afterward, she returned home to England to her task of carrying wealthy vacationers to the Norwegian fjords until mid-September, when she was again assigned to the London-Australia run.[24]

DRAFTED INTO THE ROYAL NAVY

The *Otranto* remained on the London-Australia route from late 1911, through 1912, 1913, and well into 1914. Then, on August 4, 1914—the day war was declared and the same day that the British Admiralty gave the signal to begin hostile action against the German navy—her owners received the following telegram:

> Admiralty to Anderson & Co. Urgent and Confidential. *Otranto* is requisitioned under Royal Proclamation for service as armed merchant cruiser STOP Owners required to supply coal full bunkers engine room and deck stores for four months . . . and utensils for full complement STOP Admiralty [will] prepare ship but will require all assistance possible from you also in obtaining engine room complement which will be signed on from mercantile STOP Captain Hunt RN c/o P & O Tilbury appointed to superintend fitting STOP Please acknowledge STOP Letter follows.[25]

Thus it was that on the very first day of the war, the British Admiralty requisitioned RMS *Otranto* for conversion into an armed merchant cruiser (AMC).[26] To get her ready for war, she was fitted with eight 4.7-inch guns with the decks beneath the gun platforms shored up and strengthened; a range finder was placed on the bridge, and areas in the line of fire were cut away; and ammunition storage areas were fitted in the fore and aft holds. To give her a better chance of surviving a combat engagement, half-inch steel plating was attached to the steering area; cabin bulkheads and glass ventilators were removed. Then,

HMS Otranto *as an armed merchant cruiser of the Royal Navy. Imperial War Museum.*

all the furniture was removed to make space for the large mess decks presumed necessary for carrying large numbers of sailors and soldiers. Then, amidships, the most stable part of the vessel, an operating room was set up along with a large sickbay equipped with cots. This work was begun on August 4, 1914, and completed only nine days later.[27]

The day after work was completed, August 14, 1914, the Royal Navy commissioned RMS *Otranto* as one of His Majesty's Ships (HMS), and thereafter she was referred to as HMS *Otranto*.[28] The *Otranto* was now an AMC, ready for assignment to convoy-protection and commerce-raiding missions. Unfortunately, like her German counterparts, little could be done to change her characteristic appearance, and she would always be vulnerable to severe damage when engaged in combat because she had comparatively poor fire control and far less armor than was needed for protection.[29]

Nevertheless, on August 17, 1914, she was ordered to sea.[30] Aboard her were many of her peacetime officers and crew who had volunteered to serve for the duration of the war. These men were, in turn, joined by officers and sailors assigned by the Admiralty from the Royal Naval Reserve.[31]

HMS *Otranto* was the second AMC to leave England after hostilities began.[32] Once at sea, her captain reached into his safe and pulled out and read their sealed orders. He was surprised to learn that HMS *Otranto* was ordered to cross the Atlantic and join the Royal Navy's South Atlantic Squadron operating along the Atlantic coast of Argentina.[33]

After brief stops at Sheerness, Dover, and Portsmouth, the ship and crew headed south, stopping first at St. Vincent in the Cape Verde Islands, where they replenished their coal supply. Then, they continued onward, along a southwesterly course, until they joined the ships that comprised the South Atlantic Squadron off the coast of Brazil on August 27.[34]

After her captain consulted with the squadron commander, HMS *Otranto* was ordered to join the armored cruisers HMS *Good Hope* and HMS *Monmouth* and the light cruiser HMS *Glasgow* in patrolling the waters off the southeastern coast of South America. Their mission was to sail between Montevideo, Uruguay, and Cape Virgin, Patagonia, to track down and destroy any German raiders they came upon. These enemy ships had been preying on British merchant shipping all along that coast for some time, and the Royal Navy was determined to protect this vital supply line.[35]

Their patrols were soon expanded to include ranging around Cape Horn at the southern tip of South America and cruising up along the coast of Chile and back. It was a difficult assignment, and as the weeks passed with no enemy action, their principal enemy became the weather. Depending on where they patrolled, conditions encountered ranged from the most beautiful weather one could imagine with clear skies and glassy seas to storms that had HMS *Otranto* pitching and rolling in high winds and heavy seas and her crew battling for their lives through sheets of icy rain and bone-chilling cold.

The officers and crew of HMS *Otranto* had their first scare of the war in mid-October, when—just after they had taken on coal and supplies at Port Legunas, Chile—the ship struck a rock while heading out to sea. A crewman recalled that the ship first "gave a mighty jerk, and [then] shook like a leaf."[36]

Luckily, a diver from the HMS *Monmouth* was nearby and readily available. He was lowered alongside and carefully checked the hull for damage. When he returned to the surface, he reported that the damage appeared to be very slight, so the ship and crew were allowed to continue with their duties.[37] Two weeks later, however, the monotony would end in blood, death, and horrific tragedy.

The morning of October 31, 1914, began just like any other for the men aboard HMS *Otranto*. They loaded coal, got the engines running, and sailed out of Port Montt, Chile. They headed north and, on the following day, caught up to and rejoined the men and ships that comprised the now somewhat worn-down South Atlantic Squadron.[38]

The squadron was under the leadership of Adm. Sir Christopher Cradock, a seasoned veteran who had, early in his career, taken part in British campaigns in Egypt and the Sudan. During the Boxer Rebellion in China, he had commanded HMS *Alacrity* during the assault on the Taku Forts in July 1900 and later headed the force that relieved the Tientsin Settlement. A highly decorated veteran, Cradock had been an admiral since 1910.[39]

It should be mentioned here that ever since HMS *Otranto* had joined his fleet, Admiral Cradock had been expecting more ships as reinforcements. Unfortunately, the Admiralty was short of ships, and those it had were assigned to protect the country's home ports. As a result, only the armored cruiser HMS *Defence* and an elderly battleship, HMS *Canopus*, had been dispatched to join the force, and both were unfortunately still far away.[40]

The morning of November 1, 1914, found the admiral's ships, including HMS *Otranto*, sailing on a predetermined course, intending to rendezvous with HMS *Glasgow*. The *Glasgow* had sailed ahead of the main group to gather intelligence at Coronel, Chile, and was waiting for the rest of the convoy to catch up.[41] During that afternoon, while participating in maneuvers with some of the other ships of the squadron and sailing toward HMS *Glasgow*, HMS *Otranto* lookouts reported seeing smoke from one or more unknown ships on the horizon.[42] Then, as they closed in, they identified the ships as being from the German navy's China Fleet. The German commander, Vice Adm. Graf Maximilian von Spee, had learned that HMS *Glasgow* was nearby and set out with five ships of his fleet from Valparaiso, Chile, to find and sink the British vessel.[43]

THE BATTLE OF CORONEL

Admiral Spee's fast armored cruisers *Scharnhorst* and *Gneisenau*, along with three light cruisers, the *Nürnberg*, *Leipzig*, and *Bremen*, had been cruising south and were now directly in the path of the *Monmouth*, *Glasgow*, and *Otranto*.

Many believe that by the time the German commander spotted the British ships, the battle was already won because he held every advantage: he knew the approximate location of the British ships, he had greater firepower, he held the element of surprise, and his crews were far more competent. Indeed, whereas "most of Cradock's men were recently mobilized reservists, [who] . . . through the British Admiralty's fear of wasting ammunition had not fired a shot since the opening of hostilities," the German ships had been together for two years, and their crewmen were highly trained, excellent marksmen.[44]

Some naval historians believe that Admiral Cradock could—and should—have escaped by sailing in the fading light toward the HMS *Canopus*, some three hundred miles south.[45] Instead, he made the fatal decision to maneuver his outnumbered and outgunned ships to meet the opposing force. They were just off the coast of central Chile, near Coronel, when the *Monmouth*, *Glasgow*, and *Otranto* met up with their flagship, the armored cruiser HMS *Good Hope*, and began to maneuver into position to fight.[46]

A November 6, 1914, *Washington Post* report, compiled from statements by victorious German naval officers who "commended the bravery of the British in the uneven combat," describes—from the German perspective—the horrific ensuing sea battle:

> The engagement was fought in the teeth of a norther that assumed almost hurricane proportions. . . . The heavy weather militated against the larger ships, and the *Good Hope* found her guns almost useless because of the ship's roll. . . . It was 6 o'clock Sunday night [November 1, 1914] when the Germans sighted the three British ships.
>
> The latter attempted to alter their course, evidently with the intention to approach the coast and gain territorial waters and so avoid an unequal match. The Germans, however, headed them off and forced the battle. At the moment that the German guns were trained, the *Good Hope* was seen coming at full speed, and through good seamanship she managed to join the other British ships. The British had come about, and the two squadrons sailed southward in parallel lines, the Germans being nearer the coast.
>
> Gradually the two lines came nearer to each other and the *Scharnhorst* and *Gneisenau* simultaneously let go their twelve 8-inch guns, which they concentrated on the *Good Hope*. The firing continued for several minutes without damage. The German shots fell short and the *Good Hope* had such a roll that she could not reply. The smaller cruisers were far out of range.

Slowly the sea fighters drew in nearer and when the two units were only 6,000 yards apart the *Good Hope* . . . was still unable to use her eight 6-inch guns. . . . [Because of the way] the vessel rolled . . . [the waves were so far above] the waterline that [the guns were almost] awash. A terrible broadside from the *Scharnhorst* and *Gneisenau* crippled the British flagship and her engines stopped.

The *Monmouth*, recognizing the distress of her companion, made a dash to cover the *Good Hope*, but by that time the distance separating the two squadrons had been reduced to 5,000 yards. The Germans were able to bring all their ships into action and to use all the guns of the five vessels. These were directed first against the *Monmouth*, *Glasgow* and *Otranto*. The *Otranto*, badly damaged, escaped in the gathering darkness and soon afterwards was followed by the *Glasgow* which also had been put out of action but continued apparently seaworthy.

The five German ships continued their attack on the *Monmouth* and *Good Hope* until in a few minutes the former sank. By this time only 4,500 yards separated the fighters. The *Good Hope*, badly damaged, hung on until an explosion occurred on board her. She withdrew to the westward at 7:30 o'clock. As she disappeared, flames were seen. . . . Whether her crew was able to stop the fire or if an explosion finally sunk her is not known. The flames died down and she was not seen again.

The *Nürnberg* searched until daybreak for the wounded ship; when the German officers concluded that she had been lost with all her crew.

It was impossible to save any of the crew of the *Monmouth*, as the Germans could not put over their small boats in the face of the gale and the *Monmouth* could not have lowered her boats.

Contrary to the first reports, the *Glasgow* did not reach Coronel or Talcahuano, nor did the *Otranto* find a Chilean port.[47]

While this contemporary account states that the *Otranto* was "badly damaged," she was not. In fact, she had retreated unscathed. At 7:35 p.m., just as shells from the German ships straddled her, officers aboard both the *Otranto* and the *Glasgow* received orders from Admiral Cradock—aboard the nearly destroyed and burning *Good Hope*—to get away at full speed.[48]

It was a brutal engagement. According to the *Otranto*'s captain's log, the German commander opened fire at 7:12 p.m., and within twenty-eight minutes both the *Good Hope* and the *Monmouth* were afire and disintegrating amid a series of explosions.[49]

In a vain attempt to distract the Germans' attention from their bombardment of the *Good Hope* and the *Monmouth*, the crew of HMS

Glasgow had forced flames up the funnels of their ship, hoping they would seem an easier target in the coming darkness. They did everything they could to attract fire intended for the other, now very badly damaged ships and save their comrades. But the captain of the *Monmouth*, knowing that his ship's situation was hopeless, signaled to the *Glasgow*, "I can't get away, my ship is taking on water rapidly forward. I shall go back and engage the enemy and endeavor to ram or torpedo one of them."[50]

Unspoken was the true meaning of his message. He intended to place his ship, and the lives of his 650 officers and sailors, between HMS *Otranto* and HMS *Glasgow* and the approaching Germans so that those vessels might have the opportunity and time to escape.

A crew member of HMS *Otranto*, N. W. Douglas, in a letter he wrote home to his parents on November 11, 1914, provides an eyewitness account of what happened next:

> No doubt you have heard by now of the battle off the coast of Chile last Sunday (November 1). We were in the thick of it for the first twenty minutes. We sighted smoke about 3:30 p.m. and reported it to the flagship. The *Glasgow* was sent to see what it was, and reported four cruisers.
>
> We steamed up to them in line—*Good Hope, Monmouth, Glasgow,* and *Otranto*—turned and steamed parallel with them for about an hour at a distance of 12,000 yards. When the range got to 10,000 the guns opened fire at 7:12 p.m. The first two Germans had four funnels and could each fire a broadside of 6 x 8.5" guns. The *Good Hope* only had 2 x 9.2" and all the rest of our guns were 6".
>
> The first salvo of the Germans fell about 200 yards short. I think from the time I saw the first flash from the Germans until the shots dropped in the water was the most awful moment I have ever spent. The second salvo from the Germans fell in a line about 100 yards ahead of us and took the *Good Hope*'s forward 9.2" [gun emplacement] clean off the deck and set fire to her. The third went over the top of it with such a rotten whistling noise, caught the *Monmouth* on fire amidships, took the *Good Hope*'s foremast away.
>
> At this time we were a little out of line and the *Good Hope* was just making a signal for us to leave but she never finished it. All we got was "*Otranto* leaving—keep out of range." All the time the fight was on we were steaming 15 and the range was 2,000 yards, more than our guns could reach. The fighting went on anyhow—*Good Hope*'s one 9.2 and 6" firing—*Monmouth* and *Glasgow* firing 6". We could not use our lower deck guns as the sea was too high.

At 7:40 the *Good Hope* and *Monmouth* blew up. It was an awful sight. It was just beginning to get dark and a big red glare lit up the sky with bits of iron, funnel etc. We think it must have been her forward magazine as she had a fire on her foredeck all through the action. The *Glasgow* had shots falling round her like rain [but] she was only hit in three places on the waterline and four of her crew wounded. The *Monmouth* caught fire in three places and half an hour after we started she was well alight.

At 7:55 p.m. the Germans fired their last shot and the *Glasgow* replied with two—6″. By this time we were getting well away from the scene. The *Glasgow* made off down the coast to Port Stanley to wireless [the news] home and the *Canopus* was 200 miles away at 8 p.m., so she was no use, and she can only steam 10 knots. We steamed a zig-zag course all night and were in fear of our lives until morning as the fourth cruiser suddenly disappeared and we thought she was after us.

The *Monmouth* had ten cadets from Dartmouth [aboard] all about 15 and 16. It does seem rather a shame as they were not much use on board her. . . . We were awfully lucky to get out of it at all, as the shots were dropping all round us.

We don't know what we have done to the Germans but it can't be very much. The first ship is the "Blue Ribbon" ship of the German Navy, one of the best ships for gunnery. The latitude and longitude for the fight was 25°.33′S–76°.40′W.[51]

Another British crewman aboard the *Glasgow* related,

It really was awful. You see the engagement started at five minutes after 7 and finished about fifteen minutes after 8—that's near enough the truth—and nearly all that time firing was on. We fired incessantly for 55 minutes, but the light was so bad. As the sun went down, we were beautiful targets for the Germans, whilst all their smoke was being blown to us.

Salvo after salvo hit the poor, decrepit old *Good Hope* and the *Monmouth*, and they say the sight, as the four funnels of the *Good Hope* were blown up by the explosion, was awful. The ship's side was red hot, and even after that, with all her midships blown out of her, she continued firing. Somehow or other, she had got quite close to the enemy in the darkness, and we think her steering gear was shot away. . . . After the *Monmouth* went back to cover our escape, she had about 76 more shots fired at her.[52]

G. M. McCarthy, another eyewitness aboard the *Otranto* wrote,

Looking out on the horizon we could plainly see five German cruisers all in a line and we all knew that we were going to fight against overwhelming odds but we were going to show them the proper "Bulldog" pluck in every Englishman. . . . The weather during the battle was terrible and the wind was howling and raining hard and a very heavy sea running. It seemed a proper death's night. . . .

After the battle had been raging for 20 minutes, the *Monmouth* caught fire, then there was an explosion with flames [that] leaped up a height of 200-ft. It was one of the finest but most awful sights it was my lot to see. Our captain signaled the flagship to ask if we could come a bit nearer, as we all wanted to fight, one and all, but the reply came back: "Tis no use *Otranto*, t'would be murder to sacrifice any more lives; clear out and make the best you can."

We started away and from a distance we could see that another explosion had occurred and the flames lit up the skies. We heard afterwards that it was the *Monmouth* that had blown up and all the lives lost. . . . [No one] in that battle off the Chilean coast will ever forget the night of November 1st.[53]

During the time it took the *Otranto* and *Glasgow* to escape, the *Monmouth* and the *Good Hope* had indeed gone down with all hands, a devastating loss for the Royal Navy. In retrospect, however, because the British had entered the battle with several serious handicaps, the disaster was a foregone conclusion.

First and foremost, the British force was seriously outgunned by the German ships.[54] And whereas the German commanders had seasoned crews, the British admiral had many who had, until fairly recently beforehand, been civilians. Indeed, HMS *Good Hope* had nine hundred inexperienced reservists and cadets aboard.[55] Yet another consideration was the wind; British officers had only brief glimpses of the opposing German ships because they were obscured by the thick heavy smoke that poured from their funnels, the same smoke that later blew onto the British ships and obscured the sight of their gunners.[56] Meanwhile, the British ships were clearly silhouetted against the setting sun for the German gun crews.

Yet another factor was the excellent marksmanship of the German crews. They were simply superb. After opening fire at 7:12 p.m., the German force had—with only their third salvo—set both the *Good Hope* and the *Monmouth* on fire.[57] The end came for the men on the *Good Hope* at 7:50 p.m., when her magazine exploded and what was left of the ship sank. There were no survivors.[58] The end was hellish; crewmen of HMS *Glasgow* could only stand by helplessly as they watched debris and British sailors being "blown high into the air."[59]

The *Nürnberg* then moved in and, finding the *Monmouth* ablaze and unable to fire her guns, "finished her off with point blank gunfire." Officers aboard HMS *Glasgow* counted seventy-five gun flashes.[60] Then, like her sister ship, the *Good Hope*, the *Monmouth* went down, carrying with her every single member of her 650 officers and crew.[61]

It was a dark day for the British Empire. Within a single hour, the Royal Navy lost two of its finest ships—the *Good Hope* and the *Monmouth*—along with sixteen hundred officers and crew. Among them was Admiral Cradock, who was aboard the *Good Hope*.[62] Their German opponents got away relatively unscathed. The *Scharnhorst* had received two hits, and the *Gneisenau* four; none of their crew were killed, and only three sailors were wounded.[63]

HMS *OTRANTO*'S ESCAPE

As for HMS *Otranto* and HMS *Glasgow*, during the heated battle they had reluctantly followed Admiral Cradock's orders and had broken formation and escaped—the *Otranto* with no damage at all and the *Glasgow* after sustaining five hits.[64] According to another contemporary account, however, the *Otranto*'s commander disobeyed orders, turned around, and began zigzagging toward the German ships in an effort to provide Admiral Cradock time. Only when the *Gneisenau* turned her guns in the *Otranto*'s direction and bracketed her with two salvos did she turn and leave the scene of action.[65] In the wake of the *Otranto* and *Glasgow* as they left the area, all five German ships then trained their guns on the sinking HMS *Monmouth*, annihilating the ship and all her crew.

After the brief battle, the German fleet returned to Valparaiso, Chile, where it received a rapturous welcome from the German population.[66] It was Britain's first naval defeat since 1812, and—fairly or not—anguished British families back home attributed the disaster to Admiral Cradock. Public opinion tarnished his reputation as many considered him reckless to have to have engaged a German force so obviously superior to his own.[67] It was a sad and bleak time as the English people wondered if the battle was an indication that their country's command of the seas would now be tested further with equally catastrophic results.[68]

In London, however, while they initially greeted the news with shock and disbelief, the leaders of the Royal Navy chose to redouble their efforts to seek out and destroy the German fleet to avenge the humiliating loss. Winston Churchill, then first lord of the Admiralty, quickly assembled a huge naval force under Adm. Sir Frederick Charles Doveton Sturdee for the sole purpose of seeking out and destroying Spee's naval force.[69]

Meanwhile, HMS *Otranto* steamed south in order to put as much distance between herself and the German force as possible. She rounded Cape Horn on November 7, 1914, and sailed on to Montevideo, Uruguay, where she arrived on November 10. There she found and joined her new flagship, HMS *Defence*, along with HMS *Orama* and other ships of the fleet.[70] Before returning her to patrol duties, however, the admiral sent HMS *Otranto* and her crew to Sierra Leone, in West Africa, for shore leave. She arrived there on November 26, and her crew had their first shore leave since leaving England in August of the previous year.[71]

After eight days of rest, HMS *Otranto* headed west on December 3 to scout around the Falkland Islands for signs of German warships. By the time she arrived two weeks later, however, the Battle of the Falkland Islands had already been fought, and naval forces under Admiral Sturdee had decisively avenged the losses that the Royal Navy had suffered off Coronel on November 1.

British warships had met the German fleet on December 8, 1914, just as Admiral Spee approached the Falkland Islands with the intention of raiding the British coal and radio communications center at Port Stanley.[72] It was a beautiful day, and his fleet enjoyed smooth seas and a light breeze as it closed in on the base. Spee, certain that he had an overwhelming force, was confident that the raid would be an easy victory. As his ships approached, however, two of England's most modern battle cruisers were in port—HMS *Invincible* (Sturdee's flagship) and HMS *Inflexible*—and their observers spotted the German force.

This time the British fleet, sent by Winston Churchill, held the advantage. The two cruisers had eight 12-inch guns, which were more powerful and had a much longer range than the 8.2-inch guns on Spee's cruisers.[73] To make matters worse for the Germans, the British also had the pre-dreadnought battleship HMS *Canopus* and six other ships: the armored cruisers HMS *Carnarvon*, HMS *Cornwall*, and HMS *Kent*; light cruisers HMS *Bristol* and HMS *Glasgow*; and armed merchant cruiser HMS *Macedonia*.[74]

For reasons unknown to historians, Admiral Spee stopped to have breakfast—an act we can only attribute to overconfidence. By doing so, he missed the opportunity to trap and destroy Sturdee's fleet while the ships were tied up and taking on coal and supplies. British lookouts saw the Germans first and sounded the alarm. British officers then used the time Spee gave them to get their vessels out of the harbor. One after the other, they got their engines running and headed into the open sea. The *Bristol* exited at 9:45, followed fifteen minutes later by the *Invincible*, the *Inflexible*, the *Kent*, the *Carnarvon*, and the *Cornwall*.[75]

It was only after his lookouts reported seeing the "capital masts" of British battle cruisers coming out of the harbor that Spee realized that he was about to confront a sizeable enemy force. Then, as the number of ships was reported, he understood that he was in a world of trouble and that the odds were now overwhelmingly against him.

Spee immediately ordered his ships to head out—at full speed—to the safety of the open sea. Initially, they held a fifteen- to twenty-mile lead, but before long, the faster twenty-five-knot British ships began gaining on them.[76] Realizing that his twenty-knot ships could not outrun the pursuing British, Spee ordered his armored cruisers to provide covering fire to try to hold off the British ships in order to give his light cruisers the time and opportunity to escape. However, this strategy did not work, and the German fleet was soon in a hopeless situation.[77]

At 12:55 p.m., the British began firing from extreme range, and the sea battle divided into separate engagements: the *Invincible* and *Inflexible* took on and sank the *Scharnhorst* at 4:17 p.m., then the *Gneisenau* at 6:00 p.m. Soon thereafter, the *Cornwall* and *Glasgow* engaged and sank the *Leipzig* at 9:00 p.m. During these engagements the crew of HMS *Kent* pressed forward after the *Nürnberg*. They chopped up everything on board that they could burn to push her speed and—rapidly firing salvo after salvo—closed to within four thousand yards of her, then blew her out of the water at 7:27 p.m.[78]

To add to the victors' tally, that same morning, in a separate engagement, two other German ships had appeared off Port Pleasant, the *Baden* and the *Santa Isabel*, and both were promptly sunk, after their German crews had been removed, by HMS *Bristol* and HMS *Macedonia*.[79] Thus, by day's end, except for the *Dresden*, which had escaped, Sturdee's fleet had destroyed Spee's entire squadron of four cruisers—his flagship SMS *Scharnhorst*, the *Gneisenau*, the *Nürnberg*, and the *Leipzig*—and two colliers, all with little damage to his own ships.[80]

The British tried to save as many German sailors as possible, but fewer than one hundred of them had managed to tread water in the frigid waves long enough to be rescued. It was a devastating blow for the German navy, one that would never be forgotten. Twenty-two hundred German officers and sailors went down with their ships that day, including their commanding officer, Admiral Spee, and both of his sons. For the British, casualties were light; they lost only ten sailors.

When news of the battle and its outcome reached England and Germany, the British were ecstatic while the Germans were, of course, horrified. The German navy was deeply wounded, and German citizens could only honor the memory of her dead, including Spee, for whom they would name a battleship, the *Admiral Graf Spee*, in 1934.[81]

Indeed, the destruction of the German fleet was completed three months later when, on March 14, 1915, HMS *Kent* and HMS *Glasgow* trapped the *Dresden* at Juan Fernandez off the coast of Chile. With no avenue of escape, the German crew scuttled their ship and ended, once and for all, German commerce raiding for the remainder of the war.[82, 83]

In the meantime, HMS *Otranto* rejoined the British force at Port Stanley to serve as a guard ship for the Falkland Islands. She fulfilled this responsibility until ordered home in mid-February 1915. When she arrived in Liverpool, the Royal Navy thanked and paid the P&O Line crew for their dedicated and heroic service and sent the ship in for a long-overdue overhaul and replacement of her 4.7-inch guns with 6-inch guns.[84]

Three months later, in early May 1915, the refurbished *Otranto* headed out once again to patrol the Atlantic and Pacific coasts of South America.[85] Before she sailed, however, she needed a new crew. A. B. Campbell, one of her officers, recounted some years later how he managed to hire the thirty-five men the captain needed in the engine room.

Knowing that he had to recruit mercantile marine men for the bulk of the crew, Campbell went ashore to work the port's bars, telling everyone he met that he was looking for experienced sailors to make up a crew for a ship going on a short run from Liverpool to Glasgow. Paying for drinks all around, he bragged about the premium wages they'd earn for this brief voyage.[86] Within hours, he had a wide variety of drunk and passed-out prospective crewmen, whom he and a fellow conspirator loaded into waiting taxis and marched onto the ship. In all, Campbell said that he filled thirty-three of the thirty-five slots in this manner. As the ship slid out of port and the men came to their senses, they learned that they were now "sailing under sealed orders, destination unknown." They did not to return to England for nearly three years.[87]

HMS *Otranto* went back on patrol, and because she could not stay in a neutral country's port for more than twenty-four hours, her crew seldom got leave. Further, traveling in the tropics with hatches closed each night to darken the ship's lights made for miserable and monotonous life aboard the ship.[88] The crew's only entertainment came when they met up with other ships for coaling. A. B. Campbell wrote about a time they came upon the HMS *Vindictive*, HMS *Celtic*, and HMS *Edinburgh Castle* near the Abrolhos Islands off the coast of Brazil. The men entertained each other with singing, storytelling, and a mass swimming party in an inlet with about six feet of water protected from sharks by a rocky reef between it and the ocean.[89]

Life continued in this manner, with the men stopping and searching suspicious ships on the open sea for months on end and patrolling eighty-five thousand square miles of ocean with only their shipmates as companions. The monotonous routine was punctuated only with brief layovers now and then at the Falkland Islands. Sometimes, when the opportunity presented itself, they picked up mail at Valparaiso or landed on an uninhabited island so the crew could run down rabbits for food and exercise.[90] To amuse themselves, the crew arranged boxing, fencing, and gymnastics competitions and developed and produced a ship's company variety show, starring a Royal Marine whose magic act featured a disappearing monkey.

Finally, in December 1915, the *Otranto* and her crew were ordered to Sydney, Australia, by way of Easter Island, for another retrofit. She arrived at the dockyards on January 14, 1916, and remained there until March 5 when she was ordered to return to her patrol duties off South America.[91] Then, from March 1916 until April 1918, she continuously patrolled the coasts between Patagonia and Vancouver Island.[92]

Several months later—from October 13 to December 29, 1916—HMS *Otranto* received yet another overhaul in Esquimalt, Canada. There, the crew managed to enjoy Canadian hospitality for Christmas, followed by nine more months patrolling the Pacific coast of South America. This stint was followed by a return for more engine repairs and armament retrofits in Canada, from October 2 to December 21, 1917.

When HMS *Otranto* left Canada in December 1917, she did so with a largely new crew. The war, which many had believed would last for only a few months, had now dragged on for more than three long years.

And for the crew now back to patrolling off South America, the duty had become tedious.[93]

Finally, in late April 1918, HMS *Otranto* was sent to Rio de Janeiro to escort a convoy of ten decrepit tramp steamers full of food to England.[94] The ships left Rio on May 8, 1918, and even though some of the tramps were slow, while others kept breaking down in mid-ocean and were easy targets for enemy submarines, their luck held, and the convoy arrived at the Royal Dockyard at Devonport, on June 16, 1918.[95]

JOINING THE NORTH ATLANTIC TROOPSHIPS

After the ship and crew enjoyed a layover of a few weeks in the Royal Dockyard, they left again on July 8, 1918, for New York under orders to serve as a troop transport ferrying American soldiers from New York to Liverpool.[96]

HMS *Otranto* arrived in New York on July 20 and docked at Pier 95 at the end of 55th Street, where she remained—taking on men and supplies—until August 8, when she departed for England with a full load of American troops. She arrived in Liverpool on August 20, stayed several days, and left yet again for New York on August 28, arriving on September 8.[97] Docking again at the foot of 55th Street, this time at Pier 99, her crew immediately began preparing for their next crossing, this time with a dozen other ships that would make up the convoy designated as HX-50.[98]

Unbeknownst to the captain and crew, they were preparing HMS *Otranto* for its last voyage.[99]

2

AMERICA
JOINS THE WAR

A MURDER ABROAD

On June 28, 1914, the day Archduke Franz Ferdinand, heir to the throne of the Austro-Hungarian Empire, and his wife Sophie, Duchess of Hohenberg, were shot, few in America could have imagined what the implications would be. Indeed, until the actual events unfolded, it is doubtful that even the most clairvoyant State Department diplomat could have foreseen a future in which the murder of two members of the nobility in a small Bosnian town on the other side of the globe would—due to a rise in militarism, nationalism, and economic imperialism, as well as a series of interlocking treaties among nations—result in a catastrophic world war that would kill nearly 19 million people.

However, today we know it to be true, as for the two and a half years that followed the assassination, events and the changing views of Americans ever so slowly pulled the nation into the war. Among the principal reasons were: the insult to American pride caused by the sinking of the *Lusitania* in May 1915 (10 percent of the casualties were American), Woodrow Wilson's support in 1916 for "preparedness," and—when Germany resumed unrestricted submarine warfare—his urging of active participation in the war. Yet another factor was public opinion resulting from Gen. John Pershing's excursion with four thousand American troops into Mexico in 1916 to defeat Pancho Villa's forces. Many Americans believed that Villa was part of a Mexican-German alliance against the United States and that Germany had brought the war to them.[1]

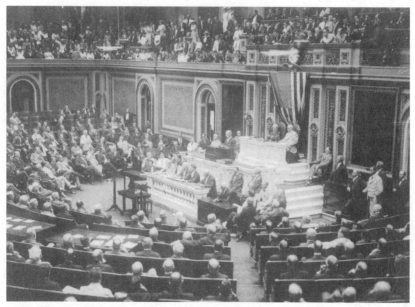

President Woodrow Wilson before Congress announcing the break in relations with Germany, February 3, 1917. US National Archives at College Park, Maryland.

The inevitable finally occurred in April 1917 when, nearly three years after the conflict had begun in Europe, America officially entered the war. It was then that Woodrow Wilson, who had only a few months earlier been reelected with the help of many antiwar supporters, reluctantly asked Congress to declare war so that America could join the Allied countries in their efforts to defeat Germany and the Central Powers. Of the 531 members of Congress who voted, only 56 objected.[2]

As for the citizens of the largely rural state of Georgia—many of whom would soon be drafted and crossing the gangplank of the British ship HMS *Otranto* to cross the Atlantic to fight—they largely supported the decision to go to war. As in the rest of the country, however, a significant minority of citizens resented the prewar military-preparedness campaigns and saw them as being in direct contrast to their own view of "states rights."[3]

Most of these soon-to-be-soldiers of Georgia and the rest of the nation were of the naïve opinion that the United States would easily defeat the enemy. Members of the Georgia National Guard, for example, who had recently returned from Pershing's Mexican Border Campaign, boasted that if given another ten-day furlough, they could go and "take care of the Kaiser" as well.[4]

The reality, however, was that in April 1917 the nation was not prepared to participate in a war of the scale being fought in Europe. The United States had only two hundred thousand men in uniform, and of these, eighty thousand were National Guard troops. As such, American leaders knew they would have to rely on volunteer enlistments for the near term and that they would have to work hard and develop a national draft to build a military force to send in the long term.[5]

DRAFTED INTO THE CAUSE

With America's entry into the war, the Allies hoped that the balance would quickly shift in their favor through the infusion of desperately needed ships, supplies, and weapons for their arsenal. However, "loyalty pledges and flag-waving not withstanding," when it came down to volunteering, many Americans felt little enthusiasm for leaving their wives and children for military service.[6] Thus, only with Wilson's passage of the Selective Service Act of May 18, 1917—six weeks after the declaration of war—were American military planners able to mobilize men successfully to make up the 4 million man "National Army" contemplated by the General Staff's contingency plan.[7]

By war's end, there would be three draft registrations, each including all men residing in the United States of various ages, "whether native born, naturalized or alien."[8] The first, held on June 5, 1917, included all men between twenty-one and thirty-one years old.[9] The second, held June 5, 1918, included all those who had attained age twenty-one after June 5, 1917. Included in that registration was a "supplemental registration" for those men who would turn twenty-one between June 5 and August 24, 1918.[10] Finally, the third was held September 12, 1918, and included men who were eighteen to forty-five years old.[11] Many of the men who would later board HMS *Otranto* were part of the September Automatic Replacement Draft (SARD). This call-up—intended as a way to supply men more rapidly to the front lines—also converted soldiers drafted into or enlisted in the US Cavalry, the Quartermaster Corps, or the Coastal Artillery into regular infantry.[12]

During the course of the three registrations, about 23 percent of the American male population (about 24.2 million men) registered.[13]

And of the 4.7 million mobilized, almost 2.7 million were furnished by conscription. The number of volunteer enlistments was over three hundred thousand.[14] Of the total forces supplied, 4 million were placed into the army, six hundred thousand into the navy, and seventy-nine thousand into the Marine Corps.[15]

Down in Georgia, 26,501 men voluntarily enlisted, along with 238 women, who joined the Army Nurse Corps. The state then supplemented these enlistments by drafting and sending another 68,820 men.[16] By the time the war ended on November 11, 1918—when the armistice was signed between German and Allied forces—America had sent 2,057,675 troops abroad and had another 2.4 million "in the pipeline" training.[17]

Although the United States suffered the smallest percentage of casualties among the nations participating, the impact was still devastating back home: 320,710 American husbands, fathers, and sons were killed or wounded.[18] Georgia lost 1,589 of its citizens—including 140 of Fort Screven's Fifty-fourth Artillery Replacements, who went down with HMS *Otranto* in what would be the worst disaster to befall American troops at sea during the war.[19]

A CONTINGENT FORMS AT FORT SCREVEN, GEORGIA

Among the hundreds of thousands of men being trained to be sent to France during the summer and fall of 1918 were those ordered to report to Fort Screven, Georgia. They included a mixture of volunteers who were not going to get their chosen assignments and men called up as part of the regular 1918 drafts. All were being processed and placed in a group officially designated as September Automatic Replacement Draft Units I and II.

Men in Georgia were being called up by local draft boards at regular intervals. For example, one contingent of forty soldiers from Screven County, Georgia—whose county seat of Sylvania had a population of only a few thousand—had been part of a county draft pool comprising two thousand men. Of 364 who were called in August 1917, all but 96 had either failed the physical exam or were exempt for one reason or another (e.g., they were farmers).[20]

However, on a bright Tuesday morning in mid-September 1917 in Sylvania, five months after war was declared, the men selected found themselves honored by "thousands of citizens, relatives and friends and well-wishers."[21] To see them off, local schools were closed, and more than five hundred schoolchildren joined friends and families of the men to celebrate their departure. They first marched to the Courthouse Square, where the county sheriff and several hundred more townspeople were waiting. There, the men, mostly self-employed farmers, loggers, and laborers, were treated to music from a brass band playing in their honor. Then, after their names were called and each was recognized, the men listened to patriotic speeches and were treated to a "barbeque spread the like of which has never been excelled."[22]

Among the incidents that day was Judge J. E. Brannen's offer "of a reward of $25,000 to the Bulloch County boy who should bring back with him the head or scalp of [the] Kaiser."[23] And at the close of ceremonies, as the band began playing "Dixie," "Hon. B. L. Robertson of Hubert, Georgia, a veteran of the Civil War, arose with a whoop and began to dance a jig in the crowd. He was [then] joined by Judge Brannen in the step, and their graceful movements caused quite a little merriment."[24]

As the men prepared to board a train that would take them to Camp Gordon, Georgia, for induction, their families and friends could only observe and wonder to themselves about how many of their husbands and sons standing amid the American flags before them that day might never return.[25]

Ten months later, on July 15, 1918, yet another contingent left Sylvania, including forty of the men who would be aboard HMS *Otranto*.[26] Again, a large group of family, friends, and neighbors assembled at the depot to see them off as they boarded the Sylvania General Railroad train. This group was met by another large group of family members at the siding in Rocky Ford, Georgia, as they transferred to a Central of Georgia train bound for Fort Screven on Tybee Island, just outside Savannah, to join the US Army's Coast Artillery.[27] A local paper reported, "Rev. W. S. Johnson [had] made the boys a splendid patriotic talk," after which a local farmer, Josh Daugherty, presented them "with a wagon load of 40-pound Watson water melons," which "the boys greatly appreciated and enjoyed."[28]

Fort Screven, Georgia, was a coastal artillery station built on Tybee Island during the Spanish-American War. Intended to guard the water entrance to the City of Savannah from possible attack by the Spanish fleet, the fort was situated at the mouth of the Savannah River on an island two and a half miles long and two-thirds of a mile wide.[29] Named for Revolutionary War general James Screven, it stood on land originally purchased in 1875 for the construction of a lighthouse.[30] The fort consisted of state-of-the-art reinforced concrete batteries with twelve 3-inch to 12-inch seacoast guns, along with eight 12-inch rifled mortars. Other guns were placed across the river near Fort Pulaski to provide a cross fire against any enemy forces that might appear.[31]

Home to the 61st and 64th Coast Artillery Regiments, Fort Screven was also the "control post for protecting the southeastern seaboard in the event of a coastal raid by enemy war craft" and the "headquarters for the artillery elements of the National Guard of Georgia when they became Companies 4, 5, 6, and 7 C.D.C."[32] Its grounds consisted of barracks, parade grounds, a mess hall, a recreation building, stables, storerooms, an infirmary, a machine shop, and an impressive row of nine two-story officers' quarters all situated on three hundred acres.[33]

Unfortunately, due to the increasing number of casualties on the Western Front and the pressing demand from Allied commanders for immediate replacements, orders were issued on September 10, 1918, to use SARD guidelines to convert many thousands of the men who had enlisted in or been drafted into the Coast Artillery to serve, instead, in the infantry. As a result, most of the recently drafted men were to be rushed through an abbreviated infantry training. Indeed, many would be provided only a short rifle-training course, if that.[34]

Only days after the new soldiers' arrival, officers at Fort Screven were directed to issue P1917 Enfield rifles and to prepare the men for travel to a northern port, where they would board the troopships that would carry them to the war.[35] Thus, while a few of the men received training on the heavy guns of the Coast Artillery, most—when they shipped out—had been in the army for only a few weeks and barely knew squad formations, let alone artillery work.

Joseph E. Hewell, who was inducted on July 6, 1918, was typical. He described in his journal how, after arriving at Fort Screven on July 8, he was issued two blankets to use on a canvas-covered cot in the barracks and spent his time drilling and participating in rifle practice while waiting to go overseas.[36]

Another soldier, Pvt. Leholmes Wells of Sylvania, Georgia, who had enlisted on August 13, 1918, because "I felt my country needed me and that I was going to have to go anyway,"[37] recalled of his training that summer, "The weather was real hot—I mean *hot!*—some of the boys in the outfit often fell by the wayside because of the heat. Those of us that were used to plowing by a mule stood the heat better."[38] Like many of the other soldiers, though he had enlisted specifically to get into the Coast Artillery, he never had the opportunity to fire any of the big guns at Fort Screven. Instead, Wells spent most of his time there marching on the beach and firing his rifle on the nearby rifle range.[39]

Another soldier, Edgar Sheperd of Augusta, Georgia, observed at the time, "There is a great difference between the regulars, who are volunteers, versus the draftees." He was young, standing about five feet, seven inches and weighing only about 130 pounds, while many of the older draftees weighed 180 to 250 pounds. Sheperd recalled after one march down Tybee Beach, "a mile on the double," that a number of the "middle-age obese draftees" fell out in the hot sun. After watching this situation unfold, he concluded that if he were commander in chief, he would demand volunteers.[40]

Anti-German paranoia peaked in 1918, and there were always concerns that spies might be lurking about the fort. As a result, on quite a few occasions, "hapless holiday tourists were . . . detained and interrogated for photographing the huge artillery guns."[41]

ORDERS TO CAMP MERRITT, NEW JERSEY

On Sunday, September 15, 1918, preparations for sending the men off to war came to an abrupt end as the camp commander received urgent orders to select and send four officers and 580 enlisted men to Camp

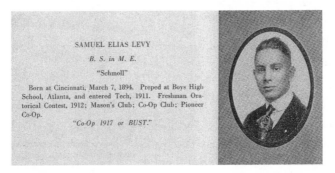

Samuel Elias Levy as a student at Georgia Tech, 1917. Georgia Institute of Technology, 1917 student yearbook, The Blueprint.

Merritt, New Jersey. There the men were to be outfitted with battle gear, supplies, and the other equipment needed for their voyage to Europe. The commander selected 2nd Lt. Samuel Elias Levy of the Coastal Artillery Corps to command the men and then pulled enlisted soldiers from a variety of companies on base to form two units he identified simply as "Detachments A & B." Each detachment consisted of 280 to 290 soldiers, who were brought together into common barracks.[42]

With dark hair and piercing eyes, Lieutenant Levy was the very opposite of the comparatively uneducated, mostly rural farm boys placed under his command. Born in Cincinnati, Ohio, on March 7, 1894, Levy had prepped at Boys High School in Atlanta and entered Georgia Tech as a co-op student in 1911.[43] There, the medium-build young man—nicknamed "Schmoll" by classmates—spent six years, alternating terms working and attending class, until he graduated with a bachelor of science degree in mechanical engineering in 1917.[44]

Lieutenant Levy was a near-perfect match for service with the Coastal Artillery Corps as Georgia Tech's mission was to graduate men "able to grasp and solve mechanical problems," who were trained to be "expert draftsmen" and "thoroughly familiar with shop processes and limitations." Levy had completed thorough and demanding courses in mathematics, physics, chemistry, and mechanical drawing, along with electives in "machine design," "engines," and "mechanics."[45] Of particular interest was the emphasis Tech placed on developing leadership skills and character:

> It is not sufficient for a course in engineering to turn out technical experts. . . . It must do much more; it must turn out men. While the schedule of subjects in this course does not indicate it, it is the prime object to send out young men to engage in the commercial work of the world with high ideals and a keen sense of moral responsibility.
>
> Good character is of more importance to the young engineer than engineering ability. . . . An earnest effort is made to fit our young men for the responsibilities of citizenship and to impress upon them the fact that the useful life, the life worth living, is a life of service.[46]

Assigned to assist Lieutenant Levy were 2nd Lt. F. A. Perkins, 2nd Lt. William H. Papenfoth, and 2nd Lt. David R. Sutton.[47] For four days after receiving their orders, the men continued drilling and participating in rifle practice while their officers oversaw the issuance of equipment.[48]

On the following Thursday morning, September 19, the troops were ordered to stand for inspection and to prepare to march out of the camp to board a twenty-one-car passenger train bound for Savannah. It was an unusually hot day, so hot that several of the men fainted during the final inspection.[49] After their inspection, the troops began marching through and off the post to the waiting train.

As the men passed the Fort Screven Hospital, a soldier wearing a full pack stood watching. He had not been selected as one of those leaving and was hoping that, somehow, he could find a way to join them. Then, as one of the units was marching past, a soldier in the ranks fainted. The observing soldier saw his chance; wasting no time, he ran out to Lieutenant Levy, who was assisting the fallen soldier, saluted, and asked permission to go in the man's place. Surprised but impressed by the young soldier's enthusiasm, Levy granted his request, and the young man quickly fell in and marched off to war.[50]

Edgar Sheperd later recalled that once they arrived at the siding where the train was waiting and had lined up,

> their names were called, [and, the] Articles of War [were] read [to them]. . . . Questions [were then] asked to [identify] those opposed to fighting on foreign soil other than U.S. possessions, as a soldier whether volunteer or draftee, could not be compelled to fight on other than the mainland or its possessions.
>
> Then . . . there being a pause before the troop train pulled out, good-bye greetings were said to wives, mothers, fathers, sons, sisters, brothers and sweethearts. I did not have anyone to cry over me.[51]

Afterward, under the watchful eyes of their officers, the soldiers boarded the train car to which they had been assigned. Then, at 7:00 p.m., the troop train left the siding at Fort Screven and began its journey—first to the rail yard in Savannah, where the cars were hooked to two huge Seaboard Coast Line locomotives. Then, later that night, with military police stationed in each coach, they began their journey northward along the Atlantic coast, destined for Camp Merritt, New Jersey.[52]

Soldiers on such trips were usually assigned to a sleeping car, but this contingent had to make do with day coaches. As a result, the men had to endure the discomfort of trying to sleep upright with their gear stowed in baggage cars.[53] It did not take long for them to become cramped as they tried to sleep in the increasingly uncomfortable seats. After the cars filled with cigarette smoke, the men opened the windows;

Soldiers en route to Camp Merritt, New Jersey. US National Archives at College Park, Maryland.

instead of enjoying cool, fresh air, however, they now had to contend with cinders and dirt flying through the cabins from the fast-moving locomotive's smokestack.[54]

Joseph Hewell recalled that the trip took two days and three nights. During most of that time, he was wide awake because there were three men for every two seats turned together, making it nearly impossible to sleep. He remembered that on Friday they stopped for lunch in Hamlet, North Carolina; later that evening they had supper in Raleigh. On arriving in Washington, DC, on the following morning, they were allowed to disembark and get coffee from a Red Cross canteen. After stopping at around 6:00 p.m. in Philadelphia, where they were allowed to walk around downtown a bit, they traveled the last leg of their trip to Camp Merritt, New Jersey, arriving very early on Sunday morning, September 22, 1918.[55]

Once the train arrived, it remained on a siding until after reveille and through breakfast. Finally, at 8:00 a.m., the train was given permission to proceed to the beautiful Victorian-style terminal at Tenafly Station. The soldiers then stepped off the train, gathered their gear from the baggage car, and marched in formation to barracks assigned to them on post at Camp Merritt.[56]

The men found themselves—still in their just-issued summer uniforms—confronted with cold, early-winter temperatures. Pvt. Lonzon Sheley recalled later, "When we reached New Jersey, it was freezing, [with] icy, cold streets and we were in our B.V.D.'s and thin uniforms."[57]

Camp Merritt was a large army post—for many of the men, it was as large as, or larger than, the towns they had grown up in. Completed just a year before at a cost of $11 million, it was one of the few army posts with painted buildings and paved streets. Conveniently situated ten miles north of transatlantic port facilities in New York City, the post boasted 143 miles of concrete roads; 39 warehouses; 4 fire stations; 93 hospital buildings; 1 athletic field; 611 two-story, sixty-man barracks; 40

Drawing clothing at Camp Merritt, New Jersey. US National Archives at College Park, Maryland.

two-story officers' quarters; 165 company kitchens and mess halls; 15 post exchanges; and a 2,500-person-capacity theater.[58, 59] The camp was massive and capable of accommodating more than 40,000 soldiers at a time. Indeed, by the end of the war, more than 579,000 soldiers had passed through its gates on their way to Europe, and another 510,000 men had passed through on their way home.[60, 61]

As the young soldiers were escorted to their assigned barracks and allowed to rest for a few hours, their officers met with camp personnel to prepare for the distribution of heavy clothes and overseas equipment. Unit officers and sergeants worked through that day and into the night, drawing supplies from the warehouses and issuing to the men everything from underwear to overcoats, all to make sure that the men would have the rifles, clothing, and everything else they'd need to fight.[62] Worn equipment was turned in and replaced; summer khakis were traded for winter uniforms; tan shoes were swapped for hobnail boots; and campaign hats were turned in for "overseas caps."

It was a busy, hectic time of typical army "hurry up and wait." Between periods of standing in line for meals and equipment, the soldiers were questioned by intelligence officers to make sure there were no saboteurs among them and hurriedly examined by medical staff to determine whether each was healthy enough to proceed.[63] Haircuts were part of the process as well. Joseph Hewell recalled that the men were called out in small groups and received "quite a hair clipping" as "six men clipped about 570 heads" using horse clippers. He was particularly impressed by the efficiency, noting that "one fellow would turn the handle while the other would handle the clippers" and that the whole process "only took about 2 or 2 1/2 minutes per man."[64] Another soldier commented, "We all looked like freshly denuded sheep. Bumps, depressions and scars, hitherto hidden by comely locks, now were pitilessly revealed."[65]

The men were lucky, however, to be processed through Camp Merritt, because that camp's medical staff went to great lengths to make sure that soldiers entrusted to them received the best care possible. This was an important factor, because during the time the men from Camp Screven were being processed, the world was experiencing a worldwide influenza pandemic that was killing hundreds of thousands of Americans and millions of others worldwide. Camp Merritt, with thirty-eight hundred hospital beds, was praised for having the lowest "sick rate" of any camp in the United States as well as the lowest death rate (from influenza).[66]

Finally, after the officers had double-checked the equipment allocation checklists their sergeants had compiled and signed off on the equipment they were responsible for, the Fort Screven contingent was ready to proceed to the point of embarkation.[67]

HEADING DOWN THE HUDSON RIVER

Wasting no time, the soldiers were assembled during the early-morning hours of Monday, September 23. The men lined up silently in "heavy marching order" with full seventy- to ninety-pound packs.[68] Then, after standing around for one or two hours, they finally received orders to begin the three- to four-mile march from the main area of the camp down to Alpine Landing on the Hudson River.[69]

The men from Fort Screven did not know it, but during the previous few days, while they had been going through processing, another eight to twelve thousand troops had already been gathered from various units at Camp Merritt. Divided into columns of two to three thousand, those troops had marched down before them to the landing and had

Soldiers take a ten-minute rest during the hike from Camp Merritt to Alpine Landing. US National Archives at College Park, Maryland.

already been sent down river to board ships docked in New York Harbor. The men had been marched out between one o'clock and six o'clock in the morning with their departure times staggered so that they could be processed and boarded onto the waiting ships in an orderly manner.[70] Because the troops from Camp Screven had been hastily added to the list of those to be shipped out, unbeknownst to them, they would cause the whole contingent to leave a day later than scheduled.

It was a grueling hike for the Fort Screven contingent as dust rose up from the road and hung over the men all the way down to the landing. The newly issued hobnail boots gave many blisters; some were too tight, and others were too large. For many, it seemed that the road would go on forever. Some of the older men fell out of the line and had to stop to rest before going on. Other soldiers—having been in the army for just a couple weeks—refused to obey their noncommissioned officers' orders to stand up and continue marching. The men who could not, or would not, hike any further were eventually picked up by large trucks following behind the column carrying their heavy equipment.[71]

Others experienced discomfort from the pack straps cutting into their shoulders and were frustrated that their clumsily rolled packs were coming apart. There was much cursing among the men who thought they were being treated too harshly after the long, uncomfortable train ride from Georgia.[72] Lonzon Sheley recalled, "Most of us had [already] contracted colds [and] such a walk across the New Jersey hills made perspiration roll down our backs. . . . I was wet with it as we [marched]" down toward the ferry.[73]

At last, the men reached the edge of a hill that marked the brow of the Palisade Mountains, where the narrow dirt road they were on began twisting and winding sharply downward, through woods and underbrush, to a pier extending out from the edge of the Hudson River.[74] Eventually they all arrived at the landing, where they waited to board a ferryboat that would take them twelve miles down to the North River, to the piers in Manhattan where their transport ship lay waiting.[75]

Alpine Landing was a historic spot. It was there, in 1776, while British troops were making preparations to occupy the Hudson River Valley, that the British general, Lord Cornwallis, made his headquarters in an old farmhouse that had at one time been an old Dutch trading post. Also nearby was a marker indicating where patriots of the American Revolution were killed by German mercenaries hired to fight for the British.[76] It is probable that many of the thousands of soldiers—including the contingent from Fort Screven—who marched past the marker pondered the cost of freedom as they headed out to fight in a war to help their country's former enemy, England, fight the German army.[77]

The ferryboats departed every half hour, each loaded with soldiers for the trip down the Hudson River and on to New York City.[78] The soldiers from Fort Screven were joined on the ferry by another group that had marched behind them under the command of Lt. Bernie J. Coffman. These were men from loosely formed units designated as Casual Companies 406 and 410, made up mostly of soldiers from previous units who had deserted in New York City.

The deserters had been confined at Camp Merritt until there were enough of them to form the two companies; they were then ordered to ship out. It was expected that once they arrived in France, they would be court-martialed for desertion. The soldiers were hard-talking, tough men, and while one of their own sergeants had been put in charge of them temporarily for the voyage, their orders placed them, their sergeant, and Lieutenant Coffman under Lieutenant Levy's command.[79]

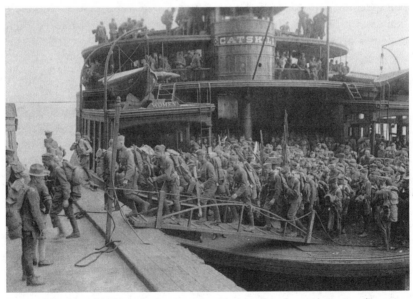

Leaving the ferry that brought them to New York Harbor from Alpine Landing, New Jersey. US National Archives at College Park, Maryland.

The ferry cast off, and as Pvt. Lonzon Sheley wrote later, "Down the Hudson affords some beautiful scenery, so we started out on the deck in the damp, cold air."[80] Two hours later, after passing upper New York City, all the men disembarked at Pier 95, just off 55th Street. From there, they stared in awe at the scene before them: a dozen or more troop transport ships, in various stages of taking on men, were lined up before them, ready to cast off and form yet another convoy bound for France by way of England.[81]

As the men in the Fort Screven contingent and Casual Companies 406 and 410 stood around waiting for their orders to board ship, they were treated to coffee and donuts by American Red Cross volunteers.[82] Then there was more "hurry up and wait" as they went through more medical and equipment inspections, were again questioned by intelligence officers, and received other "instructions of many sorts."[83]

During this time, each soldier was also issued and ordered to wear, suspended from his neck, two metal identification tags bearing his army serial number. These tags were often the only way a soldier, killed either at sea or on land, could be identified.[84]

Finally, all the rituals had been completed, and the men marched in formation for several blocks, down city streets lined with applauding spectators, to Pier 99. There, on that cool afternoon of Monday, September 23, 1918, the men lined up in single file and boarded their assigned ship—Transport No. 641—HMS *Otranto*.[85]

CONVOY HX-50 LEAVES FOR ENGLAND

THE TROOPS BOARD HMS *OTRANTO*

As the men lined up to board her, their first view of HMS *Otranto* was of a large, two-funnel ocean liner whose gleaming colors had been painted over with a dirty-grey color scheme.[1] The drab colors were intended to help her profile blend in with the sea, making it more difficult for enemy submarine commanders to track her.

After each soldier's paperwork was double-checked, he was waved aboard. Then, as they were shown to their quarters, many talked with members of the 380-man British crew, asking questions about the ship's guns, whether they had sighted any submarines on the way over, and so forth. The seasoned crew patiently answered their questions and re-assured them that they were not boarding an ordinary troopship—they were boarding an armed merchant cruiser of the Royal Navy.[2]

Of the wide variety of other large ships nearby, most of those making up their convoy, designated HX-50, had taken on troops the day before and were now anchored in the channel waiting for orders to hoist anchor and proceed out into the open ocean.[3]

In command of the *Otranto* as acting captain was Cpt. Ernest G. W. Davidson, assisted by Lt. C. D. Simmons.[4] Davidson was a seasoned and respected British naval officer whose career at sea had spanned decades.[5] In deference to his experience and ability, he was appointed commodore of the convoy with the responsibility of leading the ships to England.[6]

As mentioned previously, this was not the *Otranto*'s first journey across the Atlantic to ferry soldiers to Britain. Just a month before, in early August, well-known American actor Buster Keaton had sailed aboard her from New York to Liverpool as part of Company C of the 40th Division, 159th Infantry.[7, 8]

Davidson had planned to lead the convoy out to sea on that day (September 24), but he had received a communication a few days earlier from American authorities notifying him that a late train had arrived at Camp Merritt with the several hundred men from Fort Screven who needed to be accommodated.

After checking with the commanders of all the ships in the convoy, he determined that his own ship, HMS *Otranto*, was the only one left with the capacity to carry the extra soldiers. To do so required him to delay the convoy's departure by twelve hours, so he notified the other ships of the change of plans and set to work.[9] Thus, while the men from Fort Screven were being processed at Camp Merritt, Davidson and his crew were hurriedly making arrangements, bringing extra stores aboard, and cleaning the cargo areas needed to accommodate the men.[10]

The rush was on because HX-50 was designated as a "fast convoy," a category reserved for those capable of attaining thirteen knots and comprising no more than fourteen ships carrying troops.[11] Because "HX" convoys sailed for the west coast of England from New York every eight days, a delay by Davidson's convoy might have a ripple effect on the next.[12]

A standard procedure for the soldiers—just before they actually boarded their ship—was to drop a "safe-arrival postcard" into a mail bag along with any last letters they wanted posted. Then, they would march up the gangplank, receive their billet indicating the deck, hatch, compartment, and bunk number to which that had been assigned and be given instructions as to which areas would serve as their "parade" and "weather" decks.[13] Enlisted men were typically quartered down the companion stairways located on both sides of the ship from the well deck, in the cargo holds forward and aft.[14]

As soldiers from Fort Screven went below, they could not help but notice that just about all the interior furnishings had been ripped out, and every nonessential piece of woodwork had been cut away. HMS *Otranto* was a ship pared to her bare bones.[15] Instead of plush cabins, the men were shown to rows of tables running crosswise the length of

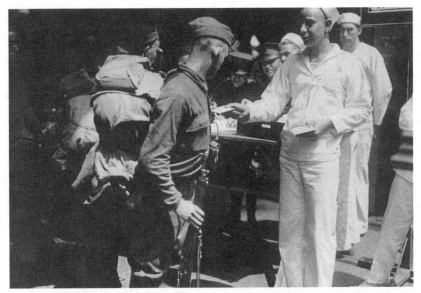

Soldiers being issued "I have arrived safely" cards to be signed and placed in mailbags at the gangplank before boarding. US National Archives at College Park, Maryland.

the interior of the ship. Over the aisles between the tables, hammocks hung from hooks, where the men would sleep. Off to the sides of the sleeping areas were wooden, pen-like enclosures, where the men could toss their hammocks for storage during the day. However, because so many left their hammocks hanging, there was usually only a couple feet of headroom for those walking through the area.[16] Each bunk area—referred to as a "standee"—took up a six-by-three-foot area. The men were to use their life preservers as pillows.[17]

Ventilation below deck was provided by means of stair doors and the skylights between them. In stormy weather these would all be closed.[18] Once below deck, the men were met by a strong odor of phenol, an ingredient used in disinfectants. The odor, which reminded many of them of a hospital, seemed to pervade the whole ship.[19]

Leholmes Wells recalled, "It was the stinkingest ship, you couldn't stay below deck long."[20] He believed that HMS *Otranto* had brought cattle over in its holds during its previous voyage because the men could smell the ship from the dock. While the bunk areas had been thoroughly cleaned, the crew's overuse of disinfectants to counter the smell of cow manure made for a nauseating combination.[21, 22]

Observing that the commissioned officers and two "YMCA men" who joined them in coming aboard had been assigned cabins, and knowing that the ship was designed to carry more than a thousand passengers, there was much speculation among the enlisted men as to why they were not allowed to occupy some of the cabins as well. What they didn't know, however, was that while it may have appeared that many of the *Otranto*'s staterooms appeared vacant and available, most had been dismantled before the previous voyage.[23]

Amidships, on the port side of the *Otranto*'s upper deck, was a canteen where the men could purchase extra rations if they had the money. And below, near the aft-end, was another. While these were intended for use by the ship's crew, American soldiers were allowed to buy from them as well.[24]

Trouble began during that first night, while the *Otranto* was still tied to the pier. Dozens of soldiers began coughing and getting chills. Their symptoms were a bad omen as the United States and the rest of the world were in the middle of what experts would later refer to as the greatest disease event of the twentieth century: the Spanish Flu pandemic.[25] The influenza virus is often mild, but in 1918 a strain had mutated into a devastating killer. Unlike other strains, this one stalked the youngest and strongest men, such as those aboard the *Otranto* and other ships that made up the HX-50 convoy. The pandemic was so deadly that 20 to 50 *million* people worldwide died from it before it ran its course two years later.

That night, however, the doctors walking through the *Otranto* were not fully aware of the world's health crisis. While many men were ill, doctors determined that only nine showed symptoms serious enough for them to be ordered off the ship and admitted by a nearby hospital.[26]

Lonzon Sheley was only slightly ill, so he volunteered to accompany one of the soldiers who had been ordered to report to a local hospital. While there, the doctor also took his temperature, gave him a few cc's of penicillin, and ordered him back to the ship. Sheley later learned that the young man he took to the hospital that night died a few days later. Sheley believed that many of the men were suffering from exhaustion and from the extremes of weather to which they had been exposed before sailing, commenting later, "The entire crowd was sick, with few exceptions, when we left New York."[27]

Except for the men ordered to the hospital and those assisting them, none of the other soldiers were allowed to leave the ship that night.

Guards were posted and given instructions that no one aboard was to leave the ship without an authorized, signed pass. Despite this precaution, three men from Coastal Artillery Corps (CAC) Casual Company 406 and two from Casual Company 410 disappeared and were reported "absent without leave." These soldiers had deserted previously and were scheduled for court-martial. One had already deserted three times.[28] It was believed that he and the others had evaded the guards and either hand-walked their way down the ship's hawsers to the pier or jumped into the water and swum ashore.

While some contemporary accounts differ slightly from an official "Composite Report" submitted by Lt. Sam Levy on October 16, it appears that, at sailing, on Wednesday, September 25, 1918—after the removal of the nine sick soldiers and accounting for the five deserters—in addition to the 380-man English crew and two American YMCA officers (T. L. Campbell of Memphis and C. A. Carpenter of Waukesha, Wisconsin), there were 701 American troops of all ranks aboard.[29, 30] Thus, the total of all aboard—based on these calculations—would be 1,083 men (see table 3.1).

Besides the four officers from Fort Screven (Lt. Sam Levy, Lt. Frank A. Perkins, Lt. William H. Papenfoth, and Lt. David R. Sutton), other officers aboard included Cpt. Charles A. Dickson and Cpt. Fred Heimer of the US Army Medical Corps; and 2nd Lt. Bernie J. Coffman, DMA, and Lt. Harry M. Conwell of Company M, 355th Infantry, who were responsible for the 406th and 410th Casual Companies.[31]

On Tuesday night, September 24, the evening before sailing, some of the American soldiers mingled with the British sailors and spoke of their inexperience with the ocean. Being so far away from home, with many never having learned to swim, they were anxious and concerned. However, they were reassured by the crew's comments that they were aboard a "lucky" ship and regaled with stories of how Captain Davidson

Table 3.1.   Lt. Sam Levy's Account of American Troops at the Time of Sailing

	Officers	Enlisted	Less Those AWOL-NY	Present
Fort Screven, SARD	4	570	0	574
CAC Casual Co. 406	1	62	3	60
CAC Casual Co. 410	1	66	2	65
U.S. Army Medical Corps	2	0	0	2
Total US Army Troops Aboard	8	698	5	701

and the crew had avoided disaster time and again. The American soldiers focused on the comments and stories that emphasized that their chances of being sunk by a U-boat—"tinfished," as the sailors called it—were slim.

Indeed, the *Otranto*'s crew truly felt that their ship was "a favorite of fortune." After all, they had escaped the Coronel disaster, done light duty on the fringes of the Falkland battle, run aground twice without serious damage, and come through three years of arduous and dangerous duty unscathed.[32] As one of the ship's officers later said, "We were almost boastful about our luck."[33]

In retrospect, perhaps it was better that neither the American soldiers nor the British crew had any idea of the enormous danger they would soon face.

IOWA TROOPS BOARD HMS *KASHMIR*

Meanwhile, as preparations to get underway continued aboard HMS *Otranto*, a sister ship in the convoy that would play a significant role in this story—HMS *Kashmir*—had already pushed off and was waiting for the *Otranto* to form up and lead the convoy.

Unlike the men aboard the *Otranto*—who were mostly new recruits and draftees—the men on board the *Kashmir* were from an experienced battalion of the Iowa National Guard Field Artillery that had been expanded into a regiment at full war strength. The unit's original batteries were mustered into federal service in June 1917 at Fort Des Moines, Iowa, and the affiliated troops were sent to Fort Logan H. Roots, Arkansas, the following month, where they too were inducted into federal service.[34]

Two months later, in September 1917, the regiment was transferred to Camp Cody, in Deming, New Mexico. There it was designated the 126th Field Artillery and joined the 125th Minnesota and the 127th Nebraska to become the 59th Field Artillery Brigade of the 34th Sandstorm Division. Because the soldiers from Minnesota and Nebraska had all been infantrymen, there was a year's delay in sending them to Europe due to the need to retrain them as artillerymen.[35]

On July 3, 1918, the 59th Field Artillery left Camp Cody for Fort Sill, Oklahoma, where they would receive their final artillery training. A regular army brigade arrived at about the same time, but because the

59th made a better showing in training and competition, it was allowed to leave for France first. It was under those circumstances that the men boarded a train in mid-September for Camp Upton, New York, where they would make final preparations for their voyage abroad.[36]

Unfortunately, upon arrival at Camp Upton on September 17, their officers found most of the camp under quarantine for influenza. Despite the difficulties the quarantine presented, however, like the men of the *Otranto*, they continued to prepare for their departure, exchanging equipment and uniforms and receiving the horse-clipper haircut intended to prevent lice.[37]

Finally, six days later, on the morning of September 23, the men marched to a train that carried them from Long Island to Brooklyn. There they took a ferry to the Hoboken slip where the *Kashmir* was docked.[38]

The twin-screw steamer *Kashmir* was a bit smaller than the *Otranto*.[39] At 8,960 gross tons, she was 480 feet long, had a beam of 58.2 feet, and a depth of 33.7 feet.[40] Her two seven- to nine-thousand-ihp quadruple-expansion engines gave her a maximum service speed of up to fifteen knots.[41-44]

Designed to carry seventy-eight first-class and sixty-eight second-class passengers, the *Kashmir* cost £185,396 to build.[45, 46] With three decks and twenty-one masts, she was fore and aft schooner rigged, with an elliptical stern, clincher built.[47] As a K-class ship, she was designed for secondary intermediate services with a limited number of passengers for the sake of comfort because of her large cargo capacity.[48] Launched and turned over to the Peninsular & Oriental (P&O) Steam Navigation Company on February 16, 1915, she was considered so sturdy that she was used on her maiden voyage to carry the Royal Mail to Bombay.[49]

Before the war, the *Kashmir* was used for the P&O's Far Eastern route with occasional voyages on the Australian mail service run. Then, in December 1916, she was drafted into military service and assigned to carry troops around the Mediterranean.[50] Like HMS *Otranto*, she had also endured a few close calls, including one in June 1917 in which she had barely escaped an enemy submarine while carrying almost twenty-one hundred troops. It was only by expert helmsmanship and being able to make a run for it at sixteen knots that she managed to escape.[51]

HMS *Kashmir* continued to serve in the Mediterranean until 1918, when she was reassigned to the North Atlantic to join the *Otranto* and other ships in ferrying American troops over to England.[52] By the time the American troops of the 126th Field Artillery had marched aboard, she and her skipper, Cpt. Edmund Burton Bartlett, had already made two trips to and from New York carrying troops.[53]

Just before noon on September 23, the men of the 126th marched up the *Kashmir*'s gangplank, and after finding their quarters, they could not help but notice the ship's cold, sweaty, sloping sides, the long wooden mess tables flanked by benches, and the canvas hammocks set up for sleeping. Like the men on the *Otranto*, each soldier was issued a heavy life belt to fasten around the upper part of his body and ordered to wear it constantly during the voyage or suffer punishment.[54] Looking around at their spartan quarters, the men realized there would be little comfort during the crossing.

After depositing their packs in their quarters, soldiers typically went back up to the top decks to get some fresh air. There some observed a commotion down on the pier. Some detachments of African American troops from Georgia had just arrived—soldiers from Overseas Casual Companies 391 and 403 and the 404th and 345th Labor Battalions. The men had obviously received very little training, as their leggings were carelessly wrapped, and many had unbuttoned their shirts. Even some of their packs had come undone, and the soldiers were seen trying to balance their loose clothing, banjos, and other musical instruments while walking onto the gangplank to board. They, too, were guided to their quarters, areas similar to the Iowa troops' sections but—as was typical of the times—in the back of the ship.[55]

African American soldiers endured significant racial discrimination during the First World War. When war was declared, the US Army only had about ten thousand African American soldiers in uniform, most serving in segregated regiments stationed at remote posts in the Southwest. However, by war's end, some two hundred thousand had served.[56, 57]

In Georgia, where many of these troops were from, the African American population endured enormous economic and physical oppression. Their occupational choices were limited, and members of the Ku Klux Klan continued to shoot, hang, beat, and burn many African Americans who dared to cross them.

For example, Walter White of the National Association for the Advancement of Colored People documented the lynchings of 510 African American citizens in Georgia between 1882 and 1927.[58] And despite

Georgia's passing laws in 1893 to prevent such mob violence, it is very likely that many more such murders took place than those documented by White. Indeed, such deaths were so common in Georgia during these years that some historians refer to this period as "the Lynching Era."[59]

In July 1918, Army Intelligence officers sent to Georgia to investigate problems related to the draft status of African Americans reported back to their superiors in Washington that "night riding and negro-baiting around Athens, Georgia [continues] without hindrance from local authorities. [And] local policemen and Internal Revenue officers [are] reported to be members of the Klan."[60] One telling example regarding the high status of membership in the Klan at this time is the presence of photographs of members of the campus's "Ku Klux Klan Club" in the "Student Clubs" section of the Georgia Tech yearbooks for 1917 and 1918.[61]

Race was also a factor in the draft and in the gaining of deferments throughout Georgia. White landowners sometimes would not allow their black sharecroppers to register or report when called up and often did not pass along the mailed notices ordering black farmhands to register. Other landowners bribed local sheriffs to look the other way and not arrest their workers for not registering or reporting for duty during planting and harvesting season. As a result, many African American farmhands were jailed for failure to report for duty.[62] Georgia historian Todd Womack writes, "Local draft boards 'resisted sending healthy and hard working black males' because they were in need [of their labor] in the cotton fields and by the naval stores industry."[63]

Despite the fact that members of all-black divisions such as the 92nd and 93rd would prove very capable and hard-fighting soldiers—and eventually play a prominent role in defeating the Central Powers—the majority of African American soldiers were assigned to hastily organized, inadequately trained, and poorly equipped labor battalions such as those boarding HMS *Kashmir* that day.[64, 65] Yet, these men performed an important role as part of Quartermaster Corps labor units and pioneer infantry regiments as they completed the difficult work of enlarging port capabilities; building roads, bridges, and gun emplacements; digging trenches; and unloading the millions of tons of supplies and equipment that helped the French, American, and British armies win the war. As one writer commented, "These laborers in uniform [were] . . . the first Americans to arrive and the last to leave. They performed difficult and essential work and never received the recognition they deserved."[66]

While one source states that HMS *Kashmir* left with 2,055 soldiers aboard, another indicated that—with 700 African American troops in units of Overseas Casual Companies 391, 403, and 404, plus those in Naval Battalion 345 and 1,368 white soldiers from the 126th Field Artillery—she was carrying 2,068 troops.[67–69]

Thus it was that during the late afternoon hours of September 24, 1918, the captain of HMS *Kashmir* steered her out into the lower bay and dropped anchor near several other troop transports. There she waited, within sight of the Statue of Liberty and the New York skyline, for HMS *Otranto* and the rest of the convoy to lead them out of the harbor the following day. As mentioned previously, the HX-50 convoy had been scheduled to proceed into the open ocean on September 24, but their departure was delayed so that the *Otranto* could take on the late-arriving troops from Fort Screven, Georgia.[70]

A few days earlier, senior officers of the ships of the HX-50 convoy had attended the required convoy meeting. There shipmasters of vessels assigned to sail as members of the HX-50 convoy and commanders of the British and American naval vessels serving convoy escort duty gathered in the office of the port convoy officer. These meetings were regarded as of such importance that the port convoy officer would not permit any vessel to sail unless its shipmaster had either attended or the port convoy officer had stopped by and personally instructed and examined the shipmaster regarding the procedures to be followed.[71]

Every relevant detail and concern regarding the convoy's operation was discussed. For example, during the meeting, the convoy officer drew a diagram of the convoy's formation on a large blackboard and indicated where HMS *Otranto* and all the other ships were to be situated as they headed out to the open sea. This briefing was important because it allowed everyone present to see exactly how his ship would be positioned in relation to all of the others. Captain Davidson and the other ships' officers were then given a slip of paper indicating the exact time and location at which his ship was to assemble with the others and a sealed envelope containing route instructions to be opened if their ship became hopelessly separated from the rest of the group during the voyage. With these top secret instructions, any of the captains—with the assistance of his navigator—would then be able to plot a path to the convoy's destroyer rendezvous point and rejoin the convoy off the coast of Northern Ireland.[72]

Chief radio operators of each ship in the convoy were also required to attend and—regardless of how experienced or familiar they were with their responsibilities—were briefed on the radio procedures they were to follow while at sea.[73]

THE VOYAGE BEGINS

The early-morning hours of Wednesday, September 25, 1918, were cold, raw, and foggy.[74] However, preparations were now complete; all of the American soldiers aboard were accounted for, and it was time for HMS *Otranto* to head out and lead the HX-50 convoy out to sea.

Just before noon, Captain Davidson gave the order to cast off the mooring lines and then carefully observed the harbor tugboats as they slowly pulled and pushed HMS *Otranto* into the channel. Then, at 12:40 p.m., the big ship, along with her destroyer escort, began to move slowly through the harbor on its own power.[75] Most of the American soldiers had gathered topside, where they stood silently along the ship's rails peering through the thick fog at the outline of the Statue of Liberty, which was barely discernable as they passed. For most of the men, this was their first view of the famous landmark; for many, it would be their last.[76]

As HMS *Otranto*, which served as the convoy's flagship and primary reference point, passed the last channel markers and entered the open sea, she picked up other ships to her left and right. Soon, most of the ships comprising the main body of HX-50 had joined up and were passing the Lightship *Ambrose* located twenty-three miles east of New York Harbor.[77, 78] Shipmasters joined the convoy by flying position signal flags and using those of other ships to move their own vessel into its proper place in the formation. They formed into three lines, four ships abreast.[79]

While the troopships were getting underway and moving into formation, the New York Harbor Entrance Patrol was hard at work. To detect possible enemy submarine activity, the patrol boats *Natoma* and *Bagley* and the Coast Guard ship *Gloucester* headed out towing observation balloons above and behind them. They were assisted by the US Navy, which also sent up a dirigible balloon and three seaplanes to patrol the channel.[80]

HMS *Otranto* approached and moved through the final assembly area at a slow speed, guiding her sister ships along the first leg of their predetermined base course. Captain Davidson looked left, right, and behind him, straining his eyes to make sure that all the vessels of HX-50 were in their proper place. Once he was confident that all was well, he gave the order to slowly pick up speed.[81]

They were now underway, albeit a day later than originally planned. The convoy consisted of HMS *Otranto*, twelve other troopships, two American cruisers (the USS *St. Louis* and the USS *Louisiana*), and one American destroyer (the USS *Dorsey*).[82, 83] Because the German navy was doing all it could to sink British and American transport and supply ships, the escorting US Navy ships were placed in screening positions to protect the convoy from U-boat attacks. The USS *St. Louis* and USS *Louisiana* were following orders to accompany them for a predetermined distance across the Atlantic just in case they encountered enemy battleships or heavy cruisers. Only the American destroyer USS *Dorsey* was to stay with the convoy until it met the British destroyers near Northern Ireland that would escort the ships into port.[84]

Having escort ships accompany the convoy was only one of a number of precautions taken that day. Earlier that morning, the patrol boat *Tarantula* had been sent out from the Lightship *Ambrose* with an array of microphones to listen for submarine activity in the area. She traveled over the same route that the troopships would follow later that day, steaming at ten knots and stopping every now and then to listen for submarines. Then, once the *Tarantula* reached a point twelve hours out to sea, her commander stopped her engines altogether and remained there until the convoy had passed by.[85]

That same morning at dawn, six minesweepers left from the Lightship *Ambrose* to clear a path two miles wide and eighteen miles long for the convoy to use as a safe passage out to sea. The minesweepers worked their way eastward from the lightship, marking the path by dropping buoys along the northern edge of the proposed route every two miles. It made for a long day as the minesweepers did not return to the lightship until late that evening, after the convoy had steamed past them and out over the horizon. Only then could they retrace their path, pick up their buoys, and head home.[86]

Later that same day, the patrol boat *Xarifa* was sent out with an observation balloon. Her job was to serve as a point ship and to travel in front of the convoy with observers aloft using binoculars to search for

U-boats. The men in the balloons then communicated with the crew below by telephone, and the *Xarifa*'s radio operator communicated with ships in the passing convoy group by wireless radio.[87]

The *Xarifa* started out from the lightship around noon, three hours ahead of the convoy. With the tug of the observation balloon overhead holding her back, her speed through the water was limited. Her orders were to steam with the convoy until it was too dark to continue or the convoy's ships had passed her and crossed the horizon.[88]

By three o'clock that afternoon, the ships were even farther out to sea.[89] With HMS *Otranto*, under Captain Davidson, leading one of the columns, they moved in a formation of six columns, three cable lengths apart, with each shipmaster keeping a uniform distance from the other ships and staying in line with his column.[90] The HX-50 convoy—carrying more than 18,343 American enlisted men, 568 US Army officers, and thousands of British sailors and ship's officers—was on its way. Just to the *Otranto*'s left was HMS *Kashmir*. The rest were in the order shown in table 3.2.[91]

As previously mentioned, the convoy was surrounded by their screening escort ships: the USS *Louisiana*, USS *St. Louis*, and the USS *Dorsey*.[92] Twelve of the troop transports were British, and one, the *La Lorraine*, was French. All were bound for Liverpool except the *Briton*,

Table 3.2

Column 1		*Plassy*	SS *Saxon*
		(P&O)	(Union Castle)
		1,320 troops	1,454 troops
Column 2		SS *Oxfordshire*	SS *Briton*
		(Bibby)	(Union Castle)
		1,403 troops	1,825 troops
Column 3		*City of York*	SS *Kashmir*
		(Ellerman)	(P&O)
		1,530 troops	2,063 troops
Column 4	SS *La Lorraine*	SS *Teuger*	HMS *Otranto*
	(French)	(Blue Funnel)	(P&O, convoy commodore)
	179 Troops	2,024 troops	701 troops
Column 5		SS *Rhesus*	SS *Oriana*
		(Blue Funnel)	(PSN Co.)
		1,311 troops	857 troops
Column 6		SS *Orantes*	SS *Scotian*
		(P&O)	(Allan)
		1,836 troops	2,410 troops

Saxon, and *Plassy*, which were destined for Glasgow. The SS *La Lorraine* was scheduled to leave the convoy on September 26 and take a southern course directly to Europe.[93, 94] As a naval officer recounted later,

> As the group, with its ocean escort of one destroyer and three cruisers, left the lightship, the destroyer *Perkins* of the coastal escort ranged out to starboard of the group at the head of the column. Farther back, on the right flank was the submarine chaser 52-58-89. The left flank of the column, the shore side, was guarded by the S.C. 57-61-88. The submarine chasers kept on with the group until they reached the 100-fathom curve, where they turned back. [Only] the *Perkins* accompanied the convoy throughout the night and [it] turned back to port at daylight [of] the following morning.[95]

Several airplanes accompanied the convoy for some distance out to sea.[96] Then, as the convoy left its last fixed checkpoint behind—the Nantucket Lightship—Captain Davidson received an urgent message that two German submarines might be in the convoy's path. He had to make a decision.[97, 98]

While his convoy would follow a route very similar to those of the first troop convoys of the war, he had some choices. The western terminus—called "Position 1"—of his convoy lane was positioned about 250 miles east of the American coastline. His first task was to lead his ships on a direct line from New York Harbor to this position. From there, the convoy lane proceeded across mid-ocean, through at least one more fixed position, to a final position that served as the eastern terminus of the convoy lane. This fixed position was considerably west of the actual war zone. Thus, from a navigational perspective, the next position through which Davidson's HX-50 convoy must pass after Position 1—no matter how much zigzagging he ordered or how often—was the rendezvous point north of Ireland where the convoy would meet the destroyers sent out to meet them. Thus, the decision to be made was what route to take from Position 1, a more direct route or a great, circular northern route, then east until they reached the destroyer rendezvous point designated by the Admiralty in London and wired to Davidson four or five days before the HX-50 convoy sailed. Convoy lanes were usually off the regular shipping routes, going through parts of the ocean normally deserted. These lanes were sixty miles wide to allow for zigzagging and other maneuvers by the ships within it.[99]

Davidson considered the situation, consulted with his navigation officer, and then ordered a signal hoisted directing the convoy to take the predetermined northern course.[100] While his decision meant that the ships would have to deal with the treacherous weather typical of the North Atlantic at that time of year, such difficulty was preferred to the possibility of losing thousands of troops to submarines.[101] The submarine threat was serious, as Germany was determined to sink as much Allied shipping as it could to deny the British people food, weapons, and the raw materials needed to maintain their war industries.[102]

Once the convoy crossed over the edge of the continental shelf—that region where the sea floor dropped from about six hundred to thousands of feet in depth—it entered one of the most dangerous areas for German submarines.[103] So, as an added precaution, Captain Davidson ordered the convoy to begin zigzagging, the maneuver by which ships would proceed along a given course for a certain period, then change to another course, and then another, at predetermined intervals.[104]

Rules for zigzagging were detailed in a lead-weighted volume (for easy disposal), titled *War Instructions for United States Merchant Vessels*. It contained illustrated "directions for thirty-three standard zigzags," each numbered so that a convoy commander could throw a formation into a zigzag by simply signaling the pattern number. Typically, the speed and composition of the convoy's ships were taken into account, with the pattern selected based on whether the ships were operating in submarine-infested waters.[105] There was a skilled preciseness to this process. As one naval historian wrote,

> Every American ship that ran in the convoys was equipped with a zigzag clock, a chronometer with electrical contact pins set around the dial so the minute hand would touch them in passing and close an electric circuit that rang a small bell.
>
> The master of the ship could set his clock for any desired zigzag by screwing in pins at their proper minute holes. The clocks of a group were synchronized so that all the turning bells would ring on the second, notifying the helmsman [in each ship] simultaneously to make the turn.[106]

As a general rule, "the shorter the zigzag legs and more abrupt the turns, the more protective they were." But the shorter zigzag legs were usually reserved for use in only the most dangerous waters because the mean distance gained by such a course was much shorter.[107]

HX-designated convoys—such as Captain Davidson's HX-50—which sailed every eight days, were expected to cover three hundred miles per day. So, more often than not, their zigzag legs were long with less abrupt turns.[108]

To further confound any submarine commander who might be trying to track the convoy, soldiers and sailors were under strict orders *never* to throw anything overboard. Because such items could become a trail for submariners to follow, any soldier or sailor seen throwing anything overboard was subject to immediate arrest. Trash was always placed in containers whose contents were regularly emptied and delivered to the ship's fire room to be burned.[109]

A similar precaution was taken for smoking. The men could smoke on the open deck during the day but were prohibited from smoking at night. As one naval officer cautioned at the time, "[At night,] the glow of a cigarette can be seen at a distance of a half mile." Davidson and his crew wanted HMS *Otranto* and the other ships of the convoy to be as invisible as possible at night.[110]

Once the convoy was out in the open sea, the men—who surely discussed the 1912 sinking of the *Titanic* and the possibility of seeing icebergs themselves—were kept busy learning how to break down and clean their rifles, participating in cleanup details, serving on lookout teams, and making sure that all the ship's "retch buckets" remained empty and clean.[111]

4

PRELUDE TO DISASTER

SEASICKNESS

The HX-50 convoy was barely clear of land when difficulties began. Encountering strong winds from the northwest, heavy seas, and poor visibility, Cpt. Ernest Davidson was forced to reduce speed from fourteen to ten knots to keep the convoy together. Then, conditions for the men below deck—difficult under the best of circumstances—turned truly hellish as the pitching of the ships caused most of them to become violently seasick.[1]

To the few who were not affected, it was a joking matter, but the victims found their plight anything but humorous. The soldiers' nausea was such that just the sight of food—typically "mutton, fish, cheese, white bread, and black tea"—mixed with the smell of the phenol and retch buckets in the close quarters, made them want to vomit.[2] The ill appeared exhausted with bloated features, and their skin took on a slight greenish-yellow hue. When asked, one soldier replied that he "felt like hell and wouldn't mind if the damned ship sank and ended all [his] misery."[3]

The seasickness seemed to help spread influenza among the troops. Pvt. Lonzon Sheley remembered that a company of English marines aboard had already made one or more transatlantic trips, and even they "could not stand the shimmy of the old boat" and "fed the fish." He remarked that the men's continuous vomiting weakened them so much that many could barely make it to sick bay, which is where they were "when the crisis came."[4]

ENTERTAINMENT AT SEA

In an effort to bolster the morale of the troops, the two YMCA officers set up a projector and showed movies in a dining salon, played music on a phonograph, and distributed books and magazines among the men. When Lt. Samuel E. Levy learned that there were several musicians with instruments among his contingent, he asked them to practice and play a couple of concerts. The men enjoyed these enormously, but Levy's plans for more were interrupted when the musicians became ill.[5] However, those who were not sick appreciated these efforts to help them pass the time.

As for the men aboard HMS *Kashmir*–steaming alongside the *Otranto*–their only entertainment was provided by some of the African American soldiers aboard. Several formed a musical group, and accompanied by a banjo, "they sang and danced for tips for money to patronize the canteen."[6] Unfortunately, as with those aboard HMS *Otranto*, seasickness and influenza soon put an end to their efforts.

The healthy men were content to find some secluded space, out of the wind and weather, where they could relax without being bothered. Often, however, just as one would find a nice comfortable spot, a British sailor would come along and say, "You'll 'ave to move along soldier. Y'ere roight in our wye." Then there was nothing left to do but roam the ship or look out to sea for a school of porpoises or flying fish. Thus, for those still healthy, the early stage of the voyage was somewhat monotonous.[7]

COLLISION WITH THE *CROISINE*

Six days and six nights passed—nights when the sky and sea merged in a deep blackness—as the *Otranto*, the *Kashmir*, and the rest of the convoy's ships sailed eastward amid the mist and fog with their lights out. Then, at 9:30 p.m. on Tuesday, October 1, with the convoy sailing through high westerly winds but smooth seas, its course suddenly crossed that of twenty-two large French fishing boats loaded with dried cod.[8] The French fishermen were homeward bound after fishing along the Grand Banks. As luck would have it, all the convoy's ships passed safely through the fishing boats except HMS *Otranto*.[9]

Rick Hollingsworth of Sylvania, Georgia, recalled that it was a "black, foggy night," and the fishermen, also fearful of being targeted by German U-boats, were running without lights too.[10, 11] Considering the circumstances, it was a miracle that only one of the fishing boats, the *Croisine*, was struck.

The *Croisine* was a three-masted schooner that had spent the fishing season off Labrador. The ship and its thirty-six-man crew had left their home port in Saint-Malo, France, on March 26; stopped in Lisbon, Portugal, to take on salt; and proceeded on April 30 to the North Atlantic fishing grounds. Then, four months later, in late September, with 338,000 cod in its hold, the *Croisine* and a number of her sister fishing boats began the long trip home to Brittany.[12] They were headed east, like the HX-50 convoy, when their journey home was abruptly interrupted by HMS *Otranto*'s ramming them off Newfoundland at 48°N, 36°W.[13]

At the time, many of the soldiers on the *Otranto* were watching movies in the salon when they felt a sudden jolt as the ship momentarily lifted, then fell and moved ahead.[14, 15] The soldiers and British sailors scrambled out onto the deck just as the masts and yards of a sailing vessel swept by along the port side, taking all the *Otranto*'s lifeboats and davits in that area with them.[16]

Captain Davidson immediately stopped the *Otranto* and passed an order for the rest of the convoy to go on at half speed until they were clear of the fishing fleet and then to proceed on the predetermined course. Once the rest of the convoy had passed, he watched as a crew member used a searchlight to locate and examine the damaged vessel.[17] One of the ship's officers remembered, "This was a risky thing to do, for the glare was sure to advertise our presence to any enemy ships or submarines" that might be in the vicinity.[18]

Once they located the *Croisine*, the *Otranto*'s officers could see that she had been rammed in the side and that her spars were broken and swung around. The badly damaged vessel was now drifting to the stern and off the portside of the *Otranto*.[19] Lonzon Sheley recounted that he had just climbed into his hammock when he heard a crash. Thinking they had been torpedoed, he jumped out and, as instructed during their lifeboat drills, went to his assigned lifeboat. There he was told that they had rammed a fishing boat.[20]

With HMS *Otranto*'s engines throttled down, Captain Davidson ordered the ship's emergency boat to be lowered and instructed its crew to seek out and pick up any fishermen who might have been thrown into the water.[21] As the searchlight picked out the outline of the *Croisine* in the distance, Davidson could see men excitedly running about. The two vessels then slowly drifted out of hearing range just as the *Otranto*'s boat was lowered over her side.

Lt. F. R. O'Sullevan was in charge of the rescue crew.[22] He and his men rowed over to the *Croisine* in a light swell as Davidson and everyone aboard watched and waited. Soon, the creaking of oarlocks could again be heard in the darkness, and O'Sullevan shouted his assessment of the situation to Davidson on the bridge. Realizing that leaving the French fishermen aboard the seriously damaged, sinking boat would doom them to drowning in the cold North Atlantic water, Davidson directed O'Sullevan to return to the *Croisine* and bring her thirty-seven man crew back to the *Otranto*.[23]

Considering what had occurred, the *Otranto* would have made an easy target for any lurking submarine, had one been in the vicinity. She was drifting with her engines off—except when she turned them on occasionally to keep near the *Croisine*—and her searchlights could be seen for miles. The muted conversations of the crew focused on the possibility of being torpedoed.[24]

Soon the rescue party returned to the *Otranto* with the *Croisine*'s crew. It brought thirty-six crewmen aboard along with their captain, Jules Lehoerff, and his beautiful Newfoundland dog. The dog stayed at Lehoerff's side, and in conversation, some of the fishermen related that the dog had saved several lives back in France and had been awarded a medal for heroism from the French government.

To the American soldiers, Lehoerff had a striking appearance, as one later wrote, "much like the old-time sailor one reads about in stories of the days of sail: a huge, rather grizzled man wearing a full beard."[25] A. B. Campbell, one of HMS *Otranto*'s officers remembered,

> The shipwrecked men were huddled together on our deck. They were scared nearly out of their lives. Some fell on their knees and seemed to beg for mercy.
>
> None of us could make out what language the castaways were talking. French, German, Spanish were tried on them, but they shook their heads. 'Excuse me, sir,' said a quartermaster to me. 'Them blokes seem to be slingin' the same lingo as our Jock Ferguson and Bill Mackay use when they're yarnin' private.'
>
> 'Fetch one of those men along—or both!' I said.

Jock Ferguson was available. He was a Royal Fleet Reserve man, in pre-War days a fisherman in the Orkneys. He had little difficulty in making the shipwrecked men understand him, for they were Breton fishermen, and Jock's Gaelic was akin to their speech.

All of the crew of the fishing-vessel were saved. They had been fishing off the cod banks, and, as is their custom . . . had turned in at sunset with all the lights dowsed. Well off the track even of fishing craft, they had felt quite safe. The collision had badly holed their bark. It had been filling rapidly when they took to their one lifeboat.[26]

With his own men and the French crew now safely aboard, Captain Davidson ordered his gun crews to sink the now derelict *Croisine* as she was a menace to navigation. The gun crews on the forward end and on the starboard side started shelling her. The first shots fell short and long, for the *Croisine* presented a somewhat difficult target in the light swell of the sea. Then, soon enough, the gunners found their range, and shells began decimating the boat's wooden hull.

About twenty-five shells were fired in all, leaving the boat burning fiercely, lighting up the whole sky with red and gold flames. The *Croisine* also had a 3-inch gun aboard, so when the flames reached its ammunition, a series of explosions flung pieces of the boat and a shower of sparks high into the night sky.[27] For the soldiers lining the *Otranto*'s railings, it was a sight they would never forget. As one remarked, "It was *some* scene of explosions. Looked like a tri-state fair fireworks."[28]

At 2:20 a.m. on October 2, satisfied that the *Croisine* was sinking fast and would no longer pose a hazard to other ships, Davidson ordered the *Otranto* to get underway and proceed at full speed to catch up with the convoy many miles ahead to the east. Plowing through the worsening weather conditions and now stormy seas, they finally caught up at daybreak and were back in position by noon.[29]

INFLUENZA STRIKES!

By the next evening, the American soldiers aboard HMS *Otranto* were feeling a bit uneasy.[30] Pvt. Leholmes Wells recalled that as he lay in his bunk that night, he and many of the other soldiers were beginning to think the *Otranto* was jinxed. The boat smelled like cow manure, they were thousands of miles from home, the sick bay was full of men with influenza, and having seen the other ships flying their flags at half mast after burying soldiers at sea, the ramming of the fishing boat seemed to top off the reasons for feeling depressed.[31]

The weather grew stormy with a hard-blowing wind and driving rain from the southwest as the American troops—now sealed below decks—became increasingly miserable. Most were still severely seasick and could not go topside to throw up over the rail. Conditions turned hellish with the men vomiting all over the floor near where they all ate and slept.[32] Pvt. Edgar A. Sheperd wrote some years later that a British sailor on watch was washed overboard and that conditions below deck were so bad that an American soldier became severely depressed, went topside, and jumped off an upper deck into the ocean, but his recollections are not substantiated by the historical record.

During a brief lull in the storm, it was reassuring for the crew to finally see ships in positions around them again, but by then, the *Otranto*'s officers realized that they had yet another battle on their hands: influenza. In late 1918, a deadly new strain of the virus was sweeping across the world like a tidal wave, and it now stalked the men and crew of every ship in the convoy. Medical facilities aboard each ship began filling with men afflicted with the most lethal strain of influenza ever known.[33]

Referred to as "wrestler's fever" by the Japanese and "sand fly fever" by the Italians, the name "Spanish Flu" stuck because Spanish authorities were among the first to divulge casualty figures to the world press. During the summer of 1918, approximately 8 million Spaniards caught the new form of influenza.[34]

Many of the men in the convoy had become infected during their training. One camp after another—Camp Kearny in California, Camp Johnson in Florida, Camp Lee in Virginia, Camp McClelland in Alabama, Camp Sevier in South Carolina, Fort Oglethorpe in Georgia—were all hard hit in mid-1918 with this virulent flu strain.[35]

The pandemic struck America in three waves: the first, from March to August 1918, was mild compared to the second and third; the second, and most lethal, wave lasted from August until mid-November 1918; and the third wave, "milder than the second but deadlier than the first," struck in late 1918. The virus finally dissipated during the spring of 1919.[36]

It was a devastating event in American history, as 43,000 American soldiers and 607,000 civilians died from the Spanish Flu during this time.[37] And, globally, the numbers are even more horrific as epidemiologists now believe that this highly contagious virus killed 50 to 100 million people worldwide during this period.[38]

Just as they worried that family members back home might be contracting and dying of the virus, the men aboard HMS *Otranto* and throughout the convoy were now encountering influenza during its last phase. The illness struck suddenly; victims would find themselves strangely exhausted, suffering with headaches, a high fever, a dry cough, and a sore throat, along with congestion and severe body aches.[39] Unfortunately, men who contracted the virus were contagious before the symptoms manifested themselves, and they stayed contagious until all the symptoms disappeared. Even if the soldier survived, he usually required care for another week or two.[40, 41]

It was a sad and difficult situation, for the overcrowded training camps served as an ideal breeding ground. When the second wave of the pandemic hit with the lethal, deadlier strain of the disease, the results were horrific. Doctors and nurses worked around the clock tending to thousands of men who were in a ghastly condition. Many died, sometimes within only twenty-four hours of falling ill, gasping for breath with bloody foam erupting from their noses and mouths, their skin turning blue-black from lack of oxygen.[42] A doctor treating soldiers at an army post wrote home to a friend in September 1918 his observation that his patients rapidly developed a viscous pneumonia that—within two hours of admission—left them with mahogany spots on their cheeks, as cyanosis began near their ears and then spread over their faces. Then, in just a matter of a few more hours, the men suffocated and died. He conveyed the emotional impact on the medical staff with the comment, "It is horrible, as one can stand to see one, two or twenty men die, but . . . we have been averaging about 100 deaths per day."[43]

Doctors were shocked by what autopsies revealed. Instead of lightweight lungs with some slight damage, they confronted "dense masses of flesh, soaked like wet sponges with [a] frothy, blood-stained fluid . . . [that] had replaced the oxygen in the soldiers' lungs."[44] Patients bled from their ears and coughed so hard that they tore abdominal muscles and rib cartilage. Nothing could be done; doctors could only stand by and watch helplessly as the men writhed in agony. Some who survived described headaches so severe that "it was as if someone were hammering a wedge into their skulls behind their eyes" and they "had body aches so intense they felt like [their] bones [were] breaking."[45] Victims drowned in the liquid that filled their lungs while their bodies battled the influenza virus and pneumonia.

During September and October 1918, 17,000 men were stricken at Fort Devens, Massachusetts, and of these, 787 died. Then, as a second generation of the virus spread through the Northeast and mid-Atlantic states—the region stretching from New Hampshire to Virginia—twelve thousand more died during the single month of September 1918.[46] It was a nightmarish time.

Whole families died, and children were orphaned in hours as first one parent, then the other passed away. In Philadelphia, while HMS *Otranto* was at sea, the influenza virus spread uncontrolled. On the single day of October 10, 1918, 759 men, women, and children died in that city from influenza and influenza-related pneumonia. A medical student at the University of Pennsylvania trying to assist in an overwhelmed hospital was horrified by the "dreadful business" of the dying process, noting, like the army doctor mentioned above, that patients' "lungs filled [with fluid and they] became short of breath and increasingly cyanotic." Then, after gasping for breath for hours, they would become delirious and incontinent, eventually dying as they struggled to "clear their airways of a blood-tinged froth that sometimes gushed from their nose and mouth."[47]

Thus was the nature of the beast stalking the men and crew of HMS *Otranto* and the other ships of the HX-50 convoy. The medical staff aboard the *Otranto* and other ships had known that an influenza outbreak was possible since a number of military training camps had just recently been placed under quarantine. And nationwide, concern that the epidemic was getting out of control was so great that the October 1918 draft—scheduled to call up another 142,000 men—was cancelled. So many soldiers were already ill and so many had died that exposing thousands of new recruits to the virus was considered too deadly a risk.[48] In many of the cities back home, embalmers were in short supply, and undertakers had run out of coffins. In cities throughout the country, bodies had begun to rot in overwhelmed mortuaries. To make matters worse, the virus had decimated police, nurses, firemen, and other professionals and emergency service workers, making the process of getting civic help even more difficult.[49]

Now, with nearly nineteen thousand American soldiers and nearly four thousand British sailors packed aboard the thirteen HX-50 troopships, the virus was spreading and infecting not only the American troops but the British officers, marines, and other crew members as well. They were sailing during the time that 30 to 40 percent of the pandemic deaths occurred, between mid-September 1918 and early December.[50] As the influenza cases multiplied, Captain Davidson had no choice but to turn the *Otranto*'s main dining room into a hospital; American officers assigned the men in the "casual companies," those due for court-martial, the duty of cleaning the latrines and medical areas.[51]

Official reports later indicated that there were more than one hundred severe cases of influenza aboard HMS *Otranto* alone and that this number was probably only a percentage of the actual total since her sister ship, HMS *Kashmir*, steaming nearby, had several hundred cases.[52] Within just a few days, thousands of the men aboard the various convoy troopships were gravely ill. Medical doctors on each vessel were overwhelmed as they tried to differentiate those stricken with influenza from those who were violently seasick. Extra sick bays were created wherever there was space, and privates were detailed to act as attendants, or orderlies.[53]

On the same day that the *Otranto* was racing to overtake its convoy, October 2, 1918, the first influenza-related death occurred aboard ship. Pvt. Lonnie L. Smith, in Unit 2 of Fort Screven's group of September Automatic Replacement Draft soldiers, died from influenza-related pneumonia. His body, which was kept until the following day, was gently sewn into a canvas body bag and then draped with an American flag.[54] Mr. C. A. Carpenter of the YMCA assisted Lt. C. D. Simmons in conducting Smith's service, which was brief but impressive. As the service began, Smith's body was brought out and placed on deck near the forward end of the *Otranto*'s port side. British sailors hauled the Union Jack halfway down in his honor, and Captain Davidson ordered the ship's engines to be throttled down to almost zero. After the short service, "Taps" was sounded by the *Otranto*'s bugler, a detail fired three rifle volleys, and with most of the soldiers and ship's crew looking on, Smith's body was then dropped over the side.[55]

One of the ship's officers, A. B. Campbell, recounted of Smith's and other funerals at sea, "It was ghastly to see the corpse, unstiffened from being so recently dead, slide off the gratings. They would double as they fell, and, instead of plunging smoothly into the deep, [they would] hit the surface with a resounding thwack."[56]

A sad postscript to this event occurred after the war: in June 1921, Pvt. Lonnie L. Smith's family in Quitman, Georgia, received a body, which they were told and assumed was that of their son. Not knowing the details of Smith's death and burial at sea, they reverently interred the body in their family plot only to learn, two months later, that it belonged to another soldier with the identical name. The other Lonnie L. Smith, a member of Company F, 6th Ammunition Train, had died in France of pneumonia on October 9, 1918.[57] The family was quite understandably heartbroken when, in October 1921, a War Department special agent, D. H. Rhodes, arrived to disinter and claim the body.

Rhodes retrieved the body, the aluminum strip that had been removed from the lid of the casket, and the American flag that had been presented to the family at the time of the funeral. Then, on October 11, 1921, he traveled with the body, flag, and casket plate to Greenville, North Carolina, where he was met by several members of the soldier's family, who accompanied him and the body to the soldier's home. The following day, Rhodes attended the soldier's funeral held in nearby Chicod, North Carolina, amid a large gathering of relatives and friends.

Agent Rhodes's report of this sad incident and his notes on his discussions with family members of the two soldiers are all located in the US National Archives.[58] One of the archival files there contains a carbon copy of the letter, dated August 9, 1920, notifying the Georgia family, erroneously sent the wrong body, which they buried as their beloved son, of what actually happened to him:

> There is no grave location on file in this office for your son who is shown by the records of the Adjutant General's Office as having died on board the Steamship *Otranto* and was buried at sea previous to the sinking of that vessel. . . . In all probability, therefore, there will never be a grave location for your son recorded in this Office inasmuch as he was buried at sea.[59]

From the day that Private Smith was buried at sea, doctors aboard HMS *Otranto* battled the flu while the officers and crew contended with a worsening storm that battered the ship about with heavy seas and blowing gales. On Friday, October 4, as scheduled, the USS *Louisiana* left the convoy for home, followed by the USS *St. Louis* the following night.[60]

An officer aboard HMS *Otranto* later wrote that there was not a single day—after being two or three days out—that at least one of the ships in the convoy did not ask to reduce speed for a burial service.

When a ship lost a man, its captain would order that a red flag be raised at the vessel's stern.[61] Soon, nearly every ship was flying a flag at half mast since, by then, "thousands lay ill in holds converted into emergency sick bays, while many more, unnoticed by the busy doctors, lay untended on deck all the way across."[62]

Doctors aboard their sister ship, HMS *Kashmir*, were so overwhelmed that they could not accept a man for treatment unless his fever had reached 104 degrees. Those meeting the stringent criteria were hospitalized in the after-end sick bay of the ship in space originally allocated to the African American soldiers. The storekeeper aboard HMS *Kashmir* later wrote,

> Many of the troops got wet, and then they got colds, after which influenza set in and it spread all over the ship. . . . We could do nothing about it.
>
> At one time there was a queue of dead soldiers waiting to be buried, in fact the American padre could not leave his position on the gun-platform, he was too busy.
>
> It turned out that we were not the only ship in trouble, as when a body was dropped over the side the flag at the stern was dipped . . . and stern flags all around on other ships were being dipped with a sad regularity.[63]

In one unverified story, an American sergeant with the Headquarters Company of the 126th Field Artillery from Fort Screven recounted that when he had a high-enough fever to be admitted to the hospital, he crawled in on his hands and knees. However, after he returned to his fellow soldiers, he stated that soon after he was admitted, the hospital staff had laid him out on a mess table with another soldier—an African American—who was also very ill. He said that his legs straddled one of the other man's, so that they would each have enough room to rest his head on an end of the table. When he awakened out of a half-delirious doze and glanced down toward his feet at the other soldier, he saw two eyes staring glassily back and realized that the young African American had died. Then, as he looked around for a doctor, the sergeant saw another dead soldier on a wooden bench to his right and yet another on the table just to his left. This was too much for his nerves, so he told his friends, "I'd rather take my chances up here."[64] The records, however, do not reflect these deaths due to influenza.

Still, the extent of the influenza outbreak among the ships of the convoy was so bad that the captain of one, HMS *City of York*, in an effort to save twenty-eight soldiers aboard who were on the verge of death, diverted course just so he could land at Belfast instead of Liverpool. While there, he also unloaded the bodies of several other soldiers who had died during the previous few days so that they could be buried on land. The dying soldiers, along with others less ill, were sent ashore immediately and hospitalized. Unfortunately, of the twenty-eight, seventeen died within just a few days.[65] The *City of York*'s situation was likely similar to that of every other ship in the HX-50 convoy. A historian at Yale University was to write after the war,

> Thirty-eight troopships carried nearly 130,000 men across the ocean during the epidemic. The scenes aboard some of these vessels helped to make this phase the most terrible of the whole undertaking. Nearly 15,000 cases of influenza and pneumonia developed during the voyages. Nearly 3,000 sick men were removed from our transports at Halifax. Several hundred died there, and several hundred others died in France after being carried ashore, moribund. It is conservative to estimate that the influenza at sea cost, altogether, 2,000 lives. Many of the victims were buried at sea.[66]

The situation was no better back home. In Savannah, Georgia, near the *Otranto* soldiers' home base of Fort Screven, influenza had become epidemic. By mid-October, the city's hospitals were overflowing with more than twenty-five hundred active cases and many deaths.[67]

Aboard HMS *Kashmir*, having heard that lemons were helpful to seasick men, the chaplain of the 126th had brought a crate full of them aboard. Then, as the men became ill, he began cutting them up and offering slices to those most in need. The men were eager to try anything—effective or not—to help their condition. Soon, however, with his supply being scant, his slices became thinner and thinner, until he could give what he had left to only the worst cases.[68]

Meanwhile, back aboard the *Otranto*, during the evening of October 5, Pvt. Benton Edenfield of Screven County, Georgia, died of influenza. Because there is no record indicating that he and other recent casualties were buried at sea, his body was likely still aboard the next day when disaster overtook the ship.[69]

The official records in the US National Archives may be inaccurate in terms of influenza casualties tallied, as they do not reflect stories recounted by a number of soldiers about flu-related deaths on the

Otranto. For example, ship's officer A. B. Campbell, who served on that last voyage of the *Otranto*, recounted in his book, *With the Corners Off*,

I was stopped one morning by a gum-chewing dough-boy. 'Say, Cap,' said he (anyone in uniform was 'Cap' to a dough-boy), 'there's a guy been lyin' on the smoke-room floor for three days, and he's never moved.'

'Let's go and look,' I said, and led the way.

In the seats around the lounge and on the deck soldiers in number sprawled in the misery of sea-sickness or the first onset of the epidemic malady. Over by the piano one man lay face downward, his hands stretched out under the instrument. I stooped and caught hold of his legs to pull him clear.

At the first grasp of his limbs a faint nausea gripped me, for they were stiff and leaden. I dragged him out and turned him over.

Glazed eyes stared up at me. The dead wrists had been gnawed by rats.[70]

5

COLLISION WITH THE *KASHMIR*

THE STORM INTENSIFIES—WHERE ARE WE?

Sailing the North Atlantic in the middle of hurricane season has always been a dangerous endeavor, and the early-morning hours of Sunday, October 6, found Cpt. Ernest Davidson and the HX-50 convoy battling a massive storm with Force 11 winds and poor visibility. Large patches of sea foam were being driven before the mountainous waves. As crewman Angus McNeil recounted, "The wind increased to a hurricane blowing from the northwest, [and] the sea was mountains high, [with] spray and sleet making visibility very poor."[1, 2]

Even the color of the water changed. An American soldier, David Roberts, remembered, "The waves were like mountains . . . and when I went on deck, the sea was grass green—formerly it had been bluish black—just like the Kentucky mountains. We were like a train going [down] into the valley."[3]

The storm forced three of the convoy's ships out of formation, and they were nowhere to be seen. HMS *Otranto*'s sister ship, HMS *Kashmir*, had moved closer and was now only about a quarter mile off the *Otranto*'s starboard bow.[4, 5] Meanwhile, the ship's crew was battling waves that bashed everything about in the cook's galleys and carried every bit of loose gear off the decks. For the soldiers below, the voyage had turned into a nightmare that would soon become even worse. As one wrote later, "It seemed . . . as though no vessel could survive a storm of such fierceness."[6] Pvt. Lonzon Sheley remembered that because the storm was so bad, the men could not go topside to vomit, so they used tubs that—due to the rocking of the ship—soon overturned and made the floors slippery. Then, "tapioca pudding helped put the finishing touch to the slipperiness; one by one the men gave up and went to the hospital." Thus, many of Sheley's comrades were in sick bay on Sunday morning.[7]

As the ill men wondered in their influenza-induced delirium and seasickness if the voyage would ever end, Captain Davidson and other ship's officers throughout the HX-50 convoy worried how far they had been blown off their intended course. Because of the rough weather, navigation officers had not been able to take the necessary observations needed to determine their position accurately. As a result, they could only make an educated guess as to where they were.[8]

Thus, as the convoy approached the northern coasts of Ireland and Scotland, now believed to be only a few hundred miles to the east, Captain Davidson was proceeding by dead reckoning. It was a nervous time: not only were they taking a terrific pounding from the weather, but they were receiving wireless radio messages that U-boats were lurking near the Irish coast, and they still had not seen the British destroyers that were supposed to meet them two hundred miles out and guide them into port.[9, 10] Their screening ships were gone, too, as the battleship USS *Louisiana* had turned back for home on Friday, October 4, followed by the battleship USS *St. Louis* on the following day.[11] Then, on October 6, their last escort ship, the American destroyer USS *Dorsey*, had followed its orders and left the convoy at 6 a.m. to head for the Royal Navy anchorage at Buncrana in northwestern Ireland.[12, 13]

Captain Davidson and the rest of the ship's officers in the convoy did not know that two days before, on October 4, eight British destroyers had indeed been ordered to sea from Buncrana to meet the convoy.[14] However, they, too, had encountered the same ferocious storm as HMS *Otranto*, the *Kashmir*, and the rest of the ships in the convoy. For the safety of their own crews, their commander had decided to turn back and return to sheltered anchorage, where they arrived at 4 a.m. on October 5.[15]

Meanwhile, all through the previous night, the soldiers and crewmen of Convoy HX-50 had had a hard time of it. Hurricane-force winds with spray and sleet continued to make the helmsmen's work difficult, and heavy seas buffeted the ships to the extent that they were now scattered and strung out for miles.[16, 17] Exhausted soldiers and crew members had to hold on to anything they could as the rolling and pitching of

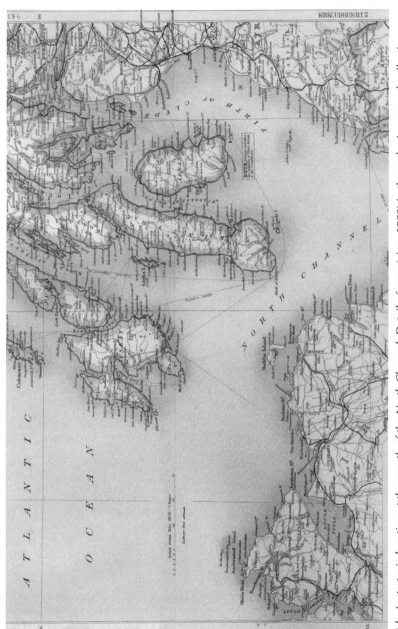

Islay's strategic location at the mouth of the North Channel. Detail of map (circa 1902) in the author's personal collection.

the ships swung their hammocks crazily back and forth with the violent motions of their vessel.[18]

Such were the circumstances that confronted Captain Davidson during the early-morning hours of October 5. He could only continue forward on a course that he hoped would bring them into the North Channel—between Ireland and Scotland—with the next dawn.[19] Sometime after midnight, however, one of the ships, the *Oriana*, reported seeing a light, which its captain thought was a lighthouse on Tory Island, situated just a few miles off the northwest coast of Ireland.[20] The watch on the *Otranto*, however, did not concur—he believed that it was another light, the one at Rinrawras—so the convoy pressed on, trusting that it would not end up on a rocky shore in the darkness.[21]

All that dark, cold, stormy night, whenever the *Otranto* was near enough to another ship, she asked for a firm position, but none of the other ships' officers knew their precise location either. As hour followed hour and the storm increased in intensity, and as the rain squalls combined with mountainous waves breaking over the ships' bows, the situation became even more perilous.[22] It later turned out that the vessels were twenty miles north of their reckoning—dangerous when approaching land at night. Finally, at last, dawn broke on the morning of Sunday, October 6. Charles Von Waldner of Savannah recalled later that there was no thought of having a chapel service as HMS *Otranto* was struggling to make headway against the powerful winds and "the tremendous waves that seemed to throw [the ship] around as though it were nothing more than a rowboat."[23]

It was a truly perilous situation. The formation was scattered and straggling for miles amid eighty- to ninety-mile hurricane-force winds, forty- to sixty-foot waves, all while traveling through haze that "hung heavily . . . [as] spin-drift sprayed the ocean."[24] With the haze, mist, and rain squalls limiting visibility to only a couple of miles, Captain Davidson continued to look for the destroyers that were supposed to take screening stations against any lurking submarines and lead them into friendly waters and port.[25, 26]

THE RAMMING—A TERRIFYING SIGHT

At a little after 8 o'clock on that same morning of Sunday, October 6, just as the mist lifted, a fragment of high, rocky land was sighted only three or four miles to the east, just ahead and to the left of the convoy.[27] The ships, blown twenty miles north of their course, were dangerously near the high cliffs that lined the northwest coast of the island of Islay, the southernmost island of Scotland's Inner Hebrides. The ships' officers, however, were not sure if the cliffs belonged to the western coast of Scotland or the northern coast of Ireland.[28]

Confusion reigned on the bridge of HMS *Otranto*. While officers aboard her sister ship, the *Kashmir*, and the other ships in the convoy correctly guessed the land ahead to be the western coast of Scotland and immediately steered south, to starboard, the officer on watch aboard HMS *Otranto*, only a half mile from the *Kashmir*, believed the land to be the northern coast of Ireland. He quickly dispatched the midshipman of the watch to run and ask Captain Davidson and the navigator—both of whom had just left the bridge for a hasty breakfast—to return immediately and help him ascertain their position. In the meantime, he ordered "a signal hoisted for the convoy to alter course to port" and directed the helmsman to turn the *Otranto* and head north.[29] Unfortunately, this maneuver put her directly in the path of her sister ship, the now oncoming *Kashmir*.

Ship's officer A. B. Campbell later wrote in *With the Corners Off*, "The wind almost blew the signal bunting to shreds. In the bad light, that silver gloom in which colors are so difficult to distinguish, the signal must have been misread aboard the *Kashmir* . . . [because] she altered course to starboard."[30]

Campbell said that he heard two blasts on the ship's siren just as the *Otranto* signaled to the other ships which way she was turning. But, for whatever reason, the *Kashmir* kept on her starboard turn, and as the two ships swung closer, collision became inevitable. When Captain Davidson arrived in the bridge and saw the *Kashmir* coming, he immediately ordered his helmsman to "put hard-a-port, and rang full speed astern on both engines, at the same time giving [another] three short blasts of the siren." By this time, the captains of both vessels realized that their ships were still swinging toward each other, and they tried to maneuver to avert a collision. Unfortunately, each maneuver canceled the other out, and the gap between the ships closed rapidly.[31]

Probably the best perspective on what happened next is the opinion written after the war by the presiding judge of the High Court in

England, Justice Hill, charged with the responsibility of affixing blame for the ensuing disaster:

> There came a time when the *Kashmir*, turning to starboard, was headed for the *Otranto*, turning more slowly to port. When they were in that position most unfortunately each began a change of maneuver. I say began, because, so far as the *Kashmir* was concerned, the change was quickly countermanded.
>
> It came about in this way: The *Otranto* at a late stage observed the *Kashmir* heading for her, and sounded two short blasts, and almost at the same time hard-a-ported and put the port engine full ahead. The two short blasts were heard on board the *Kashmir* and her helm was ordered hard-a-starboard and was actually put over, but immediately the order was changed to hard-a-port again and both engines were reversed. The collision followed soon afterwards.
>
> I am advised that but for these changes of maneuver it is almost certain that the two ships would have swung clear of one another.
>
> The effect of the *Kashmir*'s change of helm must have retarded her swing to starboard. The *Kashmir* ought to have avoided the *Otranto*. It was clear that the *Otranto*'s alteration of helm from starboard to port should have been made sooner. To delay from ignorance of the *Kashmir*'s movements and then to alter his maneuver was to throw the *Otranto* in the way of the *Kashmir* and defeat the *Kashmir*'s maneuver. It is doubly unfortunate that two short blasts should have been sounded, for it was hearing them that led to the *Kashmir* reversing her maneuver.
>
> Upon these conclusions I pronounce both to blame.[32]

At the time, however, with huge waves, high winds, and confusion reigning, it was not so easy for Captain Davidson and his crew to discern what to do. Seeing the *Kashmir* still bearing down on them despite their frantic maneuvers and shrill siren blasts, they could only watch helplessly as the nightmare unfolded. The feelings of the officers aboard the *Kashmir* were surely similar as—even though her captain had ordered them to "reverse engines"—she was still bearing relentlessly down on the *Otranto*.

The *Otranto*'s A. B. Campbell heard the siren warnings, ran out onto a deck, and began walking forward along the starboard side. Along the way he encountered an American soldier carrying a camera who asked, "Say, Cap, will it be all right for me to take a picture of that big ship?" To Campbell's question, "What ship?" the young man replied, "The one that's coming so close—on the other side now." Campbell followed the soldier and recounted later, "As I stepped from the alley-way door to port my heart—I do believe—stood still. For there, on the crest of a huge wave, not twenty feet from the ship's side, was poised the axe-like bow of the *Kashmir*." Then, just as the two ships collided, Campbell grabbed the soldier by the arm and pulled him back with him into the alleyway. Campbell would be haunted for the rest of his life by his memory of what happened next, "The whole ship shuddered as if in the throes of death. With the grinding and crashing of steel plates as they were rent apart, the wrenching of fittings inside the stricken ship, amid that dreadful clamor, were mingled the shrieks of crushed and tortured men below."[33]

At 8:43 a.m. on that cold, stormy Sunday morning, just as the two ships were closing in on each other at right angles, soldiers on the hurricane deck of the *Kashmir* turned and saw the *Otranto* lying, with its port side exposed, in a deep trough of the sea. Then they felt their own boat ride down toward the other ship along the high crest of a mountainous wave.[34] At about the same time, the troops topside on the *Otranto* looked up and saw the *Kashmir* bearing down on them. A score of them had lined up at a canteen amidships when they saw the huge liner appear suddenly. They broke and ran wildly for their lives in opposite directions, but some, not quick enough, were crushed just as a "tremendous wave lifted the *Kashmir* and flung her forward" into the *Otranto*.[35]

The *Kashmir* struck the *Otranto* on her port side, near the hurricane deck between her two funnels at no. 2 hold, just as she was rising out of a trough.[36] Men topside, aboard the *Kashmir*, looking ahead and downward, watched helplessly as they saw and felt their ship smash headlong into the other. Then, suddenly, they heard the hollow, metallic roar of ripping metal as their foredeck smashed its way into the *Otranto*.[37]

The *Kashmir* rammed the *Otranto* mid-ship. With the force of another huge wave pushing her rear upward from a deep trough, the *Kashmir*'s weight shifted forward and plunged her foredeck even further, downward into the stricken *Otranto*. In a matter of moments, the *Kashmir* was knifing even more deeply into the *Otranto*, ripping into her, just below the waterline, and continuing on down until the *Kashmir*'s foredeck was twenty feet into the *Otranto*'s boiler rooms.[38] As the *Kashmir* tore into the *Otranto* between her forward and aft stokeholds, both areas of the *Otranto* were flooded instantly, quickly drowning most of the sailors working in them.[39]

The *Otranto* then rolled into another trough just as another oncoming wave pushed the *Kashmir* back up and out of the gaping hole she had just made.[40] This action enlarged the wound, making a "slit as high as the boat deck, [while] flinging splintered lifeboats aside as a final gesture."[41] The wound in the *Otranto* was now twenty feet deep and sixteen feet across.[42] A member of the ship's crew recounted that after the *Kashmir* had hit them amidships right between the funnels, the *Otranto* heeled over from the impact. Then, he saw the *Kashmir* "jockeying in the trough of the sea with both bows gone and her forward end a tangled mass of steelwork."[43]

Amid the ringing of bells on both ships, the *Kashmir* reversed her engines and drew off, leaving the *Otranto* back down yet another trough, leaning over and looking as though she would never right herself. Finally, after a seemingly interminable time, she slowly and uncertainly came back from her precarious roll.[44, 45]

The *Kashmir* slowly backed away, leaving the *Otranto* dead in the water with a large V-shaped hole starting under her waterline and reaching all the way up to the top of her decks.[46] As she pulled away, soldiers and sailors aboard the *Kashmir* could see men aboard the *Otranto* near the gashed area hanging onto anything they could, while others were being swept into the sea.[47]

All this time an alarm sounded on the *Kashmir*, signaling the soldiers and crew to come topside and report to their lifeboat stations. It was a precarious time as the ship was now sitting lower in the water than she should with huge waves crashing over her damaged bow, and crowds of men running to see what had happened.

A crewman aboard the *Kashmir* remembered, "The sea was like green mountains on each side of us," when suddenly the ship made a tremendous roll; one moment the *Kashmir* was on one side of a wave, and the next she was pointing in the opposite direction. To his surprise, he saw that while the rest of the convoy headed south, their ship was now suddenly steaming north.[48] Their ability to turn a ship so quickly demonstrates the power and intensity of the massive waves and hurricane-strength winds HMS *Otranto* and *Kashmir* were foundering in.

Everyone aboard feared that the *Kashmir* might sink. But after a hurried survey by the ship's officers, her captain determined that—if he moved the troops aft and used their weight to keep the bow up and away from the heavy seas washing over her—he could keep the *Kashmir* afloat and make it to port.[49] The men hung onto anything they could as the ship continued to roll violently. Although they were seasick, frightened, and miserable, their discipline in staying at the rear of the ship enabled the *Kashmir* to survive and continue on to Glasgow.[50]

The last glimpse the men had of the *Otranto* as they looked back was of the huge ship wallowing in the heavy seas, struggling to stay afloat. Then, as the distance between them lengthened and seawater reached the *Otranto*'s boiler room, they saw a huge gush of steam shoot skyward, indicating that the mighty ship was probably in her death throes.[51]

THE BEGINNING OF THE END OF THE *OTRANTO*

Conditions aboard HMS *Otranto* were far worse than those on the *Kashmir*. Even though no submarine could have attacked so disastrously in such stormy weather, when the crash occurred most of the troops below thought the ship had been torpedoed. Others thought that she had been struck broadside by an unusually large wave. Regardless, they all sensed that something out of the ordinary had occurred and immediately headed topside.[52]

Soon word spread that the ship was sinking. Soldiers in some sections panicked and began running along the companionways and shoving their way up ladders to reach the upper decks. Ship's officers shouted orders to the men to stop rushing about, but few paid attention.[53] Pvt. Leholmes Wells of Sylvania, Georgia, recalled that he was on guard near the top deck that morning, and it had still been too dark to see for any distance when the two ships collided. He remembered hearing "a loud thundering, screeching, grinding noise," just before he was thrown against the side of the ship and knocked out. Wells woke up as men stepped on him on their way to their lifeboat stations. He then dragged himself to his feet just as water came rushing down the hallway; he recalled, "It soaked me completely and I realized for the first time, just how cold it was."[54]

Almost immediately after the collision, some of the ship's bulkheads began to give way. As Wells observed, water then began flooding the interior corridors of the ship, pouring through the stokehold and down through the gash below the waterline. Realizing it was imperative to stop the panic and confusion, officers pulled their guns and—as one participant wrote later—"shots were fired among the troops."[55]

Pvt. Lonzon Sheley was in a lavatory, where he was knocked to his knees. Seeing smoke rolling into his area and thinking the ship had been torpedoed, he quickly put his overcoat and life belt back on and ran out into a hallway. There, the crowd of men coming up from below literally picked him up and carried him topside, where he then saw that the ship had been rammed.[56]

Another soldier, Pvt. Joseph E. Hewell, remembered that his group had just finished breakfast—which, because of the way the ship was rocking from side to side, was not an easy task—when they felt "a terrific jar and the ship trembled all over." He rushed toward the stairs only to be told to "be quiet as there was nothing the matter." However, about twenty minutes after the men had returned and sat down, they were ordered to leave all their equipment and personal belongings behind and to report immediately to their lifeboat stations.[57]

A terrifying sight greeted the men as they came topside. Looking up and out, they could still see the *Kashmir* in the distance, riding away on a huge wave, her bow blackened and with a large hole in its front. Then, looking at their own ship, they could see the crushed bulkheads between the forward and aft stokeholds, where the ship's railing was bent inward triangularly until, at the apex, it was broken and hanging. There, many of the lifeboats were severely damaged and dangling by a rope, swinging from one side to the other.[58]

A surviving crewman remembered that as he made his way to his lifeboat station, his group had already arrived, and because the lifeboats on his side were gone, they could do little but wait for orders. He quickly sized up the situation: the *Otranto* "already had a 35-degree list to starboard and was slowly drifting before the southwest gale towards land about 16 miles distant." Further, the *Kashmir* had cut about halfway through the ship, and the *Otranto*'s boiler rooms appeared to be flooded. Then, as he walked back along the deck, he saw that the area of the ship used for sick bay had been hit badly, observing that "sick men had gone out through the hole in the ship's side and what was left was too ghastly to look at."[59]

Soon water was rushing through the gash in the *Otranto*'s side, and as the ship swayed back and forth, it ebbed in and out of the wound that dug eight feet or more into her hull.[60] The situation was dire and about to get worse—much worse. Next the engine room flooded, knocking out the ship's electric generators and lights.[61]

Ship's crewmen rushed to the damaged area with large mats and worked with precise, well-rehearsed teamwork to lower them over the enormous gash to try keep out the inrush of seawater. They soon realized, however, that the wound was too large for their efforts. A few of the surviving engine room crewmen were at that time managing to save themselves by climbing through to the top of the funnel.[62]

Pvt. Lonzon Sheley recounted, "I saw we had been rammed. There was a hole in the *Otranto* [all the way] to the hallway, about one-third through the ship. The wind was blowing at such a rate as to pick up a man and I came very near being blown overboard as I ventured out to see the hole in the side."[63] Joseph E. Hewell's recollection regarding the wind was similar: "When we came out on deck the wind was blowing at the rate of 70-to-75 miles an hour, more or less, [and] a fellow had to hold on to ropes or something to keep from being blown overboard." Hewell and the men around him initially did not know how badly damaged the *Otranto* was; he remarked, "If they had known I am sure there would have been more excitement or panic among the men."[64]

CAPTAIN DAVIDSON CONSIDERS HIS OPTIONS

Davidson immediately ordered his helmsman to turn so that the breach would be on the ship's lee side, but he found that the *Otranto* had lost her steerage and thus turning was impossible.[65] He then conferred with his officers to analyze the situation and develop a plan to save the ship and all those aboard.

With fifty-plus-foot waves and winds gusting at seventy-plus miles per hour, all realized immediately that it would be impossible to launch their lifeboats.[66] Then, looking toward shore, now only a few miles east, Davidson could see the rocky cliffs of the island of Islay, rising high above the water.[67] Scanning the coastline more closely with his binoculars, he was alarmed to see white-topped breakers between the ship and shore—a sure indication that there was a reef just below the surface.

Looking in the other direction, out to sea, Captain Davidson saw that—except for a single troop transport in the distance—they were now alone. However, he knew that even if the other transports were nearby, they could not help as a standing Admiralty order required that—in the event of a disaster—all transport ships must go on and leave rescue work to destroyers. The reason for this order was logical: if a troopship stopped or slowed enough for an enemy U-boat commander to attack it successfully, the result would likely be the loss of many thousands of lives. It was, as ship's officer A. B. Campbell later remarked, a "sanely cruel rule."[68] Unfortunately, there were no destroyers in sight to witness the *Otranto*'s plight and assist.[69]

Still, despite being in the middle of a storm in a region of the world where the waves and winds are among the most dangerous on earth, Captain Davidson and his officers were hopeful; they knew that even if two of the *Otranto*'s compartments became flooded, she would remain afloat.[70]

About that time, the chief engineer came to the bridge and reported that no more than one hundred pounds' pressure remained in the ship's boilers, and even this was decreasing steadily. And while the stokeholds had filled with water, only the engine room was awash so far.[71] He and Lt. F. R. O'Sullevan then suggested that if the bulkheads held, they might be able to keep the *Otranto* afloat long enough for her to be beached on the shore of Islay.[72] As such, they both recommended that Captain Davidson drop the ship's anchor in the hope that they could buy time until the storm's intensity lessened; then they could raise it and ride the currents and waves to shore at a time of their choosing.

The men had barely finished speaking when the sound of tearing metal rose from below deck, and soldiers and sailors came rushing up the ladders.[73] The *Otranto* then gave a great lurch to starboard: "'There go the bulkheads!' said the engineer."[74] Realizing that the boiler rooms were now flooded and that they would be unable to restart the engines, O'Sullevan and the other officers knew then that the game was up. The sinking of the ship was now inevitable.[75]

Soon afterwards all the lights went out for good, and everyone aboard could hear the deafening hiss of escaping steam. Ship's officer A. B. Campbell applauded the bravery of one of the engineers who crawled down into the engine room. Campbell reported that the man's actions "had saved the ship, beyond doubt, from immediate destruction." He had "crawled and swum about the engines, opening and shutting the essential cocks to allow free escape of the steam," and "but for this, the inrush of water to the boilers would have brought an explosion."[76]

With the *Otranto* foundering in the massive waves and high-velocity winds, her engine room flooded and unable to generate steam for propulsion, her situation was slipping quickly toward hopeless. One of the

American soldiers, Pvt. Edgar A. Sheperd, said later that he felt "sorry for the troops who were much older . . . as they were running up and down the deck crying and wringing their hands." Adding an element of uncertainty was the fact that Captain Davidson had ordered an SOS distress signal to be sent out by emergency wireless, but because the ship's dynamos had stopped soon after the crew had extinguished the fires, he was not certain whether the message had been sent successfully or not.[77]

After considering the advice of his officers and observing the subsequent events, Captain Davidson decided that the best tactic was simply to let the *Otranto* drift toward shore. While this would place her at the mercy of the howling winds and treacherous sea, there was a slim chance that such an action might eventually allow the ship to be beached or at least give the men an opportunity to swim to shore.[78]

The hurricane-force winds and massive waves slowly swung the ship around, and soon she was riding parallel with the shore and drifting toward the coast. Meanwhile, soldiers and crewmen remained at their lifeboat stations "like soldiers on parade," awaiting instructions.[79] Men standing on the port side were surely horrified by the wreckage caused by the *Kashmir* and aware that most of their lifeboats were too damaged to be launched. As they were on the ship's windward side, however, they could also see that even if the lifeboats were available, it would be impossible to lower one without the men aboard being crushed by the massive waves pounding the side of the ship.[80]

Pvt. Leholmes Wells remembered that after he arrived at his lifeboat station, he was surprised to find that the lifeboat was gone. He and the other soldiers then tried to stand around the station but found themselves washed about the deck by tremendous waves. Then, soon after an officer came running by yelling, "Men, there's nothing happened. Just be quiet," a ship's crewman stopped and directed them to take off their shoes and wraparound leggings and to tie a rope around themselves.[81]

Men on the starboard side were not much better off as, even if they could launch their lifeboats, they would obviously never survive an attempt to row the short distance to shore in such stormy seas. With each passing minute, more of the men realized that there was nothing left to do but pray and wait as the *Otranto* continued drifting toward the rocky cliffs of Islay, now only a few miles in the distance.

Survivors stated later that at this point, despite the damage and conditions, many of the men still assumed that the situation would end well. And when one remembers that most of these young men were farm boys unfamiliar with the ocean, it is remarkable that more were not more frightened by their plight. Pvt. Edgar A. Sheperd recalled, "We could see the cattle grazing on the island [Islay] and this helped lots of us to gain some hope of making it to land."

While Charles Von Waldner was impressed by "the comparative calmness with which the men took their places awaiting orders," he was dismayed by the loss of one of his close friends, William E. Gene Warth, son of Professor Warth of Savannah. They had been assigned to the same raft, and after a crew member told them to find a piece of rope to tie themselves to their raft to avoid being swept out into the open sea when their strength gave out, Warth was swept overboard by one of the huge waves breaking over the ship.[82]

Just a short time later, the force of the waves forced HMS *Otranto* into a listing position to her starboard. The men moved in small groups around the decks, seeking shelter, mostly in the lee of the cabins while the clouds overhead blew wildly past. Occasionally, they would briefly glimpse the sun breaking through, while the wind howled unnervingly. The ship rose and fell, and with each crest, the men looking out to sea could see only lines of huge waves stretching endlessly to the horizon like ridges between the furrows of a wide, plowed field.

While the American soldiers waited silently, hoping and praying for help to arrive, the *Otranto*'s British crewmen knew more fully just how bad the circumstances were. Survivors remembered seeing some of them with tears rolling unashamedly down their cheeks.[83] One crewman, when asked what he thought of the situation, replied, "I think that it looks pretty damned rotten." It would soon become apparent to the Americans aboard as well just how dire the circumstances were.

As HMS *Otranto* continued to drift closer to the shore, some of the American officers, aided by a few enlisted men, went below deck to try to get the sick soldiers still alive out of their quarters. They wrapped them in blankets and then helped them climb the steps and ladders to come topside. They hoped that this might give them a better chance of survival if the ship went down. Exactly when that time might come, no one knew, but with the ship continuing to fill with water and listing more sharply, it was apparent to Captain Davidson, all his crew, and the

American soldiers still aboard that sinking was probably the *Otranto*'s inevitable outcome.

At this time, one of the more horrific events occurred. According to ship's officer A. B. Campbell, although many of the soldiers were standing by their lifeboat stations in a disciplined manner, one of the American officers was exhibiting great distress. He did not know how to swim and had been going from one ship's officer to another, asking what he should do if the ship started sinking. Campbell remembered, "One after another of the officers had assured him quietly that the lifebelt he was wearing would keep him afloat for many hours." Unfortunately, their assurances were of no comfort as he then bitterly complained about the coldness of the water. Campbell remembered, "I myself had just left him with an encouraging word when a revolver-shot rang out." Then, as Campbell turned to see what had happened, he saw the young officer running about in circles, screaming. He had tried to blow out his brains but had managed only to take off a portion of the side of his head. His screams were awful and caused the soldiers to panic. "Word of the tragedy went along the line of patient soldiers like an electric wave. For a moment or two they wavered; then . . . their ranks dissolved." The men swarmed up companionways to take themselves as far away as possible from the horrific sight of the dying officer and the massive waves spreading out over the deck.[84]

After what seemed a long time following the collision—one survivor later stated, "it was only thirty or forty minutes [but] each minute to us who were awaiting death seemed an hour"—a miracle occurred. Far off in the distance, approaching from out of the mist, amid the massive rolling waves on the *Otranto*'s port side, just a few points off her bow, was a small ship with two funnels.[85, 86]

The *Otranto*'s crew and all the soldiers aboard her were emotionally overwhelmed, and a "spontaneous cheer rose from all the throats aboard." The soldiers and crew eagerly watched as the ship, hanging very low in the water, slowly circled the *Otranto* and approached her close to the starboard side from the stern.[87]

It was the British destroyer HMS *Mounsey*, coming to their aid. Years later, Pvt. Edgar A. Sheperd wrote of what happened next:

Now we got a close up view of the commander of the destroyer. A trim athletic looking officer who began waving two flags.

Knowing the semaphore code, I read the message to the commander of the *Otranto*: I am coming alongside to take off the American troops.

The reply to the destroyer *Mounsey* from the captain of the *Otranto* was: Steer clear as you will lose your crew and your ship.

The reply to the captain of the *Otranto*: I am coming alongside. If we go down, we shall all go down together.[88]

6

THE *MOUNSEY* TO THE RESCUE

HMS *MOUNSEY*

The British destroyers that were supposed to meet the HX-50 convoy a few hundred miles out in the North Atlantic had instead retreated from the hurricane-force wind and waves and returned to their protected anchorage at Lough Swilly along the northern coast of Ireland. They arrived back at 4 a.m. and spent the early-morning hours of Saturday, October 5, waiting for the storm to blow over. Finally, at 11 a.m., they headed out again to try to find the approaching ships and escort them into the North Channel of the Irish Sea. All of the destroyers in the group had managed to leave except one, HMS *Mounsey*, which had developed mechanical problems.[1]

The *Mounsey* was an M-class ("Moon Class") destroyer. She had a displacement of 896 tons, a battery of 4-inch guns, torpedo tubes, and a crew of seventy-three enlisted men and six officers.[2] Built by Yarrow and Company of Glasgow, Scotland, she was launched on September 11, 1915, and placed in commission six weeks later, on October 21.[3, 4] Lt. Francis W. Craven, RN, was serving as her captain. He was assisted by Lt. R. S. Stewart and Lt. Wilfrid E. Warner.[5]

Not until late that same day—at about 6 p.m.—did the *Mounsey* finally fix the mechanical problems and leave to join her fellow destroyers. Within a couple of hours, she had sighted the HMS *Minos*, and a bit later, she saw some of the other destroyers. Joining them, she cruised through the night along the northern Irish coast looking for the convoy.[6]

HMS Mounsey. *Photograph from the author's personal collection.*

The dark, early-morning hours of Sunday, October 6, found HMS *Mounsey* still searching for the convoy. Finally, at about 5:30 a.m., steering east-southeast to southeast, her crew sighted some of the ships and began shadowing one of the transports. A few hours later, Fred Robinson, who was responsible for HMS *Mounsey*'s guns, recalled that he had just taken over the bridge when, at about 8:30 a.m., he sighted land ahead—a strip just below Lossit Point. This meant that, during the night, the storm had driven HMS *Mounsey* north of her intended path, which was supposed to take them midway between Inistrail and Oversay Light on Islay. He immediately altered course southward and called for Captain Craven, who had gone below for breakfast after being on the bridge all night. After viewing the situation, Craven decided that because the troop transport they were following was having no apparent problems and two other destroyers were cruising nearby, they would strike out and search the vicinity for others that might need assistance.

Robinson recalled that they "went around the compass twice by easy stages, inspecting different transports as they came up, but as they each appeared to be all right, they left them." Then, as they passed the destroyer *Minos* struggling through the waves, Craven remarked to Robinson, "The weather can't get much worse than it is, Gunner." Indeed, Robinson recalled, "I hardly think I had seen it worse, in my twenty-six years experience at sea, and I have been in the seven of them. Except in the Australian Bight, I don't think I have ever seen worse." He logged the wind as hurricane force, southwest at Force 11, and the seas as 10, which means that waves were peaking at forty feet or more.

After searching the sector for an hour, at approximately 9:30 a.m., Robinson and Craven sighted HMS *Otranto* in the distance. Then, as they approached her, they could see that she was flying the signal flag H. 8, meaning, "Destroyer close to me." Shortly thereafter, going at about ten knots and with the *Otranto* about a mile off, Robinson took down in semaphore, "Stand by me." Craven made up his mind quickly. Robinson recalled, "He told me to get ready for going alongside, so I got the men up on deck and prepared with lines. Fenders weren't any good, so we left them." Then, as the *Mounsey* moved around the *Otranto*—with the land in the distance on one side and the *Otranto*'s stern on the other—they were drawing across her bow very close when they stopped. Craven then began using the force of the ocean waves with slight assistance of his engines to position HMS *Mounsey* parallel to the *Otranto*.[7]

CRAVEN RISKS ALL TO SAVE THE MEN ABOARD THE *OTRANTO*

Even from a distance, Craven could see that the *Otranto* was dead in the water and listing, so he knew immediately that something was wrong. Then, as he approached and saw the gash in her side, he realized that in the present stormy conditions, the *Otranto* was, more likely than not, sinking.

Though the men aboard were cheering, Cpt. Ernest Davidson sent a second signal by semaphore from the *Otranto* directing Craven not to come in too close. The waves were running high, and he feared that a huge wave would smash the *Mounsey* against the *Otranto* and place Craven's vessel in danger as well. In the meantime, Davidson ordered crew members to dump oil into the water in an attempt to calm the sea.

Pvt. Lonzon Sheley aboard the *Otranto* recalled many years later that, as the *Mounsey* approached even more closely, an officer aboard the *Otranto*—who he assumed was Captain Davidson—used a megaphone to warn Craven on the *Mounsey* to keep his distance. Instead, he heard Craven's reply, "Be calm boys, I am coming to you."[8] Craven then signaled to the *Otranto*, "Please lower your lee boats to act as fenders. I am coming alongside."[9] One of the American survivors, Pvt. Charles Von Waldner, recalled later that when the small destroyer tried to come alongside the *Otranto*, to the hundreds of men watching, the action seemed suicidal.[10]

Lt. Wilfrid Warner, aboard the *Mounsey*, recalled that Craven had "a way of thrusting out his jaw and bringing his head down when he was aroused," giving the "lean, swarthy and somewhat round-shouldered commander an air of authority that none of his crew [of seventy-three] cared to question."[11] Warner, who knew Craven well, said that while his response might be construed by some "as disobedience of an order," Craven was confident in his own capabilities and those of his ship and crew to a hair's breadth, and he believed that "disobedience of orders was a secondary consideration . . . when the saving of life . . . was involved."[12]

As the ship's crew and the American soldiers on the *Otranto* watched from their appointed stations, Captain Craven gently maneuvered the 896-ton *Mounsey* through the stormy seas to a position parallel with the 12,124-ton *Otranto*. He then waited as the two ships—driven by the wind, current, and waves—began to drift closer together.

Pvt. Harville Marsh, from Portal, Georgia, aboard HMS *Otranto* vividly recalled the scene: "The destroyer's officer stood on the deck and waved to the soldiers on the *Otranto*. He smiled to encourage them and shouted, 'Boys, we're going to get you on all right.'"[13]

Finally, HMS *Mounsey* was alongside, and the two ships slammed and scraped into each other. "There was a rending of wood as the fender boats collapsed, and then the sound of the grinding of the transport's steel side against the yielding *Mounsey*'s."[14] As Joseph E. Hewell observed, "I noticed out to the rear of the *Otranto* that a small boat [was] coming around. Sometimes it would be almost covered up by the water. I paid very little attention to it until next time I noticed it [was when] it was alongside [our] large ship." With the sea tossing the *Mounsey* about like a feather, Hewell saw how "one wave would take it some 15 to 20 feet or more away and then another would bring it back with a slam against the *Otranto*."[15]

JUMPING FOR THEIR LIVES

One of the British officers aboard the *Otranto*, Lt. C. D. Simmons, directed the ship's crewmen and American soldiers to remove their boots, leggings, and other gear to prepare to jump from the *Otranto* to the *Mounsey*.[16] The men then lined the rails on all the decks and waited for the order and opportunity to jump. Others, however, though drawn by fascination to watch, were fearful and stood back. Most were now standing in the freezing wind without their overcoats and life belts, pinning their hopes on the leap they soon intended to make.

Meanwhile, as the *Mounsey* kept working in closer to the *Otranto*, all those aboard both ships began to realize the seriousness and difficulty of the situation. Fred Robinson, on the *Mounsey*, had a narrow escape while trying to clear a rope caught on the ship's rail as one of the *Otranto*'s lifeboats came crashing down near him. He recalled, "I won't forget the first crash in a hurry. It was a rather nasty sensation, the grinding and tearing sounds, which cleared the portside from masthead, bringing down the wireless and foreyards of the *Mounsey*, smashing the portside of the bridge, and breaking all the stanchions along the deck and making a lot of wreckage."[17]

While the two ships rose and fell with the waves, Craven stubbornly continued to nudge the *Mounsey* alongside the much larger ship. Sometimes the *Mounsey*'s deck was as high as the *Otranto*'s boat deck, while at other times she would be so low it seemed that the *Otranto* would submerge her. On a calm day, the destroyer's deck would probably have been about thirty feet below the *Otranto*'s, but in this storm, the waves would raise it to where their decks would be almost level for a few seconds; then the *Mounsey* would be pushed down into a trough some sixty feet below.

Under Craven's skillful handling, the *Mounsey* rose and fell with the waves alongside the *Otranto*. Occasionally they would slip apart, but with Craven's direction and her crew's handling of her engines, they would come back together. Soldiers and sailors aboard the *Otranto* lined the railings and watched with fascination.[18] Pvt. Leholmes Wells remembered that as "ropes were thrown [down] to the destroyer and tied, men began to hand walk the ropes to the destroyer, but the monstrous waves knocked them into the sea." Still others were caught between the two ships, and the onlookers could only watch in helpless horror as the men dropped into the churning sea below and were then mangled beyond recognition as they were smashed between the two ships. Wells recounted, "It made us all sick, having to stand there and watch these ghastly sights."[19]

As the officers and crews of both ships shouted encouragement to each other, Captain Davidson gave the order to the ship's young bugler—who had stayed by his side throughout the ordeal—to sound "Abandon Ship." The boy brought himself to attention, blew the notes clearly, and then threw the bugle in a high arc out into the water, saying, "I'm through with this old bugle. Maybe I'll get me a new one."[20, 21]

Pvt. Lonzon Sheley saw the incident and remembered that the boy looked like he was only about sixteen; after he threw the bugle into the ocean, he was among those who jumped to the *Mounsey* and were saved.[22]

Captain Craven, standing on the *Mounsey*'s bridge as the two ships came within leaping distance, used his megaphone to encourage the men on the *Otranto*. He shouted over and again, as loudly as he could, "Jump men! Jump!"[23]

Joseph Hewell watched as the men began jumping, some landing safely on the deck of the *Mounsey* below, while others landed in the water between the two ships and were crushed when the two ships crashed together. After watching for a few minutes, his good friend H. E. Delaney from Nashville, Georgia, turned to him and suggested that they jump together. The two then climbed on top of the ship's railing and timed their jumps. Hewell recalled, "He made his jump first and a few seconds after he jumped, I jumped, and landed safely on the deck. I immediately caught hold of a gun . . . and was clinging to this when a large wave washed over the deck. I changed ends of the gun but still held on." Making things more difficult were the massive waves washing over the front of the destroyer, which was headed right into them. Hewell remembered, "One of the waves came over the bow and tore me lose from the gun. When I got to my feet again, I was 50 or 60 feet from the gun and very near to going overboard." Luckily, he had been swept along the edge of the deck toward a hatch where several of the *Mounsey*'s sailors pulled him in to safety.[24]

The American soldiers, British sailors, and French fishermen now began jumping in small groups, some tumbling down from the *Otranto*'s upper decks, while others simply stepped from one ship to the other. A large group of *Otranto*'s sailors were among the first to abandon ship, sliding down ropes from the *Otranto*'s A deck to the *Mounsey*. More often than not, the men who jumped landed safely. However, others who crashed onto the steel decks landed on pieces of equipment, ropes, and cables, breaking arms or legs or fracturing their skulls. Still others who landed safely were washed off the *Mounsey* and into the icy water by the huge waves. Observers agree that quite a number had the misfortune of falling in the gap between the two ships and being crushed to death.[25] Because so many of the American soldiers had never seen the ocean until this trip, the more experienced sailors of the crew had better success.[26]

Pvt. Harville Marsh recalled, "The men started to leap across the yawning chasm between the ships. Some I saw reach their mark, but others missed and they were drowned. I saw them down there drowning before my eyes." The choice was a stark one: risk jumping from the deck of the *Otranto* to the *Mounsey* and possibly drowning, getting crushed between the two ships, or suffering a fractured limb, or choose to go down with the ship. Marsh chose to jump: "I jumped fully 15 feet. It was a horrible moment. My feet just touched the edge of the deck of the destroyer. I thought I was going down, and I should have done so if I hadn't had my socks on. They gave me a moment's foothold and time to grasp a wire around the destroyer." March remembered that as he scrambled to safety, men were jumping and falling all around him. Then, when he looked back up at the *Otranto*, all he saw were giant waves sweeping men off her deck and hurling them into the ocean.[27]

Many of the survivors were haunted for the rest of their lives by the images of their friends swimming amid the massive waves while frantically waving to those aboard the *Mounsey* to get their attention so that they might somehow come and save them. But nothing could be done. They were left to swim toward shore amid the wreckage and debris of the splintered and crushed lifeboats of the *Otranto*.[28]

By this time, panic had begun to set in among those still aboard the *Otranto*. Lonzon Sheley remembered, "I saw one soldier jump and just catch [the edge of the *Mounsey*'s deck] by his hand; then the boats rammed and cut him in two." Seeing this, the officers aboard the *Otranto* yelled for the men to remain calm and try to be sure of their distance before jumping. But the men were panic stricken. Sheley said that, at about this time, he saw an American soldier run out from the crowd and jump off the side of the *Otranto* with a full seventy-pound pack on his back. "He never stopped . . . his pack just carried him down."[29]

Captain Jules Lehoerff, one of the French fishermen rescued from the *Croisine*, was among those who jumped and fell short of the *Mounsey*'s deck. Immediately afterward, his beautiful Newfoundland dog jumped in after him and was last seen by observers struggling through the water in an effort to get near enough to Lehoerff to try to save him.[30]

Ship's officer A. B. Campbell of the *Otranto* observed that sometimes the deck of the *Mounsey* would come within eight or ten feet of the larger ship, while at other times, it would quickly drop forty or fifty feet below. This meant that many of the *Otranto*'s crew, being used to the motion of ships, could exercise good judgment in their jumps, while the American soldiers, "panicky and unused to the ways of ships, could neither hear orders nor grasp the validity of instructions to wait for the word to jump." Indeed, some crashed onto the *Mounsey*'s deck when it was in a deep trough, resulting in broken arms and legs, while others struck with such force that they bounced off the destroyer's deck and into the ocean. Campbell commented later, "The fate of those unfortunates who fell between the two ships was awful, for while a lucky few managed to climb aboard as the gap closed, the majority were crushed horridly to death as the waves forced the vessels together." Campbell claimed he even saw one man throw himself down one of the *Mounsey*'s funnels and commented that he did not envy the task of the destroyer's crewmen later tasked with "ferreting through the mass of indistinguishably mingled flesh clinging to the ship's side for identity disks of what had once been separate and living human beings."[31]

Lt. Wilfrid Warner, aboard the *Mounsey*, said that Captain Craven turned to him at one point and said, "I wish to God this ship were ten, then I could get the whole lot off." His crew were working hard, pulling the jumpers to safety and moving them as quickly as they could into the cramped quarters below deck so their weight would not capsize the already burdened ship. Unfortunately, time and again, groups of ten or twelve men would jump together, and before one of the destroyer's crewmen could get a rope to them, they were washed away by the massive waves.[32]

As each group of men was pulled in, Craven would point toward the hatchway and say, "Make way lads, make room for more." According to Lieutenant Warner, "During the whole of this operation, he never showed the slightest excitement, and during the worst of it he was laughing." Warner commented, to use an "Americanism," he "scared the pants off me."[33]

By the time Pvt. Lonzon Sheley aboard the *Otranto* had pulled off his hobnail boots, put his lifejacket back on, and walked to the ship's rail, "so many had jumped and either got mashed to death, or missed and drowned, that the jumping was finally slowing up." As for the soldiers in the ship's hospital, he recalled that they had been left to die, as when they tried to walk, many were so weak they just crumbled and fell. Thus, when the order came, "Every man for himself," the men attending to the sick left them. He remembered that the situation was so frightening that one of the officers committed suicide by shooting himself, and "an officer was no more than a buck [private] in that life-and-death grapple."[34]

Meanwhile, aboard HMS *Mounsey*, Fred Robinson observed that, due to "the after part of the ship being washed by waves at least six feet in depth, and water pouring down into the engine room and stokehold hatches," several men had been carried down the ship's ladders by sheer weight of water. With every space available filled with men from the *Otranto* and water coming through the hatches, he was concerned that the ship was in danger of sinking. Robinson remembered that the ship's engineering officer had to "shut off sea suction and pump the water from the bilges, through the main circulators and condenser, to keep the water out." The situation was further complicated when "in the stoke-hold—which was badly damaged with the bulkhead being cracked and boiler slightly shifted—an oil lead pipe from a tank broke and water got into the fuel and caused the steam to drop." Thankfully, after a period, "two stoker petty officers, in changing over the oil lead to the other side of the ship, were able to get sufficient steam to go slow astern."[35]

Lieutenant Warner recalled, "Three attempts to bring the ships parallel were made. We got alongside twice. The first attempt was a failure." However, while only two attempts by the *Mounsey* to maneuver alongside and remain close to the *Otranto* for any length of time succeeded, the two vessels made contact with each other—to the extent that men from the *Otranto* were able to jump to the *Mounsey*—several times. One survivor counted eight such near contacts.[36]

The soldiers and sailors aboard the *Otranto* jumped in waves, many landing on top of those who had jumped just before them. Others landed in the *Mounsey's* lifeboats, on her guns, and on or among other equipment topside.[37] Lonzon Sheley recounted, "Sub-chasers [destroyers] are only about six feet above the water . . . and for some [jumping] it was not far, as the water picked up the chaser at times, but just as it was coming up towards the *Otranto*, I jumped and hit a stob which threw me flat on my back. I reached and got hold of a pipe beside the smoke stack, and pulled up." After Sheley landed, the *Mounsey* went out a bit from the *Otranto* with hundreds of men on her deck, plowing through massive waves. Sheley remembered, "I began to think the waves would mash me to death. Ice cold. I got strangled, but I held onto my pipe. Pretty near all that had jumped that time [with me] got washed overboard."[38]

T. L. Campbell, a Memphis lawyer and YMCA secretary who weighed about 220 pounds, also remembered standing on the *Otranto*'s rail, waiting for his chance to jump. Like Sheley, he also barely made it, for just as he leaped, the *Mounsey* lurched away. Instead of landing in the middle of the destroyer's deck, as he had hoped, he found that one of his legs had barely caught hold of the cable that ran along the perimeter of the destroyer. Luckily, he was able to pull himself aboard uninjured and grab a piece of equipment before the next wave hit.[39]

British seaman Francis Edwin Turner on the *Otranto* estimated that as the two ships rolled up and down with the massive waves, the distance of the jumps the men made to the *Mounsey* below them ranged from forty feet when the *Otranto* was in the trough of a wave to less than twenty feet when the sea rolled her up.[40] He vividly remembered watching how the force of the waves would tear the men's grip off whatever they were holding and throw them out into the water to drown, be crushed, or be "cut in half by the ship's wire rope rails" when the *Otranto* and *Mounsey* smashed against each other.[41]

As he stood at the *Otranto*'s railing watching the horrific scene unfolding before him, Leholmes Wells realized that the *Otranto* was going to sink and that he—like the others—had no other choice but to jump for his life. He remembered, "I said a little prayer, asking the Lord to show me the way." Then, suddenly, even though no spotlights were being used, he noticed a small lighted area on the deck where a rope was lying up close along the cabin walls. He commented, "I think God was pointing this rope out to me so that I would know that I had something to grasp when I jumped." Then, as the *Mounsey* edged closer to the *Otranto* and dropped down twenty feet or more in a trough, Wells saw a wave crest coming. Knowing that the *Mounsey* would soon be rising up rapidly, he got ready to time his jump. Then, with the destroyer only twelve to fifteen feet down, he jumped. He hit the deck hard and felt a pain in his foot immediately. He ripped a toenail off and bruised himself badly, but he had landed safely on the *Mounsey*'s deck. The question now was, could he find something to hang onto as the waves washed over him and the deck? Wells remembered, "I scampered quickly, in a crawling fashion, to the rope that I had seen moments before and grabbed and held onto it for dear life. I wrapped both my arms and both legs around it. A gigantic wave then swept over the deck about that time and I felt like I was drowning, but I held on tightly, just like I would hold a stubborn mule." After fifteen to twenty minutes, sailors aboard the *Mounsey* pulled him to safety through a porthole. Wells remembered, "There I found about 20 men in that little room standing in water up to their knees—ice cold seawater. They, like me, were wet, bruised and battered, just standing there, not saying a word, but thanking God to themselves . . . that they were still alive."[42]

Soon Captain Craven realized he had all the men aboard the *Mounsey* that the ship could handle, and he knew that with each massive wave crashing over her bow, his ship was in greater danger of sinking. Indeed, because of the collisions with the *Otranto*, the destroyer's side and railings were now badly damaged, and her wireless radio mast had been carried away. Down below, the ribs of the ship had been knocked loose, and all the men there were "standing in eighteen inches of water" as the pumps worked furiously to keep the destroyer afloat.[43, 44] At approximately 11:00 a.m., seeing that his ship was full and that a reef and Islay's rocky coastline were threateningly near, Craven ordered his helmsman to shove off and proceed away from HMS *Otranto*.[45]

Among the very last to jump were the commanding officer of the American troops, Lt. Sam Levy of Atlanta, and an officer of the *Otranto*, Cdr. A. B. Campbell. Both survived the plunge. While military authorities later attempted to scapegoat Levy through a court-martial investigation recommending that he be officially reprimanded for not adhering to "his duty to remain to the last" with the men in his command who chose to remain aboard the *Otranto*, the action was overturned by Maj. Gen. William Sims, Commander of the Allied Expeditionary Forces in France, who responded,

> While it is my belief that Lieut. Levy should have remained on board the ship to the last, yet, on account of his youth and inexperience, and of the fact that the officers of the ship had given the command: "Every man for himself," I think that Lieut. Levy didn't realize his obligation as commanding officer. He seemed to have kept his head and helped when possible and the knowledge he must now have that an educated soldier would have remained to the last would seem sufficient reminder of his action.[46]

As for Commander Campbell, he would go on to write a memoir titled *With the Corners Off*, detailing his recollections of serving aboard the *Otranto*, the collision, jumping "at the last possible moment," and landing "on the destroyer's foredeck just as she was pulling clear."[47]

Another member of the *Otranto*'s crewmen, saved by the *Mounsey*, commented later to a newspaper reporter, "Her commander deserves a double Victoria Cross as I have spent my life at sea, but I have never seen such a magnificent piece of maneuvering and ship handling in all my life. The destroyer was in danger of being dashed to pieces time and again . . . it was a miracle how she got alongside."[48]

As the battered HMS *Mounsey* steamed slowly away, those aboard caught a glimpse of a ship's officer aboard the *Otranto*, presumed to be Captain Davidson, standing on the bridge, waving farewell.[49] One can only imagine what he was thinking, knowing that the men's last hope of comparatively easy survival was sailing away. The only options left were either to try to beach the ship amid crashing waves against the rocky cliffs of Islay or to get the *Otranto* closer to shore so the crew and passengers could try to swim for their lives.

British seaman Edwin Turner later commented that he believed more of the soldiers did not jump because many "Americans thought they would be safer on board the larger vessel than the smaller naval craft, and that this was their undoing."[50]

Pvt. Leholmes Wells remembered his last glimpse from the deck of HMS *Mounsey*: "I looked with sadness at the foundering *Otranto*. . . . The gale winds were slowly pushing her toward the rocky coast. It was a sad and pitiful sight."[51] Pitiful indeed, as another soldier saw a man on the after-end of HMS *Otranto* "sitting on a pile of life rafts slapping his thighs and laughing as though he were enjoying a huge joke. He had cracked under the strain."[52]

T. L. Campbell, the Memphis attorney aboard the *Otranto* as a YMCA officer, and Pvt. Harville Marsh from Portal, Georgia, both later told separately of how—from their vantage point aboard the *Mounsey*—they could see eighteen to twenty men standing along the rails on the after-deck of the *Otranto* waving farewell when a giant wave suddenly swept over the ship and hurled eight or ten of them into the sea.[53] Both knew that all those men had just been sent to a certain death as the "waves [were] running sixty to seventy feet high."[54]

As Craven ordered the helmsman to move HMS *Mounsey* away from the *Otranto*, he had to guide his ship through dozens of men in the water who had missed his deck or been washed overboard from the *Otranto*. They looked pitifully small as they tried to keep their heads above water amid the blowing wind and massive waves tossing them about. Many were heard shouting and pleading for help, but Craven's crew could only throw to them whatever loose gear they could lay their hands on in the hope that it might be of help in their swim to shore.[55]

OUT OF THE FRYING PAN AND INTO THE FIRE

Craven immediately turned his attention to saving his own ship and the soldiers and sailors he had brought aboard. Noting that the weight of the additional men on the upper decks was causing the ship to become dangerously top-heavy, he ordered those who had jumped on board who were still topside to descend into the cramped quarters below.

Lt. Wilfrid Warner later recounted, "The survivors were dumb with shock, cold and the frightful noise of the storm. This was probably just as well, as never for a moment was there any sign of panic." However, it was difficult to get all of the men below because several had lashed themselves to anything they could find, and seawater had swollen the knotted ropes, making it difficult to get them free. Warner remembered, "Those worst off were the men who had landed on the fo'c'sle, and lashed themselves to the cables and anchor gear. They were being half drowned by the heavy seas coming over the bows." Under such adverse circumstances, Warner believed, "it would have been sheer foolishness to have tried to get back alongside the *Otranto* as even had we sea room to do it, we needed most of the steam from the one remaining boiler for the pumps."[56]

While Warner did not report any panic among the men, he was perhaps not being fully candid, as another stated, "Officers aboard the packed destroyer had trouble in ordering the men down from the deck, [as] they were in a panic, afraid that the small ship might sink. . . . Guns had to be pulled to get them below."[57]

As the *Mounsey* was plowing through the heavy waves with the last group of American soldiers and sailors who had jumped from the *Otranto* on the upper decks, holding onto anything they could, A. B. Campbell remembered that many could not be persuaded to come below. Recalling their precarious situation, he wrote, "With the weight atop her, every time she rolled she was in danger of turning turtle. . . . For the safety of all, the troops had to be compelled to go below, and it was done at the point of revolvers." Soon after the men were distributed into compartments below, "the destroyer regained buoyancy and—crippled though she was—she made progress."[58]

With HMS *Mounsey* seriously damaged, it was clear to all aboard that the journey to Belfast, Ireland, would be a perilous one. According to Pvt. Lonzon Sheley, "The guns of the *Otranto* had gouged holes in the *Mounsey* and the ship was leaking bad. . . . I would not go down in the hole as the officer tried to get me. I had a horror of going, as water was pouring in and air would bubble back up, like out of a jug. But I was freezing to death." Eventually Sheley realized that he could not hold on any longer, so he forced himself to make his way down into the engine room. There, he recalled, "we were far from being safe, for with all the pumps going they [still] had to dip with buckets to keep the *Mounsey* afloat as it had ripped its side running against the other boat."[59]

Ship's officer Lt. R. S. Stewart was concerned that the *Mounsey* would not make it to port as "the water was up to the floor plates of the engine room and it was all the pumps could do to keep the water under. The port side was like a concertina. It was extraordinary that the ship could stand such a hammering."[60]

Lieutenant Warner's recollection offers perhaps the most graphic description of the condition of the *Mounsey*: "The bridge had been smashed, all the oil-fuel tanks except one was punctured, two out of the three boiler rooms were flooded, boats, davits, and upper deck gear were all smashed to bits, and spare depth charges were rolling about the upper deck." Compounding these structural issues was the fact that "both masts had been carried away along with the wireless with all the signaling gear, the pumps were only just able to keep pace with the water pouring in through holes, [there were] cracked seams and wrecked ventilators, [and the] deck was full of debris [with] ropes and survivors being washed about by the tremendous sea."[61]

Returning the damaged ship to port took every bit of seamanship Captain Craven and his crew could muster. More than once, while turning in the heavy seas, the *Mounsey* was completely engulfed in water. The influx of water and the impact of the waves were such that the dynamos in the engine room were affected, and all the ship's lights went out.[62] Panicking, some of the sailors and soldiers from the *Otranto* started up the companion ladder in the engine room, but the dynamo attendants there reassured them that they would soon get the lights back on. Thanks to the crew's hard work, they managed to do so. All this time many could not help but wonder whether they had been wise to jump from one sinking ship to another.[63]

Pvt. Charles Von Waldner described his own experience. "I had jumped from the stern and landed on the deck of the destroyer, only to be almost swept away by a wave that swept across it. Wet, cold, and weary, I made my way down below deck to where the men who were being saved were gathering." There, though surprised to find himself with Clyde Benson, an old friend from Savannah, he recalled "a dead stillness among the men packed into those small quarters." He remembered that as they stood in the cold water, the destroyer rising and falling with the tremendous waves buffeting it from side to side, "no one seemed to have voice to express anything, not even a word of rejoicing that he had been saved. I think we were all semi-paralyzed by the horror of what we had seen. We hardly knew we had been saved."[64]

Indeed, getting the *Mounsey* back to port would be a challenging endeavor. As Craven later stated in his official report, "After ascertaining position, course was set for North Channel, as it was being impossible to steer further to westward, owing to a very high sea and weight of the men on board. *Mounsey* was hanging very heavily at the end of her rolls. Thus, after rounding Oversay, [we set] course for Belfast."[65]

As her engineering officer later reported, the overloaded destroyer had to be turned slowly and with great care to avoid capsizing. "I think Craven's best work was done while going to Belfast. He worked the ship across the North Channel under the lee of the Irish coast [while keeping] the water (in the engine room) down to a minimum which relieved me of a good deal of anxiety in the engine room department."[66]

Meanwhile, many of the survivors packed into the hold below became violently seasick. The stench of their vomit amid the cold seawater they were standing in, combined with the foulness of the air in the compartment's battened-down hatches, made the experience for all of them truly miserable.[67]

Like Charles Von Waldner, Leholmes Wells found that the men in his cabin had little to say. He remembered that they became so tired, they "just slumped down and sat in the cold water, all the way to Belfast."[68] To his surprise, it was not until the soldier next to him asked for a chew of tobacco that he recognized him—it was Lonzon Sheley, one of his close friends from back home in Screven County, Georgia.[69]

The men aboard were exhausted and anxious, many wondering whether they had been wise in jumping.[70] Whenever a *Mounsey* officer stuck his head into a compartment to see how everyone was getting along, he was asked over and again, "Where are we going, and how long will it take?" The men were frightened, and the tension increased as each hour passed and the *Mounsey* had still not made port.[71]

According to Lieutenant Warner, while none of the *Mounsey*'s crew was seriously injured, several of the soldiers and sailors from the *Otranto* had broken arms and legs. While others described the side of the ship as having a mass of human flesh and body parts attached to portions of it, Warner only mentioned that after getting into Belfast, they "found one dead American soldier [Private Simpson, serial number 844815, R., CAC] under the piles of wreckage" on deck. He wrote later of how badly he felt for the men taken aboard and squeezed into the compartments below, saying, "They must have suffered all the tortures of the 'Black Hole of Calcutta' crammed below, wet, sick, cold, and beaten by nature into a numb horror, wondering if they had gone from the frying pan into the fire." Indeed, he reported, "I was glad to be on deck with work to do [as] my job as navigator kept me on the bridge, in what remained of the chart-house."[72]

Craven was worried, too, because—with the serious damage to his ship—he was not sure if, or how long, they could stay afloat. He wanted to use his lamp signal to send a message to a passing vessel in the hope that it could then relay a message by wireless radio for him, but his crew found that most of their equipment had been rendered inoperable. Finally, at around 6:30 p.m. Craven managed to send a signal to HMS *Mindful*, passing nearby, whose radio operator in turn relayed the message to authorities in Belfast regarding the *Mounsey*'s situation.[73]

THE MEN ARRIVE SAFELY IN BELFAST

About an hour later, at around 7:30 p.m., HMS *Mounsey* entered the Belfast Lough and proceeded on to Spencer Basin, where, at 8:45 p.m., she tied up alongside the dock.[74] There, Craven and his crew were greeted by American Red Cross ambulances waiting to take the injured and sick to a nearby hospital and by the American consul, Hunter Sharp, who had come to look after the interests of the American survivors.[75, 76]

Leholmes Wells, who had sat in ice-cold water the entire trip, remembered, "Many of us had to be toted off the ship. I couldn't walk one step as my legs wouldn't move. Sitting in that cold water [for more than five hours] had made me stiff." He later joined a few of the soldiers who had found a warm fire at a nearby police barracks, commenting "that fire felt so good and we got so close and warmed so long that our clothes smoked and sizzled."[77]

While members of the *Otranto*'s crew were lined up and led off to the Seamen's Home, the American soldiers and French fishermen able to walk were brought up on the deck of the *Mounsey* and marched off to the Queen Victoria Barracks.[78]

As the exhausted American soldiers and French fishermen trudged along the rough cobblestone streets, citizens of Belfast came up and, walking alongside, asked why they had come to Ireland instead of England or France, where American troops usually landed. Their sympathetic remarks and concern, when they learned what had happened, were deeply appreciated by the men.[79]

Once they reached the vicinity of the barracks, the men were split up and assigned to their quarters, some in the barracks, others in a nearby church, and the rest wherever else space could be found.[80] Volunteers had been called in, and they were busy stuffing and sewing straw into casings to make sleeping bags.[81] These, along with Irish soup, dry clothing, new underwear, and "comfort kits" were given to the men by Red Cross representatives.

Joseph Hewell vividly remembered that after they landed, he had started walking, but due to his injuries he had to stop at a police guard post and wait for a ride. There, he and several others waited until "some automobiles came and [took them] to the Victoria Barracks, where they were supplied dry clothing and something hot to eat." Then, soon thereafter, "doctors came through the crowds of soldiers, examined the injured, and sent those who needed medical care on to the hospital."[82]

Ship's officer A. B. Campbell had gone with the other surviving crew members of the *Otranto* to the Seamen's Home. There, he and the others were assisted by local women who had answered the Red Cross's call for help—women who had left their own comfortable homes to minister to the men. Campbell remembered, "The smell of hot coffee and of frying potatoes soon put fresh heart into us. Plates of fried eggs and potatoes disappeared, washed down with cups of steaming hot coffee." Then, because so many of the men were sparsely clothed, one of the ladies, a Miss Cunningham, left and soon returned with a load of donated clothing. Campbell helped her distribute the variety of suit jackets, pants, shirts, vests, and boots and was heartened to see the men enjoying the sometimes strange garments. He recalled, "Some diversion was wanted to keep their minds from what lay so recently behind them. One man, a cockney fireman, found himself in clerical clothes. His antics in them raised howls of laughter among his fellows, but I'm afraid the laughter had in it something of hysteria."[83]

Meanwhile, the crew aboard the *Mounsey* was still busy. Lieutenant Warner remembered that after they docked in Belfast, Craven could not rest until all his crew had eaten a hot meal and changed into dry clothes. Then, Warner recalled, "he collapsed, and I can see him now in the wrecked and stinking wardroom, stretched in the remains of an arm-chair, asleep with a half-eaten sandwich in one hand and a cup of cocoa . . . in the other."[84]

Captain Craven certainly deserved the time to rest as, according to lists published later in the *Naval War Notes*, he and his crew had saved the lives of 597 men that day: 300 American soldiers, 266 officers and crewmen of the *Otranto*, 1 American "YMCA man," and 30 French fishermen from the *Croisine*. While the intact remains of one soldier were found under some equipment on deck, a grisly panorama of blood and body parts of many others who had been crushed between the two ships was left all along one side of the *Mounsey*.[85]

Besides those injured from their jump to the *Mounsey*, others were critically ill from influenza. Hospital records indicate that at least five of the men taken to the hospital that night died of influenza and were buried there in Belfast. Typical of those with injuries and influenza was Pvt. Leholmes Wells, who, during the morning after they arrived in Belfast, found that he was unable to speak or get up from bed. He recalled, "An officer woke me and asked if I could get up and go as those that could make it were being sent on to France for assignment. . . . I tried to speak, but discovered that I could not talk nor move my legs. . . . I had double pneumonia." He remained in the hospital in Belfast until November 25, when he was shipped back to New York. There he had the misfortune of catching the mumps and found himself confined to a mumps ward for another twenty days. Of these experiences, he could only say, "I was still lucky to be alive."[86]

As for the battered *Mounsey*, she was put in dry dock to be cleaned and repaired. Lieutenant Warner wrote, "The *Mounsey* was so badly damaged that she had to have new plating all along one side (port side) and new frames for two-thirds of her length. She was repaired, but was never used again on active service."[87]

The emotional well-being of the American soldiers in Belfast was affected too. As Lonzon Sheley wrote, "It was a lonesome day [that] next day, with so many of my lifelong friends gone. Many never had an opportunity, for the *Mounsey* was not more than 100 feet while the other was over five-hundred, [and] you could not push through the line but had to wait for a chance."[88]

A few days after the disaster, during the early-morning hours of Tuesday, October 8, soldiers who were able boarded the mail boat RMS *Leinster* in Belfast to travel to Dublin. From there, they traveled sixty miles across the Irish Sea to Holyhead, Wales. Of the trip, Pvt. Edgar A. Sheperd recounted, "An unusual experience in going across [the Irish Sea] was our being followed by a German submarine. It seemed as if I could [reach out and] put my hand on the periscope."[89] German submarines regularly shadowed the mail ships plying those waters and had tried several times to sink one, but they were frustrated by the ships' ability to zigzag rapidly and maintain a relatively fast speed. Only two days later, however, on Wednesday, October 10, 1918, the *Leinster* was hit by two torpedoes, fired three minutes apart, from the German submarine U-123. Of the 700 aboard, 300 were soldiers, and only 256 of the 700 survived.[90]

From Holyhead, Wales, the soldiers boarded a train that took them through London and on to Winchester, England. They arrived around 4:00 a.m. the following day and were immediately transported to the nearby Morn Hill Rest Camp. There they recuperated for a few weeks before the main body of the group traveled on to France on November 17.[91] Soldiers who made it to France were assigned to a variety of Coast Artillery units for duty as heavy artillerymen, and the African Americans among them were sent to various port facilities to unload ships.[92]

Pvt. Joseph Hewell was one of the American soldiers left behind in Ireland in the Ulster Volunteer Force Hospital. While admitted because of an injury to his heel, he contracted a severe cold, lost his voice, and was bedridden for a week before he was allowed to get up. He remembered, "I had shaved the day before the wreck and had gone some five or six days without shaving, so by then the hair on my face was about as long as it was on my head." He was happy when the time came that he could finally sit up, shave, and present a better appearance. Hewell was in the hospital for three weeks. After his discharge, he travelled with several others from Belfast to Dublin, across the Irish Sea to Liverpool, and then southeast across England to London. He remembered that they did not spend much time in London because it was so foggy but, instead, caught a train for Southampton. Once they arrived there, authorities assigned them to an English rest camp in Winchester, where he remained until the armistice ending hostilities was signed on November 11, 1918.[93]

7

THE SINKING OF
THE *OTRANTO*

NO CHOICE BUT TO SWIM FOR IT . . .

Nearly five hundred American soldiers, French fishermen, and British crewmen left aboard HMS *Otranto* watched as HMS *Mounsey* slowly disappeared through the ocean haze. Though the sky was beginning to clear, the wind was still blowing with a terrific force from the southwest and thirty- to forty-foot waves continued to batter the wounded ship.

There was little left for those still aboard but to pray and hold tight to anything they could. All were scanning the horizon in the hope that another destroyer might find and help them, but each passing minute was bringing them closer to the rocky shoreline. As the cliffs rose before them, and with no help in sight, the men realized that their best hope now lay in beaching the ship.

Time continued to slip by, and HMS *Otranto* got so close to shore that everyone aboard could see cows grazing in the fields over the rocky cliffs above the coastline. The sick soldiers whom Lt. Frank A. Perkins and others had managed to bring up from the hospital below deck were now being strapped onto life rafts. Soon all the men could see even more clearly the massive waves crashing against huge rocks at the base of the high cliff walls. There was no sandy beach along their trajectory to shore. Then, to make matters worse, ship's officers saw a reef just offshore, and the *Otranto* was heading right for it. Cpt. Ernest Davidson knew that their circumstances were getting worse by the minute. Even if the ship or swimmers could get safely over the reef, they would then have to contend with the massive waves smashing into the boulders at the base of the fifty-foot cliffs.

The land nearby was Rhinns Point, which lay along the western coast of the Hebridean island of Islay, off the western coast of Scotland. The convoy was believed to be situated approximately eight miles northwest of the Rhinns of Islay Lighthouse when the *Kashmir* struck the *Otranto*. They were only ten hours from the safety of their intended port of Liverpool. According to one of the *Otranto*'s crew, "The location in which the *Otranto* was drifting helplessly could not have been worse as the endless fury of the Atlantic rollers, thirty feet high, dashing against this rocky coastline during westerly gales is something to be reckoned with." Mentioning that he had spent his childhood in a village on the island, he emphasized, "I will try to explain . . . [how] treacherous [this] two miles of coast area is. . . . I am a seaman, I have rounded Cape Horn in a gale on board a four-masted bark. . . . I have weathered Cape Lewis and the notorious Bay of Biscay in a storm. None can compare with the strip of ocean at Rhinns Point."[1]

Davidson and his officers met one last time to assess their situation and develop a strategy by which they might provide the best possible outcome for the soldiers and crew still aboard. Of immediate concern was the fact that the boat deck was now resting only on the support beams of the ship's structure. The fixing bolts of the steel plates had been shorn off by the shifting weight of the damaged sections of structure, and the deck was now unstable. In the hope of getting the weight concentrated onto the lower decks to help with the ship's center of gravity, Davidson ordered the crew to send the men back down to C Deck. By this time, however, orders were not being followed, as many of the troops were now in a panic-stricken state and feared going down to a lower deck, especially those who did not know how to swim. Also, because of the storm and the noise of the situation, it is questionable whether the crew and the soldiers actually heard and understood Davidson's order.[2]

While some witnesses later claimed that they saw Captain Davidson swimming in the water among them, ship's officer A. B. Campbell observed the captain leaving the bridge to investigate the damage and see how the ship was reacting to the wind and waves. Campbell claimed that he then saw him "standing on the after well-deck when the end of the boat-deck—with its load of men—came crashing atop him." Recalling that this is exactly what the other ship's officers had predicted, he claimed that he looked on as "numbers of troops were thrown into the sea while others were smashed by the weight of the deck as it fell upon them." According to Campbell, "the Captain was immediately underneath–[stepping down a companionway]–as the crash came. The edge of the falling deck . . . almost decapitated him."[3]

The end of HMS *Otranto* then came quite rapidly. The collision with the *Kashmir* had taken place at approximately 8:40 a.m.; about three hours later, at approximately 11:55 a.m.–a half hour after HMS *Mounsey* left her–a huge breaker, even more mountainous than the rest, picked her up and dropped her on the reef.[4] Called *Botha na Cail-lieach*, or "Old Woman's Reef," the reef is located about three-quarters of a mile from shore, near the entrance to Machir Bay on Islay. Thus, as luck would have it, Davidson would not be able to land the *Otranto* on a sandy beach just north of the reef, which would have offered a safe haven for his ship.[5, 6] This was unfortunate, as just a year before, a small steamer had been washed ashore on that same beach without the loss of a single life.

One massive wave and then another lifted and dropped the *Otranto* onto the reef, time and again, first breaking her into two large pieces, then ripping her bottom clean out.[7, 8] In a matter of only a few more minutes, half of what remained of the ship lay twisted sideways along the reef. Then, yet another massive wave picked this twisted half up and, in the process of rolling it over, threw all still aboard into the sea before carrying the wreckage beneath the waves. The other half of the ship, held fast on the rocks, was then quickly pounded to pieces by the monstrous waves.

Just before HMS *Otranto* had landed on the reef, the few crewmen still aboard–realizing that they would all soon end up in the water–advised the remaining American soldiers who had not already done so to remove their heavy overcoats and shoes. Then, just as the ship hit the reef and broke apart, a ship's officer, whom many presumed to be Captain David-son, was heard to shout, "Boys, we'll have to swim for it after all."[9]

Quite a few of the American soldiers clung to the *Otranto* to the last because, as mentioned previously, many, hailing from rural farms, had never seen the ocean before sailing and had never learned to swim. As one soldier wrote of a friend who perished that day, "He could not swim, and this fact gave him a natural dread of the water [as] he knew not how to fight for his life and keep his head above the water."[10]

Other soldiers, who had more confidence in their swimming skills and sensed that nothing could be gained by staying aboard, had already jumped into the icy, debris-strewn water. Then, after grabbing any floating piece of wreckage they could, they began swimming for the distant shore. Unfortunately, they soon discovered that whatever debris they tried to hold onto would, more often than not, be wrenched from their grasp by the force of the huge waves breaking around them.[11]

William Richards, one of the survivors, remembered, "The fellows were fine. We knew that when the *Otranto* went fast on the rocks so far out we would not have much chance to save our skins, but we all seemed determined to make a good try." Richards recalled that after he was washed off the ship and into the cold water by a massive wave, he saw "three men on a mattress riding in to shore as if they were enjoying life, but then—while I watched them, and wishing I were on it, too—a big roller swept them all off and slammed them against the rocks." Later he watched as several men hanging onto a bench and others "on the tiny rafts lowered from the ship" were all "smashed to pieces" against the rocks.

Richards remembered that "the noise of the wreckage grinding on the rocks was fierce and [that] any fellow who [was swept] into the wreckage [below the cliffs] was as good as gone." Of the time he was swimming toward shore, he remarked, "I saw dozens of boys floating around me, all dead, with nothing but their blue faces [showing on the surface] out of the water." He managed to survive by riding a huge wave into the rocks, where he was one of the few to land in a place that sheltered him from the debris and other waves pounding the rocks and cliffs around him. There, someone along the edge of the cliff saw him and threw him a rope, which he tied around himself and then used to climb up the cliff hand-over-hand.[12]

Of the estimated 489 men left aboard the *Otranto* after the *Mounsey* left her, only twenty-one, including seventeen Americans, were fortunate enough to swim successfully through the stormy, debris-strewn waters, land in one of the crevices between the rocky cliffs, and survive.[13] Of that number, two—one an American—died later from his injuries.[14]

Some of the survivors believed they owed their lives to the cotton-padded collars of their life preservers for saving them from the potentially fatal blows of pieces of wreckage. As one said, "If the heads of the swimmers had been similarly protected, many others would have probably escaped" death as well.[15]

The handful of survivors who made it ashore were too exhausted to walk. One, David Roberts, later wrote in a letter to his mother,

About 9 o'clock [that morning] we felt a jar but thought it nothing more than a big wave. But the boat that had a position behind us . . . became disabled in some way and struck the port side of the ship. We thought everything was alright and we would make port, as we were supposed to that night. [But] they soon put out the rafts and told us to stand by. We were in sight of land all of the time.

Soon after, a sub-chaser came up and stood alongside, and as the waves took her against the ship, many of the men jumped on her deck. When the chaser was gone an anchor was thrown out, but the waves were so strong [that] the boat drifted within a mile of shore then grounded on a rock. The waves turned the boat over to about 60 degrees, and the big waves came over the ship and washed many of the fellows over.

We had no-one to command us, [so] it was everyone for himself. When I saw [that] the boat [was] starting to break up, I waited until it leaned over almost to the water, then I jumped over. I had on a good life belt, one that slipped on like a vest. The waves carried me away from the ship, then a wave about as high as a house came over me and whirled me around like paper in a whirlwind. I went under about three of them, but then I got hold of a raft and drifted close to shore. Another big wave came and swept me off the raft close to shore. I grabbed hold of a rock and hung on, and then I climbed. . . . [Finally, as I reached the top,] there was a Scotch lad who got hold of a sailor and me, and took us to a cottage.

All I had left on was my underwear, pants and shirt and one sock. I had taken off the other clothing before I left the ship. The wind was blowing as hard as I have ever seen it blow before. It simply carried us along. When we got to the cottage they gave us dry clothing and put us to bed. It sure was fine, two pairs of woolen blankets. The people there could not have treated us any better.[16]

Another survivor, Charles A. McDonald, of Galesburg, Illinois, was standing on deck with his back against a cabin wall with several other soldiers looking out over the water, when a wave knocked them all from one side of the deck to the other. Realizing that the ship was sinking, he grabbed a rope hanging from one of the smokestacks and used it to steady himself as he climbed and stood on the ship's railing. Then, as another wave surged around the *Otranto*, he jumped off, let go of the rope, and rode the wave toward shore. While McDonald did not know how to swim, he was buoyed by the life jacket he was wearing and a cork life ring that he found in the water. As he paddled toward shore, he shared the life ring with another soldier, each keeping an arm in the ring and swimming toward shore with his other free arm. McDonald recalled, "We paddled away as best we could, and looking back at the *Otranto* I saw Captain Davidson standing on the very top deck with blood streaming down his face where something must have struck him." Soon afterwards, they saw a portion of the *Otranto*'s stateroom floating amid the waves. They swam toward it, climbed aboard, and used it as a raft. McDonald related later, "I got on but kept the life-ring. It was hard to hold on to the raft for the waves would almost tear our arms out of their sockets. We would wash off, and I found it hard to get back on again and the air was so cold that we were compelled, at intervals, to drop into the water, which, though ice cold, still seemed warmer."

McDonald clung to the raft as long as he could but was eventually washed off by a large wave that he rode shoreward. Using the life ring as a buffer between himself and the debris floating around, he could see the outline of the dangerous-looking cliffs and rocks along the rockbound coast ahead of him. He remembered thinking, "It seemed to me that I could never get through the surf and up those jagged rocks without being dashed to pieces." His luck held, however, as an enormous wave pulled him under but deposited him in a gully amid the rocks. Then, after picking his way out from amid the wreckage, he found a way between the rocks and found himself standing on shore. He remembered, "My toes were so cramped that I fell down several times while trying to stand. Then, after working my toes for time I found myself able to walk. Going a short way I came across a lad named Earl Garver lying on the ground exhausted. I helped him to his feet and started to drag him along with me."[17]

Meanwhile, on shore, the first to arrive at the scene was David Mc-Taggart, a local farmer, who saw the seriousness of the situation and immediately traveled four or five miles to call out the island's Life Saving Crew. He then returned as quickly as he could and began helping another farmer, Donald McLachlan, who had also arrived on the scene. The two men used a long broom handle to pull three survivors out of the water. Then McTaggart went into the cold, swirling water after the men, while McLachlan held him by his jacket. As more help arrived, McTaggart—with the help of Donald Ferguson, a local shepherd—then used a rope to rescue yet another soldier trapped by waves just offshore on a rock outcropping.[18]

As word of the unfolding disaster spread, farmers, fishermen, and residents from the nearby villages of Portnahaven and Portwenyss hurried to the scene.[19] Soon the Coast Patrol's Life Saving Crew arrived. They tried to get a line out to the men so they could use a breeches buoy to rescue some of them, but the strong winds, the massive waves, and the distance to the wreck prevented them from doing so.[20]

Particularly noteworthy were the courageous actions of eighteen-year-old Donald McPhee and his seventeen-year-old brother, John. Both boys were shepherds who used their walking sticks to reach out across the water and through the driftwood at considerable risk to their own lives to rescue three of the survivors. Then, as John helped the three men walk to his home to be looked after by his sister, Margaret, and his mother, Donald remained behind and joined Andrew Stevenson, a British sailor home on leave from the HMS *Harwick*, to rescue yet another. The soldier, Pvt. Thomas A. Kelly, was seen "among the driftwood with nothing but his head showing, [and] his body absolutely jammed among the wreckage." He had landed in a narrow crevice with perpendicular walls. If he were to be saved, he would have to be hauled up the jagged cliff by rope.[21] To make matters even worse, the rescuers could see that his left arm was broken and twisted back over his shoulder.

Andrew Stevenson and Donald McPhee dropped a rope down to Kelly amid the dangerous, churning water. Kelly somehow managed to fasten it around himself with his good hand, but he was still wedged in so tightly by the wreckage that the two men could not lift him. Finally, after a small boy was lowered by another rope to remove some of the debris, both Kelly and the boy were hauled up the cliff to safety.[22]

Two other British soldiers home on leave—Archie Torrie and Donald McIndeor—were heroes as well, distinguishing themselves when they went to the aid of an American soldier on a rock just offshore. Seeing a broad chasm between the rock and where they were standing, they realized that it would be impossible for the soldier to get safely to shore due to the water rushing through the gully between them. Still, Torrie and McIndeor were determined to save the man. Realizing that the only way to get to him would be to jump across the gully, they summoned their courage, made the jump, and got to where the American had landed. Thankfully, while they accomplished this feat, onlookers found some planks and made a temporary bridge. They all made it safely back across the chasm, but if they had slipped, they too would have died.[23]

Nearby was the small hamlet of Kilchoman, which consisted only of a stone church, a parsonage, and three small homes. It was the clergyman, Rev. Donald Grant, who first saw the *Otranto* out on the reef and sent word to others on the island to come through the storm and help. Conditions that day were so severe that four of the rescuers traveling to the scene in an automobile were blown off the road and into a ditch. Many of the islanders said that the storm was the most violent they could remember.[24]

Local residents searched desperately all through that night for additional survivors but without success. Only twenty-one men were rescued; of these, two later died, including an English sailor who succumbed just after making it safely ashore. Some of the survivors were seriously injured, and all were suffering from exposure.

All of the rest of the 489 soldiers, French fishermen, and British crewmen of the *Otranto* and the *Croisine* left behind by the *Mounsey* perished that day. Some were held by the sea, never to be found; the rest were slammed over and again into boulders on the shore along the cliffs, their bodies lodged in the crevices of the rocky shoreline amid the tons of debris, provisions, and pieces of the structure of the ship.[25]

NOTHING BUT CARNAGE

On October 7, 1918, the morning following the disaster, there was no sign of the *Otranto*; she had been torn to pieces by the waves. Debris and wreckage were piled more than fifteen feet high amid the rocks for three miles as the islanders frantically searched for injured survivors. Instead, they found only bodies—hundreds of them—strewn amid the ship's debris.[26] Enormous quantities of bacon, flour, and supplies lay everywhere. As a newspaper reporter wrote, "The storm that raged at the time of the loss was so terrific that wreckage was carried by huge waves over the cliffs a quarter of a mile inland. It is regarded as a miracle that anybody escaped."[27]

Indeed, it was an awesome display of nature. Searchers found that parts of the *Otranto*'s engines had been wrenched out from the

Searching through the tons of debris for bodies washed ashore. Courtesy of Carl Reavey, editor of the Ileach, *Islay, Scotland, and the Museum of Islay Life.*

wreckage on the reef and rolled along the ocean floor by the force of the storm's waves until they were thrown up on shore.[28] Bodies were treated in a similar manner—mercilessly battered against the rocks and then scattered and buried amid the debris. Medical personnel who later examined them found that—because of the density of sand in the water and the great force of the waves—the respiratory organs of the bodies were clogged with sand.[29]

The searchers pitched in and began the difficult and heartrending task of extricating bodies from the ship's wreckage. Just eight months previously, many of these same men and women had assisted survivors of the SS *Tuscania* after it was torpedoed by a German submarine near the same reef where HMS *Otranto* now lay. While not the same scope as the loss of the *Otranto*, 210 American soldiers and 35 British sailors were lost when that ship went down. Many of these same volunteers had dug graves for the 150 bodies of the 245 lost that had washed ashore.

The *Tuscania* had been part of an HX-20 convoy commanded by Cpt. Peter Alexander McLean. She was carrying 2,156 American soldiers and 239 officers and crew when torpedoed on February 5, 1918, by German submarine U-77.[30] Unlike with the *Otranto*, however, nearby escorting destroyers and other ships had immediately come to her aid; otherwise, hundreds more would surely have been lost.[31]

Standing along the top of the cliffs amid the rain and wind and watching the *Otranto* disintegrate the day before, then seeing the hundreds of bodies strewn along the base of the ocean cliffs the next morning, was surely a traumatic experience for the men and women of Islay. Authorities took one look and knew that they would need to dig an even larger cemetery than they had for the *Tuscania*'s dead.[32]

Islanders looking for survivors and bodies from the *Otranto* were divided into groups of thirty and assigned a section of shoreline to search.[33] They were joined the following day by a Red Cross party that had come over from Belfast, then by yet another group the next day—two days after the disaster—that arrived from England.[34] The search efforts were supervised by Lt. Col. C. Heaton-Ellis, the highest-ranking British officer on Islay. Everyone on the island who was able participated and did all they could to be of help.[35]

Two days later, on October 9, Lt. R. E. Condon, representing the US Army's Office of the Commanding General, arrived on Islay. He was accompanied by two medical officers. Immediately after they arrived, they located the seventeen men reported as surviving the wreck.

The seventeen American survivors who reached shore alive were identified as follows:

Robert Brown	Emil Peterson	Charles E. Smithson
Earle Carver	Joseph S. Richards	George S. Taylor
William Cooney	William Richards	Noah Taylor
Stuart Early	David R. Roberts	Joseph Tollock
Thomas A. Kelly	Robert E. Schaun	John E. Wean[36]
Charles McDonald	Ben Smith	

Condon soon learned that of the seventeen American survivors, six had already been transported to safety by a destroyer. The remaining eleven were staying with Mrs. Isabel McIntyre and her neighbors, Reverend and Mrs. Grant, on the west coast of the island.[37]

Lieutenant Condon and the medical officers set out from Port Charlotte. Once they found the McIntyre and Grant homesteads near the Kilchoman Parish Church, they examined the men to determine the extent of their injuries. Of the eleven, six were fit to travel. Condon sent five of the six to Glasgow the following morning and ordered one, Sergeant McDonald, to stay behind and help look after the remaining five whose injuries were too severe to allow for immediate travel.[38] Lieutenant Condon then wired the list of the survivors to the Office of the Commanding General in London.[39] Despite the efforts of the civilian doctor, a nurse, and one of the British army medical officers assigned to help look after the soldiers, one of the survivors, Pvt. William J. Coney, died on October 15 of bronchitis and pneumonia.[40]

In the meantime, search efforts continued to locate and retrieve bodies amid the wreckage. By the evening of Wednesday, October 9, seventy men were actively engaged in this effort, now coordinated by several constables who had recently arrived with Lieutenant Colonel Turnbull, the chief constable for Argyllshire.[41]

On Saturday, October 12, six days after the wreck, twenty-five American soldiers and thirty British soldiers assigned to a labor battalion for this purpose arrived from the Scottish mainland. The Americans were immediately put to work building coffins, while the British soldiers relieved exhausted local volunteers who had been searching for bodies for six straight days.[42]

The soldiers and remaining local volunteer searchers were confronted by enormous piles of wreckage, almost all of which was jammed into deep gullies at the base of cliffs along the shoreline.[43] Not only were the woodwork, cargo, stores, and structural parts of the ship among the wreckage, but pieces of the ship's engines, heavy machinery, and the ship's compass and control panel were all visible in the piles as well.[44] The only way the searchers could find and get to the bodies was to pull off the enormous piles of debris from amid the rocks, an exhausting process. Complicating the task was the fact that other bodies could be seen just below the surface, amid the kelp beds—or "tangleweed," as the islanders called it—just offshore.[45]

Initially, because of the heavy surf and the difficulty the volunteers and workers faced in searching through the piles of debris along the high, rocky cliffs, the progress of the search parties was labored and slow.[46] The grisly task was further complicated by the fact that once a body was found, the men not only had to dig it out, but they had to pull it up to the top of a cliff and then carry it for two or three miles over rough terrain to the churchyard at Kilchoman to be examined and identified.[47]

Bodies of the Otranto's *victims were placed in the Kilchoman Church graveyard after the sanctuary was full. Courtesy of Carl Reavey, editor of the* Ileach, *Islay, Scotland, and the Museum of Islay Life.*

By Thursday afternoon, two hundred bodies had been recovered and brought to the church.[48] The first one hundred were placed on pews; then, after all the pews had been filled, the next group was placed on the rostrum. Once the church was full, the searchers had no choice but to place the bodies on the ground outside in the churchyard, side by side, under improvised shelters.[49]

Two or three days after the wreck, the ocean finally became calm, making the search parties' work somewhat easier.[50] Then, unfortunately, the following Saturday, six days after the disaster, the waves and wind, now "blowing strongly off-shore," swept the debris and bodies off the shoreline and back into the sea.[51]

IDENTIFYING THE DEAD

Of the first 200 bodies, authorities managed to identify 160.[52] For others, however, identification was difficult. All of the American soldiers

Police Sergeant Malcolm MacNeill, far left, examined each body for identification and corresponded with family members in the United States and England for many years after the war. Courtesy of Carl Reavey, editor of the Ileach, *Islay, Scotland, and the Museum of Islay Life.*

were supposed to have two brass identification tags around their necks, but many of the tags had been torn from them by the force of the waves or were snagged and ripped from their necks by wreckage in the water and along the cliffs on the shore.[53] Doctors examining the men's bodies determined that many more of them had been killed by the debris and rocks than had drowned.[54]

One of the principal officials involved in the identification of bodies and inventorying their personal effects was police sergeant Malcolm MacNeill of Bowmore, who meticulously recorded the description of each body, noted any tattoos or other identifying marks, and placed each man's personal effects in a small bag sewn by local volunteers. His careful and heartrending descriptions fill eighty-one-pages of a notebook that now resides in the Museum of Islay Life, donated many years later—along with his correspondence to family members in the United States and England who had lost sons, husbands, and brothers aboard the *Otranto*—by his grandson, Lord George Robertson, British defense minister and secretary general of NATO, who was born in the Port Ellen police station.

The personal effects that Sergeant MacNeill so carefully cataloged were then stored and eventually sent to each man's family. Because the American soldiers had been paid two days before the wreck, many of the still-clothed bodies had money in their pockets.[55] One body, found with both arms and legs missing, had almost $500 in a money bag tied around the waist—quite a sum of money for 1918.[56] When Captain Davidson's body was found, Sergeant MacNeill noted that his possessions included "1 pair of binocular glasses, 1 wrist watch, 1 gold ring, 1 silver cigarette case, and 1 tobacco pipe."[57]

ANOTHER FUNERAL

Within a few days, the decomposition of the bodies forced authorities to bury those already found as quickly as possible.[58] Thus, the first fu-

The funeral procession—led by two bagpipers playing "Flowers of the North"— marches from the churchyard at Kilchoman, Islay, Scotland, October 11, 1918. In Archibald Cameron, Otranto Disaster, 6th October, 1918 at Kilchoman, Islay and Burial of American Soldiers and British and French Sailors: *Souvenir Album (Bowmore, Islay, Scotland: Archibald Cameron, 1918). From the author's personal collection.*

neral was held five days after the sinking, on Friday, October 11. It was a solemn affair, conducted by Rev. Donald Grant, who, along with his wife, had played a prominent role in the search-and-rescue efforts.[59] Of the three coffins available on the island, one was used for the body of the *Otranto*'s captain, Ernest G. W. Davidson, and the other two were used for the bodies of two officers.[60] Nearly everyone on Islay turned out, many riding up to thirty miles in the uncomfortable "box carts" indigenous to Ireland and Scotland.[61]

The funeral procession began in the churchyard at Kilchoman, where the bodies had been brought, and was led by two Scottish bagpipers playing "Flowers of the North." Just behind them was a cart bearing the three coffins and an honor guard of British and American soldiers marching with their arms reversed. One of the American soldiers was Sgt. Charles A. McDonald, the survivor from Galesburg, Illinois, who had been asked to stay behind and help look after the other injured survivors. He served in the solemn procession as the American flag bearer.

Rev. Donald Grant conducts the funeral service over the coffin of Ernest G. W. Davidson, captain of HMS Otranto, *and bodies of the first two hundred casualties. In Archibald Cameron,* Otranto Disaster, 6th October, 1918 at Kilchoman, Islay and Burial of American Soldiers and British and French Sailors: Souvenir Album *(Bowmore, Islay, Scotland: Archibald Cameron, 1918). From the author's personal collection.*

Trailing behind the bagpipers, cart, and honor guard were the rest of the members of the procession. These included all three of Islay's clergy—Rev. Donald Grant of the Scotch Presbyterian Church, along with the Episcopal minister and the Roman Catholic priest—followed by American and British military officers, prominent local and Red Cross officials, and a large crowd of local men, women, and children.[62, 63]

Once at the graveyard, they were all confronted by long, wide, shallow trenches—seven feet by sixty feet—that had been dug into a level area on top of the cliff that overlooked the reef where the *Otranto* had wrecked. In the trenches, lying side by side, were the bodies of 46 British and French sailors and 120 American soldiers, all covered with blankets and flowers. Of the bodies, fifty-two had been found without identification tags or any other identifying characteristics and were being buried nameless.[64] Members of the Argyllshire Constabulary, who had traveled to Islay from the mainland, stood guard around the open-trench graves.[65]

American and British flags are dipped as an honor guard fires a six-volley salute. The American flag bearer is one of the survivors, Sgt. Charles A. McDonald of Galesburg, Illinois. In Archibald Cameron, Otranto Disaster, 6th October, 1918 at Kilchoman, Islay and Burial of American Soldiers and British and French Sailors: Souvenir Album *(Bowmore, Islay, Scotland: Archibald Cameron, 1918). From the author's personal collection.*

The service was simple. Rev. Donald Grant, assisted by his colleagues, spoke briefly and read a number of prayers. Then, as the American and British flags were dipped, the honor guard fired a six-volley salute.[66, 67] At the end of the service, the "time-hallowed custom of singing 'God Save the King' at the conclusion of every formal British ceremony was broken."[68] Instead, everyone took off their hats and stood with bare heads in the cold wind and sang both the British and American national anthems.[69]

For the American army officers, survivors, and Red Cross officials present, the singing of "The Star-Spangled Banner" was a deeply appreciated courtesy.[70] After the service—because the bodies were to be all reburied in coffins once the American labor battalion had time to make them—the bodies were all then covered with a light layer of dirt.[71]

The reburial took place six days later, when on Thursday, October 17, they were taken up, added to other bodies found and examined since the first funeral, placed in just-constructed wooden coffins and—under the direction of British colonel Neaton Ellis, US Army captain

View of Kilchoman Bay with the church and manse in the foreground. The cemetery is marked with an "X." In Archibald Cameron, Otranto Disaster, 6th October, 1918 at Kilchoman, Islay and Burial of American Soldiers and British and French Sailors: Souvenir Album *(Bowmore, Islay, Scotland: Archibald Cameron, 1918). From the author's personal collection.*

Puffer, and US army chaplain Aiken (who conducted the ceremony)—reburied.[72] The total number of recovered bodies in the trenches at the end of this reburial was 280.[73]

As other bodies were found, they, too, were brought to the churchyard, examined, and taken to the growing cemetery for burial. Reverend Grant officiated at all of the funerals, sometimes conducting services for six or eight, then three or four, and later for only one at a time, until—in the end—315 American soldiers had found a resting place in the rocky soil of Islay, Scotland.

Lt. R. E. Condon, accompanied by Lt. J. E. McDill, left Islay on the day following the reburial to escort five survivors to Belfast. There they picked up men injured from their jump from the *Otranto* onto the *Mounsey* and proceeded to a rest camp near Winchester, England, where the others had arrived previously.[74]

Meanwhile, officials back on Islay were notified several weeks later that yet another body—that of American sergeant Tom Davis—had been found on the island of Muck. Residents honored his sacrifice by making a coffin of driftwood and—after conducting a simple funeral ceremony—laying his body to rest in the ground of that remote island.[75]

A GRIM ACCOUNTING

There has always been confusion regarding the actual number of casualties. While Paul Frederiksen of the *New York Times* commented, "No one seems to know how many men met their death in the *Otranto* disaster, because no one knows the size of the *Otranto*'s crew or the number of deaths aboard from illness," he cited official reports that put the total number of American lives lost at 358. Thus, to get the total number of men lost, one would then add another 6 who had been among the crew of the French fishing boat *Croisine* and approximately 150 more from the *Otranto*'s crew (Davidson included). Thus, Frederiksen ascertained that 514 men had died in the *Otranto* disaster.[76]

A contemporary account published in the *Washington Post*, however, placed the number of *Otranto* crew killed at 164, with one less American, bringing that final tally to 527.[77] A. B. Campbell, the senior surviving officer of the *Otranto*, stated in his memoir, *When I Was in Patagonia*, that 235 of the crew perished, which would bring the final

Table 7.1. HMS *Otranto* Casualties

	Officers	Men	Marines	Total
British crew	12	84	10	106
American soldiers	1	357	—	358
French fishermen	—	6	—	6
Total	13	447	10	470

tally to 599. Yet another set of figures from the November 1918 issue of *Naval War Notes* reported that "the death roll of [American] soldiers stood at 364 or 366. The discrepancy between the figures [is] . . . due to the mixing up of two identification lists."[78]

The *Naval War Notes* also reported that, in addition to the 16 survivors in Islay already accounted for, there were 300 American soldiers, 30 French fishermen, and 266 members of the *Otranto*'s crew accounted for after being rescued by the *Mounsey*.[79] And of the thirty French fishermen brought aboard after their boat, the *Croisine*, was sunk by the *Otranto*, survivor Leholmes Wells stated, "15 later died in the [*Otranto*] shipwreck."[80] Finally, a letter written nearly two decades later in 1935 by an officer in the Office of Naval Operations to F. J. Reynolds, director of *Collier's Magazine*'s Research Bureau, provides the accounting shown in table 7.1.[81]

In the end, however, for official purposes, the US government appears to have settled on the accounting of the American soldiers aboard shown in tables 7.2 and 7.3, as provided by the War Department's Adjutant General's Office.[82]

Table 7.2. Units aboard *Otranto*, Sunk off the West Coast of Islay, Scotland, October 6, 1918

	Officers	Enlisted Men
Casual officers	2	0
Overseas Casual Co. 406th	1	59
Overseas Casual Co. 410th	1	64
SARD CAC Fort Screven, Unit 1	2	283
SARD CAC Fort Screven, Unit 2	2	285
Total	8	691

Table 7.3. Survivors, Identified Dead, and Missing[83]

	Officers	Enlisted Men
Absent without leave before sailing	0	5
Survivors	7	327
Identified dead	0	205
Died on board before collision	0	2
Died in hospital	0	1
Reported dead, body not found	1	0
Unaccounted for	0	151
Total	8	691

8

THE FAMILIES
BACK HOME

CONFUSION AND DISBELIEF

News of the deaths of the men aboard HMS *Otranto* and the uncertainty from reading incomplete news accounts regarding those lost, missing, or saved had a devastating effect on the soldiers' families back home.

As one reporter in Augusta, Georgia, wrote, "It is believed that forty men from this city were on the vessel, and there is the keenest anxiety in many Augusta homes."[1] They certainly had reason for concern, since, of the forty sons, brothers, and husbands from nearby Screven County on board the *Otranto*, twenty had drowned.[2] October 1918 was an emotional, painful, and confusing time. Lonzon Sheley recounted many years later, "Cards came back that we had landed safely . . . cards that we had mailed in New York; and a wire also went back there that we had landed safely, meaning—we were out of the danger zone—but we never landed anywhere on the *Otranto*. She landed, but at the bottom of St. George's channel."[3]

The cards that Sheley referred to were the cards supplied dockside in New York by the American Red Cross. Each conveyed a brief, simple message: "The ship on which I sailed has arrived safely overseas," followed by blank lines where the soldier wrote his name and unit.[4] For fear that vital information regarding troop movements might land in the hands of the enemy, the name of the ship typically did not appear on the card. After the soldiers filled them out and dropped them into the outgoing mail bag as they marched aboard HMS *Otranto*, the cards were then supposed to be pulled from the box and kept in a safe location until the ship had landed safely. Then, authorities were supposed to pull the cards and mail them to each soldier's next of kin to indicate his safe arrival.

However, in the *Otranto*'s case, American officials received an erroneous wireless message stating that she had arrived safely in England and—on this basis—mailed the cards to family members a couple of weeks after the men had left. Most likely the notification error resulted from an oversight, some clerk indicating that the HX-50 convoy had arrived without mentioning that the *Otranto* was not with it.

When the *Tuscania* had sunk the previous February, near where the *Otranto* had gone down, an account of the tragedy had been wired immediately to newspapers back home. By the following day, the event was front-page news across America.[5] However, with the *Otranto*, it wasn't until October 11, 1918—five *days* after the disaster—that the U.S. War Department sent a brief official cablegram to the press confirming the word-of-mouth accounts that the ship had indeed sunk after colliding with the *Kashmir*.

The cablegram gave no estimate of the number of soldiers confirmed dead or missing; nor did it identify which American units were aboard. As a result, American families back home were still in the dark seven days after the disaster, when newspapers reported on October 13 that the sunken ship was indeed the *Otranto*. Still, the US Army chief of staff, Gen. Peyton C. March, refused to identify the units on board, citing his concern that doing so would bring "needless anxiety" to relatives of men aboard the other ships of the convoy that had landed safely.[6] He changed his mind on October 19, but the announcement was then delayed again because the original copies of the passenger list had gone down with the *Otranto*. Army clerical staff had to search for duplicate rosters from War Department files and then cable them to staff in London so they could check those lists against the names of known survivors. In the meantime, General March could only assure the press, "As soon as this work is complete . . . the [names of] casualties will be announced."[7]

One can imagine the anxiety and concern that families back home were experiencing as they read news accounts of the sinking of HMS *Otranto*. Knowing that it went down with over three hundred soldiers at about the same time that they knew their husbands, fathers, and sons had sailed certainly caused great anguish back home.[8]

Their worst fears began to materialize around October 19, when cablegrams from some of the survivors began arriving in communities back home. Until that date, only a few general newspaper reports had appeared with names of survivors or those killed. In these cablegrams home, however, survivors often mentioned the names of friends and acquaintances who had been killed, friends whose families had already received postcards announcing their safe arrival.[9]

As the cablegrams trickled in, and with little information coming from the War Department, hometown newspapers began supplementing articles about the disaster with information gleaned from cablegrams shared by family members. Then, as family members realized that the postcards they had received—assuring them that their sons and husbands had arrived safely abroad—were not reliable, they spent an agonizing two to three weeks awaiting word as to whether or not their loved one had been aboard the ill-fated *Otranto*, and if he was, whether he was among the survivors.[10]

Stories clarifying the circumstances of local men were published throughout the South. For example, twelve days after the disaster the *Atlanta Constitution* reported, "Fred Johnson . . . has arrived safely overseas, according to a message received by his parents. . . . It was feared

Early news report in the New York Times *regarding the sinking of HMS* Otranto. *Print copy from the author's personal collection.*

that he was lost when the *Otranto* was sunk recently. However . . . while he was in the same convoy with the *Otranto*, the vessel on which he was a passenger escaped without any mishap."[11]

Yet another story—surrounded by articles about individuals who had died in or survived the ongoing horrific influenza pandemic—appeared in the October 28, 1918, *Savannah Morning News*. It focused on the loss of three men from Adel, Georgia (Thomas H. Holland, George Hutto, and John T. Moore), who were on board the *Otranto*: "Moore, son of Frank Moore, a well-known farmer, was married only a few weeks before entering the army. Because of the erroneously reported safe arrival overseas of . . . men who went down on the *Otranto*, uneasiness was expressed [by] persons with relatives on their way over that such reports cannot be depended on."[12]

Finally, even though the War Department was still checking original muster rolls of the units against duplicate listings and identification tags on bodies, department officials cabled to prominent newspapers and news services an incomplete list of the names of two hundred dead soldiers and twenty-nine survivors.[13] These lists were widely reported in papers on October 27 and 28, nearly three weeks after the sinking.[14]

Another example of the incomplete accounting of casualties to families back home was the fact that while the name of survivor M. L. Wallman of Macon, Georgia, was not on the October 27 official list, his wife received a telegram from the War Department that same day informing her of his death.[15] Another partial list of seventy-nine Georgia survivors appeared in the *Savannah Morning News* and other newspapers on November 4.[16]

Meanwhile, other brief reports, based on letters and other communications, continued. For example, the *Atlanta Constitution* published in its issue of November 5, 1918, that "Sergeant George H. Kennedy, [son of Mrs. William E. Kennedy, widow of the late William E. Kennedy, US Army retired] of Augusta was not on board the ill-fated *Otranto* . . . [according to] a letter received from the young soldier by his sister . . . announcing his safe arrival overseas on another vessel." The paper reported that Kennedy had been transferred to another unit just prior to the sailing of the *Otranto*.[17]

In yet another example of such reports, while the family of Pvt. William J. Cooney in Augusta, Georgia, had received a cablegram announcing his safe arrival, they read of his death in a newspaper even before the second telegraph cable arrived. The reporter wrote, "It appears that young Cooney was saved and [had] promptly cabled his father. However, before his cable reached them, he was dead from pneumonia, contracted from the exposure following the wreck." The Associated Press announced the young soldier's death and burial before his telegraph cable, sent about October 12, reached his family.[18] The same account concludes, "It is believed that at least 60 to 65 Augustans were on the ill-fated transport and the anxiety here continues to be intense. So far the War Department and Navy Department have not given out the names of those aboard the *Otranto*. . . . It is doubtful that the Washington authorities know exactly who were on the vessel when it was wrecked."[19]

With datelines from scores of small towns throughout Georgia—Sparks, Nichols, Blythe, Quitman, Alamo, Morven, Sylvania, and Moultrie—as well as the rest of the South, stories and photographs of men lost were reported in a steady stream of accounts in local, hometown papers. The stories appeared day by day, through the end of October and into November 1918, while duplicate muster rolls were being sent back and forth between England and the War Department to establish the identities of the soldiers lost.[20]

Thumbnail entries with heartrending stories regarding deaths accented the grief and anxiety of everyone concerned. For example, William P. Battle Jr., son of the assistant fire chief for Augusta, Georgia, who before going into the army had been employed in the executive offices of the Georgia Railroad, was among those killed. He was Chief Battle's last surviving child; within a brief time, the chief had lost his mother, his wife, and his daughter to influenza, and now his son had perished on the *Otranto*. He was left with only a little grandson, the son of his daughter, as his only relative.[21]

How, one asks, can a person survive such grief? Yet another heartrending story is that of Cpl. Willie Ready who had gone into the army two years previously. Only twenty years old, he had lost both parents and lived with a sister, Mamie Junkins. His brother Charlie had not been heard from in several weeks, and it was feared that he was on the *Ticonderoga*, a ship torpedoed on September 30, 1918, in the mid-Atlantic by U-152.[22] Of the 237 sailors and soldiers aboard the *Ticonderoga*, only twenty-four survived.[23]

Names of 4 additional *Otranto* casualties and 294 enlisted men who had been saved were published in newspapers on October 28.[24] The War Department continued to send cablegrams to families in small towns all through October and into November. Savannah was among the cities and towns hard-hit; for example, on October 30, three weeks after the sinking, the Savannah paper reported, "The wife of Sergeant Ralph S. Ray has been advised that he was lost on the transport *Otranto* off the Scottish coast. This is the seventh Savannah victim. . . . He had previously been reported 'safe overseas.'"[25] Ray had enlisted in the regular army and, while stationed at Fort Screven, married a local Savannah girl and intended to make the city his home after the war ended.[26]

Yet another loss was reported in the *Atlanta Constitution* on November 19: "Mrs. Jodie C. Forrester [of Savannah] has been advised of the death of her husband, Sgt. Jodie C. Forrester, on the transport *Otranto*, lost off the Scottish coast several weeks ago. He left from Fort Screven and had been in the service six years. His parents live in Pinson, Tennessee."[27]

The process of notifying families dragged out ever so painfully. The names of twelve additional American soldiers lost were announced on November 14, thirty-nine days after the disaster.[28] Another thirteen names were released on November 21, and seven more on November 23. Then, forty-eight days after the *Otranto*'s sinking and thirteen days after the cessation of the war's hostilities on November 11, the US War Department announced one hundred more names of those lost—forty-eight of whom were from Georgia—on November 24, 1918.[29-31]

It was an emotionally brutal and sad time for families. With so many declared missing and the War Department being so slow to communicate the final status of the men, their mothers, fathers, and wives began placing queries in local newspapers in the hope that someone might know whether their loved one had survived or been lost. For example, seven weeks after the sinking and two weeks after the armistice that ended the war, a mother placed the following notice in the *Savannah Morning News*:

Waynesboro Mother Seeks Information of Her Son

I ask every mother who has a surviving son from the *Otranto*, to cut out this clipping and mail it to her boy, asking if he can give any information concerning Private Edwin A. Smith, on board said ship.

I have had official information that he sailed, but he is still unaccounted for. Any one who can furnish any information whatever concerning my son please wire or cable at my expenses. Mrs. E.A. Smith 503 Jones Avenue Waynesboro, Ga.[32]

Yet another list was reported November 27, with the names of seven more men from largely rural Berrien County, Georgia. Townspeople of Nashville, Georgia, and its surrounding countryside, who had so many family members aboard the *Otranto*, now had forty-five sons, brothers, fathers, and husbands who were not coming home from the war.[33] Local citizens were already talking about erecting a monument on the town square to honor the men.[34] Savannah lost nine: Sgt. W. W. Carter, Sgt. Thomas L. Davis, Sgt. Henry E. Gaudry, Sgt. George W. Lowden Jr., Pvt. John A. Hutton Jr., Pvt. Joseph H. Oppenheim, Pvt. Charles F. Walden, Pvt. William E. Warth, and Pvt. Gordon S. Hickman.[35]

As staff in the US War Department continued to struggle with getting the names on their lists correct, one soldier, Walter T. Browner, was at his father's home in Atlanta when he read his own name in the November 24 list as being among the dead. Browner had indeed been on the *Otranto* when it was ready to sail, but he was among those pronounced physically unfit and ordered back to Camp Merritt, where he recovered in the camp's hospital. Just a month later he was discharged from the army.[36]

Indeed, even though the war was over, the cables to families continued, and there was no way to be confident that a loved one had survived his voyage aboard the *Otranto* unless a family member had received a letter from him dated after the ship's sinking. Case in point was the notification on November 29—fifty-four days after the *Otranto* disaster—of the next of kin of four more men from the small town of Quitman, Georgia, that their family member had died. These men lost were in addition to three others from Quitman whose deaths had been announced previously. So, in sum, seven of the twenty who had left Quitman the previous July would never return home. Two months after the wreck, newspaper reporters continued to report that "families of some of the others have not heard from [their loved ones] and are very anxious about them, as all of them are believed to have been in the same unit."[37]

Survivor Leholmes Wells's family had received a telegram notifying them that their son was among the dead, and until he returned home, he was uncertain as to who among his friends had survived and who had perished. His family learned that he was alive from a list of survivors published in the local newspaper, the *Sylvania Telephone*.[38, 39] The impact of the previously received telegram, however, had been devastating. Wells related some years later, "My mother said she was cooking when she got the telegram. . . . She went right out the back door sat down in a field and cried. My daddy went out on the front porch and sat for several hours without moving."[40] Wells's arrival home did not go unnoticed, however: "The teacher and pupils from Beulah, the little one-room school that I attended, marched to my house from a mile away. I can't tell you how I felt when those little children came up on the porch and hugged me, one after another." Then, the next Sunday, at his church—Greenhill Baptist—the pastor had him sit in the front row.[41] Wells remarked, "I'm sure I must have looked a physical wreck to them. The last time they saw me I weighed 180 pounds. When we were reunited again I weighed only 125."[42] The emotional scars lasted his whole life; he commented to a reporter in 1963, "For a long time I didn't want to talk or think about what happened. It was too awful. . . . I haven't been on any ships since I got home, and even though it was 45 years ago, I don't think I'd like to."[43]

Articles and announcements with names and pictures of men who were added to and taken off lists of the dead continued to be reported all through January 1919.[44] And the body of one soldier—Paul Portington—was not recovered and buried until eight months after the collision, in June 1919.[45]

THE WAR IS OVER—TOO SAD TO CELEBRATE

With the news of the disaster first suppressed, then delayed, and finally reported, but in such an incomplete manner, the joy of America winning the war and having her boys come home—for those families in communities hit hard by the deaths of their husbands, fathers, and brothers who had died aboard the *Otranto*—was overshadowed by the sadness of their losses. Many mothers, wives, and fathers were too devastated with grief to celebrate the war's end.[46]

While many celebrated the armistice, a number of ugly incidents were perpetrated against citizens of German ancestry. In Savannah, for example, a storeowner of German birth was taken from his business by a mob of several hundred who attached a sign to his back reading, "I am a Kaiser lover." They accused him of disloyalty, forced him to kiss an American flag, and paraded him through the streets until they were intercepted by the police near the police station. It was a humiliating incident, as witnesses reported that the man offered over and again to kiss the flag, stating that he was an American citizen and that the American flag was his own flag as well. When the police chief arrived on the scene and asked those in the crowd what charges of disloyalty they might want to file, no one stepped forward. The chief then offered to turn the man in to an agent of the US Department of Justice who was also present, but—there being no charges—the agent refused to take him into custody. Then Rev. John S. Wilder stepped forward and addressed the crowd. He masterfully brought resolution to the incident by having the man once again kiss the American flag and then salute it three times.[47]

Another incident described in the *Savannah Morning News* under the headline "Executed by Rumor" reported that a Scandinavian tailor—just three weeks earlier—had been brooding over accusations by someone in his South Georgia community that he was a German spy. The incident left him haunted by the feeling that others thought the same thing to the extent that he "surrendered to despair, locked himself in his little shop and slashed his [own] throat."[48] The editor of the paper, after pointing out the viciousness of his fellow citizens and the suffering that the tailor and another citizen "in a Northeast Georgia County"—who had been married to a German citizen earlier in her life—had endured, wondered if these individuals might be martyrs to the cause that America had been fighting for: "liberty, and justice for all."[49]

Still, despite the grief of so many and the dark incidents such as these, parades and celebrations took place across the nation and throughout Georgia to celebrate the end of the war. Typical of the large parades held for returning soldiers was one five months after the sinking of HMS *Otranto*, almost to the day, in Savannah, which had lost eighty men in the war, nine of them on the *Otranto*.[50, 51]

The celebration began out on Tybee Island, where a massive volley was fired by the coastal guns at Fort Screven.[52] Then, downtown, where hundreds of flags were flying, and with "the whole world out, young and old, big and little, rich and poor, all united in one big human emotion," the parade began.[53]

Marching with the returning veterans as part of an honor guard was a contingent of young cadets from Savannah's Benedictine Military School. They were followed by a group of stooped Civil War veterans, "marching in their old grey uniforms," many of them carrying small US flags.[54] Then came row upon row of returning soldiers marching in formation in front of the thousands of spectators to the gathering point for the celebration. There they stopped and, standing in parade rest formation, bowed their heads as a lone bugler played "Taps"; then they watched the flag-raising ceremony. As the gold service flag was raised, a reporter for the *Savannah Morning News* wrote, "with its eighty gold stars to honor their fallen comrades, and with the escort of honor behind them, the returning veterans faced the vast throng that looked on with tear-filled eyes, as . . . this solemn moment stood out as one never to be forgotten." Afterward, a US Marine Corps band played the national anthem, with the reporter noting, "When the last notes died away there was a moment of absolute stillness, [as] not a sound [was] heard over the vast assemblage."[55]

While such ceremonies were certainly appreciated by the wives, children, and parents who had lost beloved family members, they were still left with the age-old issue confronting family members of those who do not return from wars: Should one remain in the arms of memory and grief? Or is it best to try to move on with one's life the best way one can? While the latter is certainly the logical long-term answer, in the short term, such efforts are not so easily embraced. This dilemma of so many relatives of the *Otranto*'s dead is reflected in the words of my great-aunt, Caddie M. Scott, of Screven County, Georgia, as she reflected on the loss of her brother, twenty-six-year-old Pvt. James Frank Scott, who went down with the *Otranto*: "It seems like we cannot bear to give up dear Frank, as he was our baby boy and the light of our home. . . . Our dear brother had many friends, far and near, and [he] will be sadly missed, but mostly in his home by his devoted loved ones. How sad it is that we cannot see his sweet face again."[56]

After the war's end, US authorities spent millions of dollars to exhume the bodies of dead American soldiers and ship them home, including those recovered from the wreckage of the *Otranto*. Among the first to arrive were those of five soldiers from Screven County, each finally laid lovingly to rest in the hard red clay of their home communities.[57] Eleven years later, in October 1929—when an article appeared in the *American Legion Monthly* announcing the availability of photographs of the group of survivors who swam to shore on Islay and of the wreckage and burial services, as well as of services in their honor the following Memorial Day—only four graves of American soldiers remained on the island of Islay.[58] The other soldiers had either been brought home and buried in America or moved to the American Cemetery at Brookwood, Surrey, England.[59]

Friends, families, and shipmates in small towns and rural communities throughout the South—especially Georgia—were hard-hit. As Leholmes Wells from Sylvania remarked, "The sinking of the *Otranto* resulted in the loss of 431 lives," and "of that of that number, [it is estimated] 120 were from Georgia, and 17 of that number were friends of mine from Screven County."[60]

9

THE AFTERMATH

THE RESIDENTS OF ISLAY, SCOTLAND

The men and women of the island of Islay were caring and compassionate in their treatment of the *Otranto*'s survivors and those who came to help them search for and bury the dead.[1] The two young boys of the McPhee family—Donald and John—gave up their beds and slept in a nearby shed so the survivors staying at their house would be comfortable. And Mrs. Anderson, owner of a small store nearby, let Red Cross workers take anything they needed, to the extent that within a short time her shelves were almost empty.[2]

As a gesture of goodwill, the Red Cross sent representatives back to Islay a few months after the disaster with tokens of appreciation to those who had assisted in the search-and-rescue efforts: pipes, tobacco, and underwear for the men; chocolate and clothing for the women; and modest reimbursements for those who had incurred expenses and not been repaid.[3]

The deaths of so many men hung heavy over everyone. But were it not for the courage and resourcefulness of Lt. Francis W. Craven and the crew of HMS *Mounsey*, many more would have been lost. As such, soon after reading a press dispatch about Craven's heroism, US Secretary of the Navy Josephus Daniels cabled Adm. William F. Sims, commander US naval forces operating in European waters, to verify the reports of his courageous action and to ask again that Sims write a letter to the British Admiralty to express the US Navy's "high appreciation of the gallant achievement" of Captain Craven.[4]

Admiral Sims complied as follows:

I convey to the Lords Commissioners of the Admiralty [our] high appreciation of the gallant and courageous conduct and very skillful seamanship displayed by Lieutenant Francis W. Craven, R.N., commanding HMS *Mounsey*, which resulted in saving the lives of several hundred American troops upon the occasion of the loss of the HMS *Otranto*, and to express its very sincere thanks for Lieutenant Craven's notable services. . . .

I desire to express my own admiration, and that of the Forces under my command, for this most inspiring example of pluck, nautical judgment, and seamanship. That Lieutenant Craven was able to take a relatively frail vessel several times alongside a sinking vessel within one and a half miles of a dangerous lee shore in a gale blowing ninety miles an hour; that he repeated this dangerous operation even after his vessel was leaking badly and the presence of several hundred rescued men on board placed her in a dangerous condition of stability was, I believe, a feat equal to the best in the history of the British or any other Navy.[5]

LT. FRANCIS CRAVEN HONORED

On Admiral Sims's recommendation, President Woodrow Wilson ordered that Lieutenant Craven's bravery be recognized by the award of the Distinguished Service Medal. While intended to recognize exceptional American soldiers, the medal—which had been authorized by an act of the US Congress only the previous July—was also available for presentation "to persons other than members of the Armed Forces of the United States for wartime service . . . [but] only under exceptional circumstances and with the express approval of the President in each case."[6]

The announcement to the press of the presentation of the medal to Lieutenant Craven on February 3, 1919, included the following statement from Major General John Biddle, commander of the American forces in the United Kingdom:

The President of the United States has awarded the Distinguished Service Medal to Lieut. F.W. Craven, R.N., as a mark of appreciation for his gallantry and skilful seamanship on October 6th last.

Lieut. Craven was in Command of the *Mounsey* when the *Otranto* carrying U.S.A. troops was in collision. The accident occurred in the North of the Irish Sea in a very rough sea. By skilful handling of his ship Lieut. Craven was instrumental in taking off over 600 officers and men, comprising a part of the crew and U.S.A. troops on board.

The presentation to Lieut. Craven was made on Naval Barrack Square Chatham, by General Biddell, U.S.A. commanding the American Forces in England, General Pershing being detained in France by his military duties.[7]

The British government followed the American recognition by awarding Craven the Distinguished Service Order, often referred to as the "DSO," a military decoration presented "for meritorious or distinguished service by [British] officers of the armed forces during wartime, typically in actual combat." Instituted in 1886 by Queen Victoria, the award usually went to commanding officers of the rank of major or higher, with the exception that some awards could be given "to especially valorous junior officers" for "a high degree of gallantry just short of deserving the Victoria Cross."

During World War I, DSO award winners were announced in the *London Gazette*, the official newspaper of record in the United Kingdom.[8, 9] The description in the *Gazette* of Craven's heroism was probably taken from the following military dispatch:

Prenton Officer's Bravery
    D.S.O. for Saving 600 Americans
    Among those upon whom the honor of Companion of the Distinguished Service Order has been conferred is Lieut. Francis Worthington Craven, R.N., of Prenton, Birkenhead, who was in command of the destroyer *Mounsey*, and who by his magnificent courage and seamanship was the means of saving 600 lives from the American troopship *Otranto*, which was wrecked after being in collision off the Scottish coast on 6th October 1918, and over 500 lives lost. The official account of Lieut. Craven's deed is as follows:
    "H.M.S. *Otranto* was damaged in collision with the s/s *Kashmir* whilst carrying a large number of American troops. Lieut. Craven displayed magnificent courage and seamanship in placing H.M.S. *Mounsey* alongside H.M.S. *Otranto* in spite of the fact that the conditions of wind, weather and sea were exceptionally severe. After going alongside and embarking a certain number of men, it was reported that the *Mounsey* had sustained considerable damage, and that there was a large quantity of water in the engine room."
    "Lieut. Craven therefore, left the *Otranto*, but on finding that the damage was not so serious as had been reported, he again went alongside, though he had previously experienced great difficulty in getting away. His action resulted in the saving of 600 lives which would otherwise have

certainly been lost. His performance was a remarkable one, and in personal courage, coolness and seamanship ranks in the very highest order."

"Lieut. Craven is the son of the late Mr. Jonas Craven, J.P. of Marple and Manchester, and Mrs. Craven, Prenton. He entered the service at the then earliest age, going through the old training ship *Britiannia*. At the outbreak of the war he was on the *Audacious*, and later on the *Queen Elizabeth* at the storming of the Dardanelles Forts. It is said of him if there was any special tough job on hand the suggestion was made to 'send for Craven.' Of his four brothers, the eldest is the legal advisor in Nigeria, the second is serving with the Canadian Army, the third is a commander in the Royal Navy, and the fifth a captain in the Royal Marine Artillery."[10]

Two other officers aboard the *Otranto* were also decorated: Lt. Raymond Benson Stewart, RN, and Sub-Lt. Wilfrid Edmund Warner, RN, were awarded the Distinguished Service Cross by the British government for their heroic actions.

WHO WERE THESE BRAVE MEN?

Among the many remarkable stories of the disaster was that of Pvt. Robert F. Shawd, of Lebanon, Pennsylvania. Two of his brothers had been aboard the *Tuscania* when it was torpedoed the previous February. Both were saved and wrote to him afterwards to urge him to learn how to swim. Shawd later remarked, "If I had not taken their advice . . . I would not be alive today." He was among those who had tried to jump from the *Otranto* to the *Mounsey* but fell into the sea. Having taken his brothers' advice, he was among the few who survived the swim to shore.[11]

Another who survived was Alva J. Cochran, whose family did not learn that he was safe until two months after the disaster, when—in mid-December—the War Department notified them that he was in an American rest hospital in England recovering from shock and exposure due to the sinking.[12] Before his induction into the army, Cochran had been a member of the Atlanta Fire Department, assigned to Fire House No. 4. His family endured the war worrying about all three of their sons: Alva, who survived the sinking of the *Otranto*; his brother, Lt. Emmett Cochran, who had been rescued the previous May as the *Moldavia* was sinking; and R. B. Cochran, serving in France.[13]

There were others: Edwin A. Smith's parents in Waynesboro, Georgia, were not notified that their son was lost aboard the *Otranto* until November 24, thirteen days after the war ended and forty-nine days after the ship had gone down. A popular young man in his home community, Smith had to leave his cotton crop in the field for his father to take care of when he reported for duty. After his father had the crop picked and sold, he used the proceeds to purchase $25,000 worth of Fourth Liberty Loan Drive bonds to help support the war effort.[14]

The first of the injured Fort Screven contingent from the *Otranto* to arrive at a home hospital for treatment were James G. Wright of Adel, Georgia, and Emory D. Hall of Savannah. Both arrived at the Fort McPherson Hospital (near Atlanta) with foot and leg injuries in mid-December 1918.[15] They were followed during the ensuing months by hundreds of their comrades.

GRAVES OF THE DEAD ON ISLAY

As for the American soldiers buried on Islay, though the Scottish islanders had taken excellent care of the graves and pledged to look after them "as if they were their own until the end of time," the American

Kilchoman Military Cemetery in 2002, island of Islay. Photo by R. Neil Scott.

Graves Registration Service decided in June 1920 to exhume and rebury them elsewhere.[16] Retrieving the bodies from the small graveyard on Islay was not an easy task. The graves were situated near a cliff overlooking the ocean. As the coffins were removed, they were transported to a vessel waiting offshore. They were then transported to another vessel waiting offshore.[17] Finally, based on the preference of the soldier's next of kin, some were transported and buried in the American Cemetery at Brookwood, Surrey, England, while others were sent back to the United States. For example, the body of Pvt. Tom McDonald (Company F, 816th Pioneer Infantry Regiment) of Richton, Mississippi—whose death was attributed to influenza while aboard the *Otranto*—was shipped home. Still others were buried in Arlington National Cemetery.[18] By 1938, only three American *Otranto* victims remained buried in the Kilchoman Military Cemetery on Islay, two soldiers—J. C. Geiger and Fred J. Martin—and the YMCA officer C. A. Carpenter.

In the end, it was determined that six of the fishermen from the *Croisine* had gone down with the *Otranto*: the captain, Jules Lehoerff, and five seamen: Jean-Marie Ronsval, Jean-Pascal, Alfred Ladire, Ange Riou, and Marcel Galle. Three more—Louis Cholou, Guillaume Denier, and Jean-Marie Bougeard—had jumped to the *Mounsey* and saved themselves, but died later in a Belfast hospital.[19]

Six years later, during the summer of 1924, a French ship, the *Pourquoi Pas* ("Why Not"), was sent to Islay to pick up and transport the exhumed body of Cpt. Jules Lehoerff back to Saint-Malo, France. Back on his home soil, his friends and family celebrated a second funeral in his honor and buried him in his hometown of Cancale on July 19.[20]

During the 1920s, many mothers who belonged to the Gold Star Mothers' Association traveled to Europe to visit their sons' graves; others, however, did not have the financial means to do so.[21] For the latter, Congress appropriated funds in 1929 to authorize the secretary of war to arrange for mothers and widows of American soldiers who had died in the service of their country between April 5, 1917, and July 1, 1921, and were lost or buried at sea or interred in Europe, to travel at government expense to cemeteries in Europe.[22] Many mothers of those lost aboard the *Otranto* participated in the funded pilgrimages of 1930, 1931, 1932, and 1933.

Typical of the letters of invitation extended to them was that sent to the mother of thirty-one-year-old Pvt. Benton Edenfield from Swainsboro, Georgia, one of the Fort Screven contingent lost aboard the *Otranto*:

> Arrangements have been made for the mothers and widows of veterans who were lost or buried at sea during the World War to sail May 25, 1932, on the *President Roosevelt*. A special itinerary has been arranged which will include memorial services to be held at sea May 30th in honor of the veterans therein.
>
> The names of veterans who were buried at sea will be inscribed in memorial chapels now under construction in the Brookwood American Cemetery, London, England, and in the Suresnes American Cemetery, Paris, France. While the names may not be inscribed by June, 1932, the itinerary prepared for the mothers and widows of these heroes will include visits to both cemeteries, as well as sightseeing trips in and about London and Paris.[23]

Despite the advancing age of many of the mothers—who were typically sixty-one to sixty-five years old by the time the trips ended in October 1933—6,693 of the 17,389 eligible women made the trip.[24] Each was given a wreath to lay on her loved one's grave while a photographer took her picture. With the emotion and advanced age of the participants, "the Army expected the mothers to break down at the gravesites, [when] in fact they showed strength" as "of the thousands of pilgrims, only one mother needed medical attention at a cemetery."[25]

PLACING THE LOSS OF THE *OTRANTO* IN CONTEXT

To place the estimated 470 lives lost in the *Otranto* sinking in context, readers are reminded that during the entire war, while numerous Allied combat ships were torpedoed, only a few troopships carrying American military personnel were lost. Of those traveling eastward with troops, only the *Tuscania*, the *Moldavia*, and the *Otranto*—all British chartered ships—and one animal transport, the *Ticonderoga*, were sunk: the *Tuscania* was torpedoed February 5, 1918, by U-77 with 245 lost; the *Moldavia* was torpedoed May 23, 1918, by U-57 with 56 lost; and the *Ticonderoga* was torpedoed September 30, 1918, by U-152 with 213 lives lost.[26]

On the journey west, six ships were lost or seriously damaged: The British chartered troopship *Dwinsk* was sunk June 18, 1918, by U-151 with twenty-three dead. Three American Transport Force ships were lost: the *President Lincoln* (sunk May 31, 1918, by U-90 with twenty-six dead), the *Covington* (sunk July 1, 1918, by U-86 with six dead), and the *Antilles* (sunk October 17, 1917, by U-62 with sixty-seven dead).[27] Two other American transports—the *Finland*, "manned by a civilian crew," and the *Mount Vernon*, "manned by the Navy"—were also torpedoed but managed to navigate to port for needed repairs with no loss of life.[28]

Other American ships lost in naval combat included the *Tampa*, sunk September 26, 1918, by U-91 with 131 lost, and the *USS Cyclops*, lost with all 306 aboard in early March 1918. The *Cyclops*, a fuel ship, is believed to have disappeared in the Bermuda Triangle while returning from Brazil. Neither her wreck nor any debris was ever found. Readers interested in learning more about maritime losses during World War I are referred to *Lloyd's War Losses: The First World War: Casualties to Shipping through Enemy Causes, 1914–1918* (1990).

This modest loss record for troopships is quite impressive when one considers the number of convoys and the number of ships in each convoy that crisscrossed the Atlantic through submarine-infested waters. While certainly tragic and regrettable, the losses are light when one considers that from the beginning of the war through November 1, 1918, approximately 2,066,442 American troops were transported by troopship to France, England, and other ports on their way to the war zone, and fewer than 1,100 were lost.[29]

MONUMENTS TO THE DEAD

For the present-day visitor, there is an impressive reminder of America's losses off the island of Islay. On the southernmost tip, on a cliff jutting three hundred feet above the sea known as the Mull of Oa, stands an eighty-foot Pictish tower built by George Reid & Sons of Ayrshire. Designed by architect Robert J. Walker of Glasgow, the tower was constructed of stone gathered nearby, wheeled to the site by hand in wheelbarrows, and dedicated to the memory of the dead of the *Tuscania* and *Otranto*.

The tower, visible on a clear day for up to fifty miles at sea, was built and paid for by the Red Cross from an appropriation of $30,826 set aside for its erection and maintenance.[30, 31] It still stands today as a reminder to those who see it of the danger and death that so many

Monument to the victims of the Otranto *and* Tuscania *erected on the Mull of Oa, Islay, Scotland. Courtesy of Carl Reavey, editor of the* Ileach, *Islay, Scotland, and the Museum of Islay Life.*

men found in the nearby waters. On one side of the tower is a plaque given by President Wilson and depicting a bronze wreath; inscribed on it is the following:

> Sacred to the immortal memory of those American soldiers and sailors who gave their lives for their country in the wrecks of the transports *Tuscania* and *Otranto* February 5, 1918–October 6, 1918. This monument was erected by the American Red Cross near the spot where so many of the victims of the disaster sleep in everlasting peace. "On fame's eternal camping ground, their silent tents are spread. While glory keeps with solemn round, the bivouac of the dead."[32]

Sadly, there are no statues, towers, or other notable reminders in the United States of the fathers, sons, and husbands lost on HMS *Otranto*. Indeed, to date, I have not even identified a street, bridge, or building named for the men. Instead, one has to stop and read fading inscriptions on bronze plaques attached to the sides of a couple of World War I memorials to find any mention of the tragedy.

Spirit of the American Doughboy. *Ernest M. Viquesney's statue in Nashville, Georgia, erected in honor of the sixty men from the community lost during World War I. Of that number, twenty-five were lost on HMS* Otranto. *Photo by R. Neil Scott.*

Perhaps the most notable of such plaques is the one found in the small Georgia town of Nashville, seat of Berrien County. There, on the base of a memorial sculpted by Ernest M. Viquesney erected in memory of the sixty men from that community who were lost in World War I, are two panels of names. If one looks closely, on the panel on the north face, one will find the names of twenty-five men from that county lost on the *Otranto*.[33] Another memorial can be found 143 miles north, in Screven County, Georgia. There, in the small town of Sylvania, one will find another tablet on a small, modest stone, dedicated to seventeen local men who perished aboard the *Otranto*.

Georgia historian Todd Womack, from Douglas, Georgia, describes how Viquesney's sculpture came to be erected in Nashville, Georgia:

As the citizens of Nashville began to pick out designs for a monument, a sculptor from nearby Americus, Georgia named Ernest M. Viquesney began drawing his own design for a larger than life statue of the American doughboy in combat. The Spanish-American War veteran studied dozens of military photographs and manuals in order to accurately sculpt all of the equipment that a soldier would have carried into battle. He even had two of his friends who had just come back from the war model in their uniforms for him.

By the summer of 1919, his basic design was finished, as well as a small model of his proposed statue. He then contacted Nashville [town officials] and showed them his work. The town was so impressed that it voted to raise an additional $5,000 to purchase it.

Viquesney immediately went to work sculpting the seven foot tall bronze statue. He carefully made the M1910 backpack showing the trench shovel, bedroll and detailed stitching. The '03 Springfield rifle . with its bayonet looks real and upon closer inspection of the soldier's right hand shows that he is about to throw a hand grenade. He stands in the middle of bronze mud, amid broken stumps and tangles of barbed wire.[34]

After Ernest Viquesney finished his work, representatives from other towns and cities traveled to Americus, Georgia, to see the statue. Soon, orders were flowing in, and he found himself in the business of manufacturing and shipping copies of the statue, now renamed *Spirit of the American Doughboy*. Between 1921 and 1943, Viquesney made more than 150 of these statues for communities throughout the nation.[35] Besides the first one completed and erected in Nashville, Georgia, in 1921, others can still be viewed today in communities such as Greenville, South Carolina; Dover, New Jersey; Tyrone, Oklahoma; Palatka, Florida; and Waycross, Georgia.[36, 37]

J. A. Roquemore, in his role as commander of American Legion "*Otranto*" Post" No. 115 in Nashville, Georgia, wrote in 1930 that Berrien County, Georgia, had thirty-three men aboard the *Otranto*, and of that number, only five had survived. He wrote, "Berrien County claims the unhappy distinction of having lost on the *Otranto* more men in proportion to population than any county in the country. Twenty-eight of the men lost were from our county."[38]

When one adds up the number of men from Georgia—especially those in a triangle extending from Savannah northwest to Augusta and then south to Dublin—who died aboard HMS *Otranto*, it is surprising that there is not a notable memorial devoted to their memory. Even in Savannah's elegant Ships of the Sea Maritime Museum, housed in the

Scarbrough House, built in 1819 by the owner of the *Savannah*—with its extensive exhibit of 150 ship models and notable collection of maritime paintings and antiques—there is not a single mention of HMS *Otranto* or the men from that city who died in the disaster. This is an especially odd and troubling fact when one stops to consider that the *Otranto*'s sinking was the single greatest maritime disaster to befall American soldiers during World War I.[39]

THE BODIES ARE RETURNED HOME

Only three months after the *Otranto*'s sinking, the first bodies of the men washed ashore were being exhumed and transported to England and America for reburial. Among the first returned was the body of Maurice L. Wallnau, who had married only six months before his enlistment in the Coast Artillery. His body was returned to his wife, who saw that he was buried with full military honors in Macon, Georgia, on August 16, 1920.[40] The bodies of Sgt. Henry E. Gaudry and Pvt. Joseph H. Oppenheim were returned to their families in Savannah on August 31.[41] Soon, others came home to communities throughout Georgia, the South, and the nation, as families buried their sons, brothers, and husbands in family and church cemeteries, local community cemeteries, and Arlington National Cemetery.

When classmates of young Mack Johnson, a fifth grader at the Hill Street School in Atlanta, learned that his brother, Sgt. Jesse A. Johnson, had gone down with the *Otranto*, the children gathered together on Armistice Day 1920 and recited poems, sang patriotic songs, and planted a tree in his memory.[42] The body of another *Otranto* casualty from Atlanta, Pvt. John T. Gardner, was returned on June 24, 1922, along with the bodies of another fifteen casualties from that city, for burial in West View Cemetery.[43]

During the 1920s, survivors were encouraged to send any material they thought might be of interest to other members of the National *Otranto-Kashmir* Association to Harold F. English of Saginaw, Michigan, who had volunteered to serve as the association's historian. He assured members that the items would be "placed in the archives of the historian."[44] Unfortunately, however, over the years, whatever he may have collected has disappeared into some attic or trash bin.

In 1929, the commander of the Scotland Post of the American Legion in Glasgow sponsored the printing and distribution to family members of a series of photographs taken on Islay "of groups of survivors, of the burial services, and of the graves afterwards, [and of] parts of the coast showing wreckage and [of] services on Memorial Day, 1919."[45] Only a few of these sets of photographs are known to exist. They were printed and published by Archibald Cameron of Douglas House, Bowmore, Islay, Scotland.[46]

THE REST
OF THE STORY

FRANCIS CRAVEN IS KILLED IN IRELAND

The end of the war found the highly decorated Lt. Francis W. Craven, commander of the HMS *Mounsey*, in difficult circumstances. With the *Mounsey* badly damaged and out of service, Craven was promoted from lieutenant to lieutenant commander and placed in command of HMS *Tirade*, then HMS *Spear*. However, at this same time, issues in his personal life began to cast a shadow over his professional accomplishments. Though he was trying to support his family back home, war's end found him so deep in debt that he was being forced into bankruptcy. With no choice but to focus on resolving the financial difficulties facing him and his wife and children, he applied to be relieved of his command in November 1919, resigned his commission in April 1920, and a month later, on May 13, 1920, was placed on the Royal Navy's "Retired List."

Life then started to look up for him again, as by July 1920 he had secured funds from a variety of American friends and paid all his debts. Then, on July 27, 1920, he was notified that the US president had added the Navy Cross to the list of decorations awarded Craven for his heroic efforts in saving the men aboard the *Otranto*. Still, he had to make a living, and with the Royal Navy shedding men on its rosters by the thousands, he decided to enlist in the Auxiliary Division of the Royal Irish Constabulary, formed to help the British government suppress the Irish Republican Army in Ireland. Craven's intelligence and ability under pressure were soon recognized, as just a year later, in December 1921, he was promoted to intelligence officer. Still, it was hard going, as Craven and so many other veterans of the Great War found themselves "fighting in a vicious doomed campaign within their own country . . . in a foreign land where they could trust no one and were despised."[1]

The end for this hero came at 2:00 p.m. on February 2, 1921, when, traveling with seventeen Auxiliary police in two lorries from Granard to Longford, Ireland, Craven was ambushed at Clonfin by fifty members of the Irish Republican Army's Longford Brigade under Sean MacRoin. The men in the first vehicle took the initial blow. Two officers were killed immediately, and the rest were wounded. The other officers, in the second vehicle, then fought a pitched battle with the attackers for ten to fifteen minutes but were forced to surrender when they ran out of ammunition. Craven, among those in the second vehicle, was wounded in the leg during the exchange of gunfire. Then, as he paused to bandage his wound, he was shot in the neck and killed.[2]

Among the others who died with Craven that day were Cadet George Bush, a single man of twenty-three from Hertfordshire; Cadet John A. Houghton, a twenty-six-year-old from Gloucester who had married only two months previously and served during the war as a lieutenant with the Royal Sussex Regiment; and Cadet Harold Clayton, a twenty-four-year-old single man from Yorkshire who, like Craven, had emerged from the war a hero, having been awarded the Distinguished Conduct Medal for gallant service with the Royal Field Artillery.[3]

Craven's body was brought home to his family, and he was buried on February 5, 1921, at Dalton-on-Furness, England. Among so many of his generation who were struck down in the prime of life, Lt. Cdr. Francis Worthington Craven was just thirty-one years old when he was killed.[4] Three months later, on May 23, 1921, Francis Craven's parents were devastated again when they received news that a second son, John Hollinger Craven, had died in a Canadian hospital from wounds received during the war.

Still, Francis Craven's reputation and the heroism he had displayed on that stormy day off the Scottish coast only two and a half years before always remained in the thoughts, prayers, and memories of the hundreds of British sailors and American soldiers he saved. As one soldier remarked many years later, "Every single man among the survivors regarded his heroism with the deepest feelings of gratitude."[5]

THE SURVIVORS MEET AGAIN

As for the American soldiers from the *Otranto* and the *Kashmir*, efforts to form a "survivors association" were begun in late July 1919. Notices were published in a variety of Georgia newspapers in the hope of gathering the names and addresses of survivors who might be interested in attending a meeting in Atlanta.[6] Ten months later, on May 26, 1920, the unit's former commander, Lt. Samuel E. Levy, coordinated a sparsely attended reunion at Edison Hall on Peachtree Street in Atlanta. Attending were survivors O. K. Bourgois and James G. Wright of Atlanta; Emory D. Hall of Savannah; the mother and sister of Jesse Johnson of Logansville, Georgia; and several others.[7] With twenty-five survivors living in the Atlanta area, Levy hoped they might form the nucleus of a national "*Otranto* Club." Then, once the local Atlanta group was established, he intended to reach out to other survivors throughout the nation and expand the group into a nationwide organization.[8] Levy called the meeting to order and discussed his ideas for the association. O. K. Bourgois accepted the post of temporary secretary with the responsibility of communicating with all the Georgia survivors to arrange a meeting in June at a convenient location where the association could then be officially launched. Levy and the others present also tentatively planned another preliminary meeting for October 6—the anniversary of the wreck—to be held in Savannah.[9]

For some unknown reason, Levy was unable to garner the support needed at that time to get the organization going. Some years later, however, survivors of the *Kashmir* attending the American Legion Convention of 1939 formed the National *Kashmir* Association.[10] That group met again on October 4, 1942, in the Chamber of Commerce Building in Davenport, Iowa, with A. V. Sebolt of Davenport presiding; they met yet again the following year, on October 3, 1943, in Muscatine, Iowa.[11]

The National Kashmir Association's 1941 Executive Committee included William Adams of Davenport; Deterick Sick of Muscatine, Iowa; and Homer Larson of Kewanee, Illinois.[12] The following year, the elected officers included R. A. Grimm of Muscatine, president; Albert Hartman of Cedar Rapids, vice president; A. H. Telford of Galesburg, Illinois, secretary-treasurer; and Harold F. English of Saginaw, Michigan, historian.[13] We know survivors of the *Otranto* were present at the 1942 reunion as the minutes state that after the business session and just

Thirty-fifth reunion of Georgia survivors of the HMS Otranto *at the Mayfair Club, October 4, 1953, in Atlanta, Georgia. Photo courtesy of Grace Weeks. © Lane Brothers Photography, Atlanta, Georgia.*

following the banquet invocation given by the chaplain, A. H. Telford offered the traditional annual toast to Lieutenant Commander Craven of the *Mounsey*; then, during the round of dinner talks made by members, "David R. Roberts, of Elyria, Ohio, one of the survivors washed ashore on Islay, spoke." Fifty-four people present, and among the others mentioned were Hurluf Dahl of St. Paul and C. A. McDonald of Galesburg, Illinois. McDonald, another soldier who had washed ashore on Islay, related some of his experiences.[14]

A decade later, Lieutenant Levy made arrangements for a thirty-fifth anniversary reunion of the Georgia group of survivors. Held at the Mayfair Club in Atlanta on April 3 and 4, 1953, it was attended by seventeen survivors and their wives from various Georgia cities, including Garfield, Augusta, Savannah, Rome, Twin City, and Atlanta. Out-of-state attendees came from places like Greenwood and Moore, South Carolina; Akron, Ohio; and Memphis, Tennessee. Leholmes P. Wells attended with his daughter, Trudy.[15]

Then, in early 1968, Sam Levy, now a real estate broker in Atlanta, placed a notice in the American Legion magazine *The Torch* to encourage survivors to contact him in regard to attending a possible fiftieth anniversary reunion.[16] Some months later, in August, he followed up with telephone calls to survivors and their families, inviting them to attend the reunion set for later that year in Sylvania, Georgia.

Mrs. A. S. Boyer, news editor for the *Sylvania Telephone* newspaper, had conceived the idea of having the reunion in Sylvania.[17] She worked closely with Mayor E. K. Overstreet, who supported her idea and sent a formal invitation to Levy to hold the reunion in Sylvania on October 5 and 6, 1968, noting that because Screven County, Georgia, had more living *Otranto* survivors than any other community in the country, it, rather than Atlanta, would be the appropriate site for the gathering.[18] Indeed, forty of the men on board were from Screven County, and although seventeen of the forty were lost, six of the twenty-three who survived were still living—these fifty years later—either in Sylvania or nearby, somewhere in the county.[19] To place these casualties in context, 120 of the 431 lost aboard the *Otranto* were from Georgia, and 17 of the 120 lost from Georgia were from Screven County.[20]

Levy agreed to hold the reunion in Sylvania, and as the day drew near, the whole community worked together to make sure the men were recognized and appropriately honored.[21] Mayor Overstreet proclaimed October 6, 1968, as *Otranto* Day, and Mrs. Boyer and survivor Leholmes P. Wells took care of local arrangements. The mayor also authorized the use of city vehicles and employees to assist the now elderly visitors and their families with transportation to and from the airports and bus stations in Augusta and Savannah.[22]

Thirteen of the seventeen local survivors brought their wives, and two brought their sons, as they joined others travelling from all over the country to Sylvania to attend. First to arrive, on Friday, October 4, was Peter Horemans and his wife, who endured a two-day bus ride to get there. They were followed that afternoon by Sam Shaver and his wife, who traveled all the way from Kalamazoo, Michigan. Shaver had received a telephone call just the previous Wednesday, inviting him to the reunion. He related to a local reporter that getting the call had left him "almost speechless" since he had not seen any of the survivors since the end of World War I.

Later that evening, after Frank Ziegler and his wife drove in from Nashville, Tennessee, Ziegler explained to reporters that since he was away on leave from Fort Screven when the men had left, he had always considered himself a "fugitive" of the *Otranto* instead of a survivor. Ziegler said he was attending to honor his many friends who had lost their lives in the disaster and talked of his disappointment in returning back to the base to find that his unit had shipped out the previous day without him.[23]

As the 3 p.m. registration time approached on Saturday, October 5, others arrived at the Sylvania Community Center: Roy Scott, who came by bus from Rome, Georgia; Sam Levy and his wife, who flew from Atlanta to Augusta, where they were met at the airport; H. A. Rouse, who had been pulled off the *Otranto* due to influenza while still in New York, and his wife from Baxley, Georgia; David Roberts and his wife, who came from Orville, Ohio; Thomas Lawther and his wife from Jeannette, Pennsylvania; J. C. Futch and his wife, from nearby Statesboro; and Perry L. Handley of Garfield and Ernest Patrick of Twin City, Georgia, who both arrived with their wives.[24, 25]

Joining these guests were other survivors from Georgia: Leholmes Wells and Ernest Lee with their wives; C. F. Lee of Newington with his son, Horace Lee of Sylvania; Virgil Rosier and his wife; Vannie Morris and his sister; Mrs. Cassie M. Lariscy of Savannah; and Kinchsley Scott, who came with his son, Wallace, from the Bethany Home in Millen, Georgia.[26]

Given the advanced age of many of the attendees, the difficulties Sam Levy had in locating and inviting guests, and the transportation issues involved in having the elderly individuals travel to such a small community in east-central Georgia, it was a good turnout. The City of Sylvania provided attendees with a picture-perfect occasion reflecting small-town America: red roses bloomed in the town's flower beds, American flags hung along all the streets downtown, and a special exhibit was on display for the men in the front windows of the Farmers Hardware Store on Main Street. As community leaders gathered to honor the men, the old soldiers stood, one after the other, and introduced themselves, as well as their wives and other accompanying family members, and then gave a brief account of their relationship to the sinking of the HMS *Otranto* and where their lives had taken them after they came home from the war.

Since the Georgia group had not met for a number of years and the occasion was their first opportunity since the end of the war to meet with some of the out-of-state visitors, they spent time sharing their recollections, photographs, and documents, and talking with others who dropped by who had lost friends or relatives on the *Otranto*.[27] As a reporter later wrote, "There were emotion-packed moments . . . throughout the afternoon" as "from time-to-time, Sam Levy, who had been a young lieutenant in command of the troops aboard the *Otranto*, called his troops to attention."[28]

That evening, the soldiers, families, and community members went to a local restaurant for a dinner sponsored by W. B. Lovett, president of the Farmers and Merchants Bank.[29] Then, the following morning, they attended a special service held at First Baptist Church in their honor. Each survivor was given a red boutonniere as he entered and was then seated in pews, decorated for the occasion, facing a large, red-white-and-blue flower arrangement placed between the American and Christian flags. Pastor Edwin Douglas's sermon that morning, titled "The Foundation of Our Nation's Strength," was followed by the congregation's singing patriotic songs in honor of the visitors.[30]

A traditional Southern Sunday dinner followed—hosted by Mr. and Mrs. C. L. Miller and Mr. and Mrs. Alex Mills of the Bank of Screven County—each table decorated with an arrangement of golden chrysanthemums. After Lieutenant Levy read a prayer, Mayor Ed Overstreet again officially welcomed the group to Sylvania and Woodrow Gibson, commander of the local post of the American Legion, presented each survivor with an engraved gold knife to serve as a memento of the occasion. Lieutenant Levy then offered brief remarks while everyone enjoyed dinner. Afterward, the men took pictures, and as they prepared to go their own ways, each promised to keep in touch. Lieutenant Levy was heard to comment that the two-day reunion marked "the two most satisfactory days" of his life.[31]

It was a good day for Levy, for as DeWeese Martin remembered, "The men were overjoyed to see the Lieutenant as [for many] there had been no contact with him since their departure . . . 50 years earlier. He addressed them as his boys and called [them] to attention as he did in the days when he served as their commander."[32] Samuel E. Levy died less than three months later in Atlanta on December 26, 1968, leaving his wife, two daughters, and seven grandchildren.

THE *OTRANTO* WRECK IS SALVAGED

Yet another interesting postscript to the story of this disaster is the work of Keith Jessop, a onetime British factory worker who struggled to make a living at, then eventually found enormous success in, the hazardous pastime of salvage diving for scrap and precious metals. In his memoir *Goldfinder: The True Story of Man's Discovery of the Ocean's Richest Secrets*, he devotes a full chapter to his diving to the wreck of the *Otranto*.[33]

Viewing the coastline of the island of Islay as a "salvage man's paradise," Jessop was impressed by the intensity of the violent storms that surge across the Atlantic to smash ships—such as the *Otranto*—against Islay's "sheer cliffs, reefs and rocks."[34] He writes of how, "after years of back-breaking effort" while "living hand to mouth," he was in the process of breaking up and salvaging the seven-ton, bronze propeller blades from the wreck of the *Floristan*—a World War II–era merchant ship that lay at the entrance of Islay's Kilchiaran Bay—when he turned his attention to the *Otranto*.[35]

Jessop relates how he and his diving partner, Peter Sellars, initially had difficulty finding the wreck and had to ask Lachy Clark, a local fisherman, to guide him to it. Then once he found it, he realized immediately that he had *finally* found an opportunity for a successful salvage effort, as the *Otranto* reflected its builders' pride in putting only the finest materials into the vessel. Here's his description of what he saw during his first dive on the HMS *Otranto*:

> I was back in the water. . . . An engine block the size of a house stood proud on the sea-bed. I swam right through it. Big connecting rods led to huge bearings, there were two large condensers, and bronze pumps and large-diameter copper piping lay strewn all over the sea-bed. I swam to the stern of the vessel and found the massive three-bladed bronze propeller. What a find![36]

Jessop immediately contacted Britain's War Risks Insurance Office and requested salvage rights. He was awarded them later that winter for only £200 and a share of the salvage proceeds. He then secured a loan from a metal broker he had previously worked with and asked two former diving colleagues to join him in the endeavor.[37]

Although the giant ship rested only thirty to forty feet below the frigid ocean waters off Islay, Jessop had to charter boats, negotiate working relationships with his diving partners, and deal with numerous other logistical difficulties before he could begin lifting the tons of metal from the ship. Finally, with weather, equipment, and financial difficulties overcome, he began reaping the rewards. Here's his description of one of his first dives:

> The water was gin clear and I could see the *Otranto*'s massive engine block as soon as I put my head below the surface. From above I could see how the ship had wrapped itself around the reef on that terrible day

so many years ago and broken almost in half; the bow section lay at an angle of 120 degrees to the stern.

I could follow the line of the twin shafts from the rear of the engine all the way to what was left of the propellers at the stern, pointing in towards the shore. There [I could see] eleven large boilers strewn at different angles around the wreck and looking down between the sections as I swam towards the bow I could see stacks of large brass shell casings, loaded with cordite. Swimming above the wreck was like looking down on a vast scrap yard.[38]

Readers will find Jessop's detailed description of his salvage work on the *Otranto* a fascinating story of determination and adventure as he overcame enormous challenges to find fortune and fame.

THE SECOND *OTRANTO*

A second P&O Line ship named *Otranto* was built by Vickers in Barrow-in-Furness, England, and launched on June 9, 1925. Like her predecessor, she was placed on a mail route and assigned frequent cruises. During one, only a year after her launch, she hit rocks at Cape Grosso, Greece, during a heavy rain storm with poor visibility. Luckily, she still managed to return to England under her own power.[39] Then, two years later, in August 1928, she collided with the Japanese steamer *Kitano Maru*, inflicting serious damage on the other ship.[40, 41]

The second *Otranto* also played a role in the rescue of 853 passengers and crew from the French liner *Georges Phillipar*, which burned and sank during its maiden voyage to China in the Gulf of Aden in May 1932.[42] Like her predecessor, the second *Otranto* served in wartime as well. Converted into a troop transport in 1939, she evacuated British troops from France in 1940 and ferried thousands of troops to and from the Middle East and India. Overhauled again in 1942, she was then converted into a large assault ship, complete with landing craft. In this role she participated in landings in North Africa and in the invasion of Sicily, where she landed troops at Salerno. With military efforts then moving largely inland, the *Otranto* was reconverted into a troop transport and spent the remainder of the war ferrying troops to and from England, India, and the Far East.[43]

Released from military service in 1948, the second *Otranto* was given a complete overhaul and put back in commercial service as a tourist-class liner capable of carrying 1,412 passengers on vacation cruises.[44] She made her last voyage to Sydney, Australia, via Cape Town in February 1957. Then, four months later, in June, she was sold and broken up for scrap at Faslane, Scotland.[45]

THE *KASHMIR*

As for HMS *Kashmir*, after the collision she slowly and carefully made her way on to Glasgow, picking up along the way a two-destroyer escort that boosted the morale of all aboard.[46] After arriving at the mouth of the Clyde River, she dropped anchor for the night. Then, the following morning, with the ship finally in calm waters, the men were fed a hearty breakfast as the crew pulled up the anchor and began the short journey up the river to Glasgow. Seeing cheering girls and young men lining the riverbank, some of the soldiers removed their musical instruments from their cases and began playing jazz tunes, including the hugely popular "Dark Town Strutters Ball." As a crewman recounted later, "And, did they let it go! Everyone let off steam, much to the joy of the crowd on the banks of the river. I don't think that any troops *ever*—during that war—went up the Clyde in such style!"[47]

Upon arrival, the troops were greeted by twenty or so ambulances parked along the dock to take off the men stricken with influenza. Finally, much to everyone's relief, their harrowing journey across the Atlantic was over. To show their gratitude, after disembarking, the Americans lined up in formation, turned toward the ship, and gave the captain and crew three hearty cheers before marching off to their temporary quarters.[48]

Soldiers from the *Kashmir*—mostly from the 126th Field Artillery—then traveled by train from Glasgow through England to Southampton. There they boarded the "old Fall River steamboat" *Narragansett* and arrived at Le Havre, France, on October 11, 1918. The men were then transported on to a camp near Bordeaux, France, where—much to their disgust—they received still more training.

Archival records indicate that most of the men never saw combat, as their training ended soon after the November armistice was signed, ending the war. Several weeks later, on December 23, the unit left to return to the United States. They arrived at Newport News, Virginia, on

January 5, 1919, and then traveled on by train to Camp Dodge, Iowa, where they were mustered out on January 20, 1919.

As for the *Kashmir* herself, her damage from colliding with HMS *Otranto* was repaired, and she was lent to the French government in support of efforts to repatriate prisoners of war.[49] Afterward, she returned to the British navy and was used to ferry troops back and forth between England and France.[50] During one such trip, in January 1919, she "dropped her port screw while leaving Le Havre, [and had to] make her way [back] to Southampton on her starboard propeller alone."[51]

It wasn't until March 1919 that HMS *Kashmir* was finally released back to her owners to rejoin the P&O Line. After spending time in the shipyard to restore her back to her civilian purpose, she sailed from Southampton to Australia by way of the Cape of Good Hope. All was found to be satisfactory, and she was assigned once again to the London–Bombay–Far East service run.[52] Ten years later, in February 1929, "in bitter conditions in the Scheldt estuary, she was rammed on the port side . . . by the Belgian collier *Alexander I* and driven aground with [her] number 4 hold flooded." Although crews managed to refloat her, and she was repaired in the local dry dock, her days were numbered.[53] Three years later, the P&O Line deemed the *Kashmir* obsolete and sold her on July 31, 1932, to the Japanese scrap-metal firm of T. Okushoji for £14,400.[54]

CHRISTMAS DAY 1919 ON ISLAY

In late December 1919, Lt. James Jeffers of the American Red Cross made a special trip to Islay with several large packing cases full of Christmas gifts. He was there to thank residents for their efforts in searching for survivors and burying the dead from the *Tuscania* and the *Otranto*. The gifts were very appropriate as there had been such a scarcity of food and other goods during the war, and with so many sons, husbands, and fathers off fighting, many of the islanders had not celebrated Christmas for the previous four years.[55]

Jeffers, a New York businessman and native of Summit, New Jersey, arrived on Christmas Day with several large packing cases full of candy and toys for the children, pipes and tobacco for the elderly men, cigarettes for the island's recently returned soldiers, clothes for the women,

Lt. James Jeffers shaking hands with Mary McIntyre watched by Maggie McPhee. Courtesy of Carl Reavey, editor of the Ileach, *Islay, Scotland, and the Museum of Islay Life.*

and safety shaving razors for the members of the constabulary who had helped with the gathering and recording of the bodies. Also in his bags were bundles of small, silk British and American flags to be placed on the graves of the men killed on the *Otranto* and *Tuscania* who were buried on the island.[56]

He also had a special gift, "selected with the utmost care by the women of the Red Cross." It was a new green dress for sixteen-year-old Maggie McPhee. Maggie had been among the spectators who, upon seeing a soldier from the *Otranto* struggling in the water, had dashed "into the surf, [and] pulled him ashore . . . unmindful of the fact that she was wearing her best Sunday dress and that her heroism [had] reduced it to a shapeless ruin."[57]

After Jeffers distributed his gifts, the children of the island were assembled at the graveyard. There, they formed a procession and placed flowers and a flag on each of the graves that had been dug along the cliffs overlooking the ocean.[58]

THE LAST SURVIVOR, PVT. DONALD COOPER

As the decades passed, each survivor's story of the tragedy of the *Otranto* passed away with him. Now all that remain are their words, written in letters and in documents filed away in the US National Archives in Washington, DC, in the Museum of Islay Life, and in the National Maritime Museum in Greenwich, England. And, as near as I can determine, neither during their lifetimes nor since—except for the single monument built on Islay's Mull of Oa by the American Red Cross—has a monument, street, or bridge been erected or named in memory of the hundreds of American soldiers and British sailors lost during this tragedy.

As time passed, but for the stories told during the reunions, the event slowly faded into the mists of time. With more wars occurring and then passing—World War II, the Korean War, the Vietnam War, and the many wars since—the tragedy of the *Otranto* and memory of the men faded even further. By 2001, there remained but one known survivor, an African American, Pvt. Donald Cooper, serial number 2655034. A farmer from Screven County, Georgia, born on September

The front side of Donald Cooper's draft registration card. US National Archives at Atlanta, Georgia.

161

14, 1896, Cooper had enlisted in the army in Sylvania on April 30, 1918, and served in a company of an all-black labor battalion.[59, 60]

I, along with my friend and colleague Dr. Mark Newell, an archaeologist from North Augusta, South Carolina, interviewed Cooper shortly before his death in the US Veterans Hospital in Augusta, Georgia. Though relegated to a wheelchair, Cooper struck us both as a friendly, soft-spoken, confident old soldier. Tall and broad shouldered, with huge leathery hands—calloused from decades of working the soil of the red-clay fields of northeastern Georgia—Donald Cooper met us with a firm handshake and a bright smile and seemed to enjoy the opportunity to meet with us. While he had difficulty recalling events of more recent years, he easily remembered and talked with enthusiasm, clarity, and detail about his early childhood and his experience in the army.

We had brought along a photograph of the *Otranto* and opened our conversation by describing our interest in the disaster. Cooper looked at the photograph, and after a pause, he began talking:

I stood right there [points to starboard rail, forward of mid-ship area]. I was with a friend of mine. He jumped first and was crushed between the side of our ship and the other little ship. I jumped next and landed on the bow. Some people grabbed me and dragged me down below.

[Realizing that he still remembered the event, we then encouraged him to tell his story from the beginning.]

When I was born my Momma already had a mess of kids. Her and her man were sharecropping on some land near Savannah. The owner came by right after I was born and said, "Sally, you already have six kids. Why don't you give me that one and I'll raise him?"

I was raised just like one of the family, tho he was a white man. I went to school an' all. [Then] when I was nineteen, he told me in the kitchen one day that boys were volunteering for the war and that he guessed I should go along with everyone else.

I went and volunteered and after a few weeks they put me on a train north with everyone else. We got to New York City and they put us on one boat and then another. . . . I had never been on the ocean before.

A lot of people were seasick right from the start as there was a lot of sickness goin' round. I was up in the front of the boat with all the other Negroes, but it smelled real bad 'cos of the sickness an' all. I would go out . . . and climb up a mast where I could sit in the fresh air. It was good up there. I would watch whales . . . right near the boat. It was something I'd never seen.

It got real stormy near the end of the trip and early one morning another boat [HMS *Kashmir*] hit ours. They said our boat [HMS *Otranto*] was sinking and we all had to get up on deck. It was real difficult to stand. They couldn't launch boats or anything [because] it was too rough. It was pretty bad, with them tryin' to keep order an' everything.

After awhile this small boat [HMS *Mounsey*] came up and went around. Each time it went around, it would come alongside our boat. We were told, "Every man for himself!" and then we had to jump for the small boat. A lot of men didn't do so good and got smashed between the boats or fell in the sea. The boat came around about nine times, I'd say. My friend and I got to the rail about the next-to-last time.

I watched my friend get smashed [between the two ships] but I got my timing right and landed on the deck of the small boat. Some men dragged me inside. After that the boat headed to port. I didn't see anything of the big ship or the men on her after that. I heard later that a lot of them had died.

Me, I was sent on to the war as soon as I got ashore. We unloaded ships mostly, but after awhile I got to go fight with a rifle. I got shot in the stomach and the man came by to look at me after about a day. He said I was gut shot and wouldn't make it. About two days later he came by again and said that since I was still alive they had better do something about me. They then took good care of me. I ended up in California and when I was well I was sent home.

I worked a lot of jobs after that, mostly workin' the land. Never did want to go to sea again. Some government man came to see me awhile back and gave me a medal. My kids [have] all died and most of their kids too. My great kids look after me now since I am too old to do much of anything.[61]

Though it was almost eighty-two years later, Donald Cooper seemed still to be haunted by the memories of his friends from back home in Sylvania who were killed in the loss of the *Otranto*. Especially disturbing was the memory of his white friend who had asked him to step aside so he could jump first, then been "mashed between the two ships." When questioned previously about the incident in 1999 by news reporter Erin Rossiter, Cooper had said, "He told me to move out of the way. 'I'll jump,' he said. And he missed. Years after, his children and grandchildren [in Sylvania] would say to me, 'You saw my daddy get killed.'"[62]

After returning home to Georgia, Donald Cooper spent the rest of his life farming the fields of his home county and driving a local school bus. He left only one last time to take a room in the Veterans Hospital in Augusta, Georgia.

We were able to verify that his story of a "government man" giving him a medal was correct too. In early September 2000, when Cooper was just shy of his 104th birthday, Jean-Paul Monchau, consul general for France, traveled to Augusta and—in a public ceremony conducted in that city's historic Old Government House—recognized Pvt. Donald Cooper by naming him a Chevalier of the National Order of the Legion of Honor. As Monchau pinned his nation's highest award on the old African American veteran's breast, his words echoed over the crowd: "We remember the sacrifice of the American soldiers who fought for freedom alongside the sons of France. . . . Mr. Donald Cooper, eighty years ago you came for us, and today I come for you."[63]

Donald Cooper lived for nine more months, passing away on June 14, 2001, at the age of 104. His body was transported back to his hometown of Sylvania, where he was buried on June 22, 2001—with full military honors—in the rich red clay of a quiet, peaceful country cemetery next to Zion Fair Baptist Church.[64]

AUTHOR'S NOTE

HMS *Otranto* Disaster
Casualties and Survivors

Compiling a list of survivors and casualties of the *Otranto* disaster is a problematic endeavor. Though there are a wide variety of newspaper accounts with listings of names, US government reports and telegrams in the US National Archives with rosters and names, and dozens of handwritten and typed lists, a comparison of these offers conflicting spellings of names, names on the wrong lists, and handwritten names that are difficult to decipher. Thus, under the circumstances, one can only sort through the data and offer the best lists and spellings possible. The appendices are offered with these shortcomings in mind. Sources consulted include the following:

1. *Savannah Morning News*, October 28, 1918, 1.
2. "Supplemental Casualty Telegram to No. 39," October 12, 1918, from Lt. Charles J. Maley to HQ Base Section No. 3, SOS AEF London.
3. Joseph M. Toomey, "His Majesty's Ship *Otranto*," in *The Legion in Georgia: Georgia's Participation in the World War and the History of Georgia's American Legion* (Macon, GA: J. W. Burke Co., 1936), 56–57.
4. "Casualty Telegram No. 39," October 11, 1918, from Headquarters Base Section No. 3, SOS AEF London.
5. "Police Report: Loss of HMS Troopship *Otranto*," Argyllshire Constabulary, Bowmore Station, October 19, 1918.

6. "List of U.S. Soldiers Missing in Sinking of the Transport *Otranto*," Official US Bulletin 27, November 1918, 8.
7. Correspondence, 2nd Lt. Samuel E. Levy to personnel adjutant, Base Section 3, AEF, October 18, 1918, in "Correspondence, War Department, O.Q.M.G., Washington, D.C. RG 165, Records of the War Department General and Special Staffs. 'Correspondence of the Military Intelligence Division (MID),'" National Archives at College Park, College Park, Maryland.

APPENDIX 1

HMS *Otranto* American Casualties

ABBREVIATIONS

SARD CAC Fort Screven: September Automatic Replacement Draft, Coastal Artillery Corps, Fort Screven, GA

[Note: Blanks in the list below indicate that the information was not available.]

Name	Service Number	Home and Unit
Pvt. Henry Grady **Allen**	2595811	Stillmore, GA/SARD CAC Fort Screven
Sgt. Leslie T. **Allen**		Shiloh, GA/SARD CAC Fort Screven
Pvt. Andrew John **Andrews**	2595876	Savannah, GA/SARD CAC Fort Screven
Pvt. William P. **Ayers**	2595856	SARD CAC Fort Screven
Pvt. Alexander **Baker**	471029	Quapaw, OK
Pvt. William H. **Baker**	2562970	410th Overseas Casual Co.
Pvt. Grover B. **Bannister**	470089	El Reno, OK/SARD CAC Fort Screven
Pvt. George H. **Barago**		
Pvt. Joseph **Barr**	4157697	Acme, LA/SARD CAC Fort Screven
Pvt. Raeford Ellison **Barry**	2595680	Oliver, GA/SARD CAC Fort Screven
Pvt. Henry E. **Barthelemy**	4157444	Grand Isle, LA

Name	Service Number	Home and Unit
Pvt. William Patrick **Battle** Jr.	2595501	Augusta, GA/SARD CAC Fort Screven
Pvt. Fred **Baumann**	2585231	Philadelphia, PA/410th Casual Co.
Sgt. Ludden E. **Baxter**	718947	Lake Helen, FL
Pvt. Peter V. **Bazzara**	627086	New York, NY/410th Casual Co.
Cpl. Willie **Beady**		Augusta, GA
Pvt. Brooks **Beasley**		Rocky Ford, GA/SARD CAC Fort Screven
Pvt. Weslie J. **Beckwith**	3236383	
Pvt. David M. **Bennett**	2595695	Woodcliff, GA/SARD CAC Fort Screven
Pvt. Hiram Marcus **Bennett**	2595848	Sparks, GA/SARD CAC Fort Screven
Pvt. Samuel F. **Bennett**	718998	Jellico, TN/SARD CAC Fort Screven
Sgt. Burroughs C. **Blackmon**	718999	Penona, FL
Pvt. Lawrence **Blashik**	2524306	410th Overseas Casual Co.
Pvt. Mathew M. **Boles**	2584038	Philadelphia, PA/410th Casual Co.
Pvt. Oren O. **Bouderman**	813847	
Pvt. Sullie **Bourque**	3005462	
Pvt. Isaac R. **Boyett**		Berrien Co., GA/SARD CAC Fort Screven
Pvt. Jim Melvin **Boyett**	2595862	Milltown, GA
Pvt. Alvin Claude **Bozeman**	2595651	Waycross, GA/SARD CAC Fort Screven
Pvt. George Harrison **Bragg**		Woodcliff, GA/SARD CAC Fort Screven
Joe H. **Bragg**		Woodcliff, GA
Cpl. Joe O. **Brasher**	470201	
Pvt. Walter T. **Brawner**	2595573	Augusta, GA/SARD CAC Fort Screven
Pvt. Anthony J. **Brescia**	1271248	Jersey City, NJ/410th Overseas Casual Co.
Beasley **Brooks**		
Sgt. Walter C. **Brooks**	719002	Sumter, SC
Pvt. Ellie Alexander **Broom**	2598784	Summertown, GA/SARD CAC Fort Screven
Pvt. Daniel Edward **Brown**	2595669	Zeigler, GA/SARD CAC Fort Screven

Name	Service Number	Home and Unit
Pvt. Fernie E. **Brown**	814338	Marion, SC/SARD CAC Fort Screven
Pvt. Robert E. **Brown**	813365	
Pvt. William F. **Brumit**		406th Overseas Casual Co.
Pvt. Martin Luther **Bryan**	2595678	Sylvania, GA/SARD CAC Fort Screven
Hicks **Burden**		Norristown, GA
Pvt. Ruel [Rhul?] W. **Burley [Burleigh?]**	3005353	Operusas, LA/SARD CAC Fort Screven
Cpl. Thomas **Burnside**	813508	
Pvt. Arthur **Butler**	779136	Jacksonville, FL/410th Overseas Casual Co.
Pvt. 1st Class Alonzo A. **Bynum**	710389	McAdenville, NC/SARD CAC Fort Screven
Pvt. Hugh **Calihan**	3241311	Normal, KY
Pvt. Charles L. **Campbell**	813364	Belton, SC/SARD CAC Fort Screven
Pvt. James V. **Capoun**	470050	SARD CAC Fort Screven
C. A. **Carpenter** [Name appears on both casualty and survivor lists.]		YMCA
Pvt. Michael **Carroll**	2790175	410th Overseas Casual Co.
Pvt. William Broadus **Carter**	2595761	Waynesboro, GA/SARD CAC Fort Screven
Sgt. William W. **Carter**	718952	Savannah, GA/SARD CAC Fort Screven
Pvt. Oliver C. **Cleveland** Jr.		Culloden, GA/SARD CAC Fort Screven
H. Lee **Clyde**	2596032	
2nd Lt. Bierne H. [Bernie J.?] **Coffman**, DMA [Name appears on both casualty and survivor lists.]		Galesburg, IL/406th Overseas Casual Co.
Pvt. Alex **Collett**	2902687	Gross, KY
Pvt. Charles Frederick **Collins**	2595652	Camilla, GA/SARD CAC Fort Screven
Pvt. Mandle A. **Collins**	2595772	Oak Park, GA/SARD CAC Fort Screven
Pvt. William **Conklin**	3672760	Patterson, NJ/406th Overseas Casual Co.

Name	Service Number	Home and Unit
Pvt. David L. **Conner**	470087	Waynwright, OK
C. E. **Cook** [?]		
Pvt. William E. **Cook**	470027	SARD CAC Fort Screven
Pvt. Edward J. **Cooney**	4071103	406th Overseas Casual Co.
Pvt. William J. **Cooney**		Augusta, GA/SARD CAC Fort Screven
Pvt. John Guy **Coppage**	2595865	Hahira, GA/SARD CAC Fort Screven
Pvt. James **Corcoran**	2081815	410th Overseas Casual Co.
Pvt. Simon E. **Corrley**	814760	Columbia, SC/SARD CAC Fort Screven
Pvt. Henry F. **Cox**	2309517	New Haven, CT/410th Overseas Casual Co.
Pvt. Pearl **Crews**	2595675	Sylvania, GA/SARD CAC Fort Screven
Pvt. Samuel O. **Cribb**	814763	SARD CAC Fort Screven
Pvt. James W. **Crowe**	2595537	Augusta, GA/SARD CAC Fort Screven
Pvt. Arthur M. **Culpepper**	2595740	Morven, GA/SARD CAC Fort Screven
Pvt. Charles B. **Currens**	2952108	410th Overseas Casual Co.
Pvt. Boyd D. **Danner**	813533	SARD CAC Fort Screven
Pvt. Early **Davis**	2595632	Fairfax, GA/SARD CAC Fort Screven
Cpl. Norman C. **Davis**	793049	Screven, GA/406th Casual Co.
Pvt. Rufus **Davis**	2595836	Sparks, GA/406th Headquarters Co.
Sgt. Thomas L. **Davis**	718901	Savannah, GA/SARD CAC Fort Screven
Pvt. Carswell **Deal** [F. **Deal Carswell?**]	2595720	Arcola, GA/SARD CAC Fort Screven
Pvt. John Lawrence **Dean**	2595946	Clermont, GA/SARD CAC Fort Screven
Cpl. Roy **Dearman**	720191	Pooler, GA/SARD CAC Fort Screven
Pvt. Millard V. **Demeyer**	3732551	410th Overseas Casual Co.
Pvt. Louis C. **Dempsey**	3200960	406th Overseas Casual Co.
Pvt. Pearl W. **Dickerson**	4706692	SARD CAC Fort Screven
Roy C. **Dilts**	813539	
Pvt. Frank A. **Dinsmore**	470675	Chrisman, IL/SARD CAC Fort Screven

Name	Service Number	Home and Unit
Pvt. Charles Paralee **Dodd**	2595539	Hartwell, GA/SARD CAC Fort Screven
Cpl. Herbert A. **Dodd**	470094	El Reno, OK/SARD CAC Fort Screven
Millard V. **Domeyer**		Fulton, KY
Pvt. William L. **Dones**	2595934	Norfolk, VA/SARD CAC Fort Screven
Pvt. George I. **Douglas**	2595579	Macon, GA/SARD CAC Fort Screven
Pvt. Robert H. **Duggar**	814907	Crawfordville, FL
Pvt. Mearle H. **Dull**	3239969	SARD CAC Fort Screven
Sgt. James C. **Duncan**	718774	Greenville, SC/SARD CAC Fort Screven
Pvt. Hicks **Durden** [**Dirden?**]	2595785	Norristown, GA/SARD CAC Fort Screven
Pvt. Mack Hilton **Easters**	2595814	Lenox, GA/SARD CAC Fort Screven
Pvt. Benton N. **Edenfield**	2595770	Swainsboro, GA/SARD CAC Fort Screven
Pvt. Harley F. **Edmond**	411283	Indianapolis, IN/406th Overseas Casual Co.
Pvt. Clarence **Epps**	2595448	Augusta, GA/SARD CAC Fort Screven
Pvt. George B. **Faircloth**	2595843	Milltown, GA/SARD CAC Fort Screven
Pvt. George **Falagan**	2595725	Jesup, GA/SARD CAC Fort Screven
Pvt. Cleo J. **Falgout**	4157285	Cutoff, LA/SARD CAC Fort Screven
Pvt. Earl B. **Follis**	718810	SARD CAC Fort Screven
Sgt. Jodie C. **Forrester**	119222	Vinson, TN/SARD CAC Fort Screven
Pvt. Jack C. **Foust**	3239971	Asheboro, NC
Pvt. Gus **Frazier**		Girard, GA/SARD CAC Fort Screven
Pvt. Henry Jerome **Freeman**	2595686	Seigler, GA/SARD CAC Fort Screven
Cpl. Paul **Fry**	1362685	Steubenville, OH
Cpl. Henry **Fulsos**	470529	Bradish, NE/SARD CAC Fort Screven

Name	Service Number	Home and Unit
Pvt. John P. **Gardner**	2595582	Atlanta, GA/SARD CAC Fort Screven
Cpl. Ira M. **Garland** [**Gerland?**]	793348	Citronelle, AL/SARD CAC Fort Screven
Pvt. Lafayette **Gaskins**	2595854	Nashville, GA/SARD CAC Fort Screven
Sgt. Henry E. **Gaudry**	719473	Savannah, GA/SARD CAC Fort Screven
Cpl. Elmo A. **Gay**	470389	SARD CAC Fort Screven
Pvt. Ernest M. **Gay** [**Day?**]	2595449	Augusta, GA/SARD CAC Fort Screven
Pvt. Charles J. **Gebert**	4096437	410th Overseas Casual Co.
Pvt. John C. **Geiger**	3372653	SARD CAC Fort Screven
Harry J. **Giffen**		
Pvt. Lewis A. **Gillis**	2595641	Millwood, GA/SARD CAC Fort Screven
G. **Gilmour**		
Pvt. William S. **Goff**		406th Overseas Casual Co.
Pvt. Millard P. **Goodwyn**		Atlanta, GA/SARD CAC Fort Screven
Pvt. Mack M. **Green**	719146	Oglethorpe, GA/SARD CAC Fort Screven
Pvt. Arthur M. **Griffin**		Quitman, GA/SARD CAC Fort Screven
Pvt. Harry J. **Griffin**		410th Overseas Casual Co.
Pvt. Dominick **Grillo**	1235149	Old Forge, PA/406th Overseas Casual Co.
Pvt. Bennie E. **Griner**	2595825	Nashville, GA/SARD CAC Fort Screven
Pvt. Harlan P. **Griner**	2595599	Sylvania, GA/SARD CAC Fort Screven
Pvt. Ivy S. **Gunter** [**Hunter?**]		Waycross, GA/SARD CAC Fort Screven
Pvt. Edgar A. **Hagewood**	2902826	Hickory Point, TN/SARD CAC Fort Screven
Pvt. Edward Russell **Hall**	1277399	406th Overseas Casual Co.
Pvt. Joseph A. **Hall**	3201757	Long Island, NY/406th Overseas Casual Co.
Pvt. Lester A. **Hancock**	2595924	Alapaha, GA/SARD CAC Fort Screven

Name	Service Number	Home and Unit
Pvt. Robert J. **Hancock**	2595927	Lenox, GA/SARD CAC Fort Screven
Pvt. Marion **Hankinson**	2595951	Girard, GA/SARD CAC Fort Screven
Pvt. Wylie C. **Harmon**	718816	Inman, SC/SARD CAC Fort Screven
Pvt. Ronald A. **Harnish** [Hainah?]	3372085	SARD CAC Fort Screven
Pvt. Arthur **Harpen**	2595935	Enigma, GA/SARD CAC Fort Screven
Pvt. Freddie **Harrison**	814276	Jesup, GA/SARD CAC Fort Screven
Pvt. William P. **Hayes** [Hays?]		Alapaha, GA/SARD CAC Fort Screven
Pvt. Jennings B. **Haywood** [Haywood B. Jennings?]	720392	Stouts, NC/SARD CAC Fort Screven
James H. **Hedrick**	814687	Statesville, NC
Pvt. Plumer L. **Henderson**	723438	Grey Court, SC/SARD CAC Fort Screven
Cpl. Wallace **Hendrickson**	470203	Green Bay, WI/SARD CAC Fort Screven
Pvt. William R. **Henrey**		Manchester, TN/406th Overseas Casual Co.
Pvt. William D. **Herrington**	2595764	Sardis, GA/SARD CAC Fort Screven
Pvt. George D. **Hersey**	2595630	Nichols, GA/SARD CAC Fort Screven
Pvt. James Bertrand **Hester**	1595474	Augusta, GA/SARD CAC Fort Screven
Pvt. David C. **Hickey**	719024	Sweetwater, TN/SARD CAC Fort Screven
Edward F. **Hickey**	470461	SARD CAC Fort Screven
Pvt. Gordon S. **Hickman**	2595450	Savannah, GA/SARD CAC Fort Screven
Pvt. Jess **Higginbotham**		McMinnville, TN/406th Overseas Casual Co.
Cpl. Robert **Hiland**	470525	Omaha, NE/SARD CAC Fort Screven
Sgt. John B. **Hill**	471004	SARD CAC Fort Screven
Pvt. Paul A. **Hirt**	3372792	Strongsville, OH

Name	Service Number	Home and Unit
Pvt. Thomas H. **Holland**	2595819	Adel, GA/SARD CAC Fort Screven
Pvt. Joseph F. **Hollis**	719028	Iron City, TN/SARD CAC Fort Screven
Pvt. Carlton M. **Hooks**	2595809	Swainsboro, GA/SARD CAC Fort Screven
Pvt. George W. **House**	3194739	Brooklyn, NY/406th Overseas Casual Co.
Pvt. Wade H. **Hubbard**	814708	Lake Helen, FL/SARD CAC Fort Screven
Pvt. Roy S. **Hubbs**	719178	Gleneaston, WV/SARD CAC Fort Screven
Pvt. Orion D. **Hudson**	2902776	Jakin, GA/SARD CAC Fort Screven
Pvt. Thomas W. **Hudson**		Early Co., GA/SARD CAC Fort Screven
Pvt. John L. **Hufft**	4161706	New Orleans, LA
Sgt. David Parker **Hughes**	719460	Ludowici, GA/SARD CAC Fort Screven
Pvt. William A. **Hunter**	2595664	Oliver, GA/SARD CAC Fort Screven
Cpl. Arthur S. **Hurr**	813592	Altona, IL/SARD CAC Fort Screven
Pvt. Lester **Hutchenson**	2595800	Covena, GA/SARD CAC Fort Screven
Pvt. George H. **Hutto**	2595883	Adel, GA/SARD CAC Fort Screven
Pvt. John Alexander **Hutton** Jr.	719030	Savannah, GA/SARD CAC Fort Screven
Pvt. Eddie E. **Jackson**	813914	Mt. Pleasant, SC/SARD CAC Fort Screven
Pvt. Stonewall Joseph **Jackson**	2595696	Sylvania, GA/SARD CAC Fort Screven
Cpl. Clifford R. **Johnson**	719181	Louisville, GA/SARD CAC Fort Screven
Pvt. Earl D. **Johnson**	720394	McAdenville, NC/SARD CAC Fort Screven
Sgt. Jessie [**Jesse?**] A. **Johnson**	718963	Fort White, FL/SARD CAC Fort Screven
Cpl. Jonas Ossian **Johnson**	813602	Galesburg, IL/SARD CAC Fort Screven

Name	Service Number	Home and Unit
Pvt. Roscoe L. **Johnson**	813605	SARD CAC Fort Screven
Sgt. Watson C. **Justus** [**Justus O. Watson?**]	718777	Woodward, SC/SARD CAC Fort Screven
Pvt. Isador **Kaplin**	718964	New York, NY/SARD CAC Fort Screven
Bernard **Kaufmann** [**Taufmann?**]	1276156	406th Overseas Casual Co.
Cpl. James W. **Kehoe**	3372275	SARD CAC Fort Screven
Pvt. John Leslie **Kelly**	2595676	Sylvania, GA/SARD CAC Fort Screven
Pvt. Joseph L. **Kesler**	720225	Salisbury, NC/SARD CAC Fort Screven
Pvt. George J. **Kessler**	396437	Co. A, 302nd Tank Co.
Pvt. Joseph **Kish**	718688	SARD CAC Fort Screven
Pvt. Ralph **Knight**	2595840	Ray City, GA/SARD CAC Fort Screven
Pvt. Raymond Russell **Knight**	2902733	Pitts, GA/SARD CAC Fort Screven
Pvt. William **Kruhm**		Baltimore, MD/406th Overseas Casual Co.
Pvt. Class Alexander J. **Kurtz**	3455021	Sheboygan, WI/SARD CAC Fort Screven
Floyd M. **Larna** [**Larma?**]	2830784	SARD CAC Fort Screven
Pvt. Louis P. **Lasseigne**	3005230	St. Martinville, LA/SARD CAC Fort Screven
Pvt. Charles J. **Lauch**	3241280	SARD CAC Fort Screven
Pvt. Phillips H. **Lederer**	1107072	Patterson, NJ/SARD CAC Fort Screven
Pvt. Clyde H. **Lee**	2596063	Halcyondale, GA/SARD CAC Fort Screven
Pvt. Furman [Tupman?] F. **Lee**	813286	Stevens Pottery, GA/SARD CAC Fort Screven
Pvt. Ira B. **Levenite**	1245292	406th Overseas Casual Co.
Sgt. Oscar E. **Little**	718910	SARD CAC Fort Screven
Pvt. Otis **Losch**	3372374	SARD CAC Fort Screven
Sgt. Frank **Loughran**	719037	SARD CAC Fort Screven
Sgt. Bernard A. **Lovell**	718912	North View, WV/SARD CAC Fort Screven
Sgt. George W. **Lowden** Jr.	718886	Savannah, GA/SARD CAC Fort Screven
Pvt. Charles **Luach**		Lockland, OH
Pvt. Michael J. **Lucyk**	3372494	SARD CAC Fort Screven

Name	Service Number	Home and Unit
Sgt. Raymond E. **Luthie**	712938	Commerce, GA/SARD CAC Fort Screven
Pvt. Fred T. **Lyle**	2595551	Sailcreek, TN/SARD CAC Fort Screven
Pvt. Eldon M. **McAfee**	3372174	Coldwater, OH/SARD CAC Fort Screven
Eugene O. **McAtee**	3239974	Brooksville, KY
Pvt. Benjamin Franklin **McCranie**	2595860	Adel, GA/SARD CAC Fort Screven
Pvt. Edward **McDermott**	2795585	410th Overseas Casual Co.
Pvt. Louis **McDonald**	2595552	Fitzgerald, GA/SARD CAC Fort Screven
Pvt. Jack W. **McFee**	3241360	Black Mountain, NC/SARD CAC Fort Screven
Pvt. Thomas A. **McGowan**	4084005	Scranton, PA/410th Overseas Casual Co.
Pvt. James P. **McKenna**	2952630	406th Overseas Casual Co.
Cpl. Roscoe **McKinley**	813643	Canton, IL/SARD CAC Fort Screven
Pvt. James M. **McMillan**	2595847	Nashville, GA/SARD CAC Fort Screven
Pvt. William **McMillan** [**Miller?**]	2595861	Enigma, GA/SARD CAC Fort Screven
Pvt. Lincoln **McNeal**	4161721	Troy, AL
Pvt. James Eddie **McNeely**	2595799	Norristown, GA/SARD CAC Fort Screven
Pvt. Thomas F. **Maher**	1749637	406th Overseas Casual Co.
Pvt. James G. **Mahoney**	2903667	SARD CAC Fort Screven
Cpl. Paul J. **Markley**	3138108	SARD CAC Fort Screven
Pvt. Fred J. **Martin**	3372198	SARD CAC Fort Screven
Cpl. James W. **Meeks** [**Maerks? Marks?**]	718836	Peizer, SC/SARD CAC Fort Screven
Pvt. Vincent **Melero**	4157228	SARD CAC Fort Screven
Pvt. Wayne D. **Mendenhall**	719046	Siler City, NC
Cpl. Horace H. **Miller**	213646	Abingdon, IL/SARD CAC Fort Screven
Vincent **Molero**	4157228	
Pvt. John Franklin **Moore**	2595844	Adel, GA/SARD CAC Fort Screven
Pvt. Denver E. **Morgan**	814234	Piedmont, SC/SARD CAC Fort Screven

Name	Service Number	Home and Unit
Pvt. Alva Orendorf Morningstar	313651	Little York, IL/SARD CAC Fort Screven
Pvt. Jasper Hamilton Morris	2595754	Blythe, GA/SARD CAC Fort Screven
Pvt. Elisha T. Moseley	2595781	Oak Park, GA/SARD CAC Fort Screven
Pvt. Philip E. Moss	470684	SARD CAC Fort Screven
Pvt. Clyde Mott	2595639	Waycross, GA
Pvt. Forest M. Musgrove	470033	Fulton, MO/SARD CAC Fort Screven
Sgt. August Nelson	470170	SARD CAC Fort Screven
Pvt. Brox Nelson	814164	Union, SC/SARD CAC Fort Screven
Patrick H. Nepalone	2299786	
Pvt. Harvey Nesmith	2595739	Barwick, GA/SARD CAC Fort Screven
Pvt. Roy C. Newsome	3371515	SARD CAC Fort Screven
Pvt. Paul A. Norrington	3372142	SARD CAC Fort Screven
Pvt. Frank J. O'Hara	371854	New York, NY/406th Overseas Casual Co.
Pvt. Joseph H. O'Neill	2792390	Brooklyn, NY
Pvt. William F. O'Rourke	375286	406th Overseas Casual Co.
Pvt. Joseph H. Oppenheim	719187	Savannah, GA/SARD CAC Fort Screven
Pvt. Griffen D. Owens	2595555	Dallas, GA/SARD CAC Fort Screven
Pvt. Frampton W. Page	2595593	Augusta, GA/SARD CAC Fort Screven
Pvt. John N. Page	2595486	Augusta, GA/SARD CAC Fort Screven
Pvt. Roco Parente	2299780	406th Overseas Casual Co.
Rivie Parker	793282	Fountainhead, TN/SARD CAC Fort Screven
Grady J. Parvin	470022	Bossburg, AL/SARD CAC Fort Screven
Pvt. Lloyd Payton	3236436	Charlotte, NC/SARD CAC Fort Screven
Pvt. Samuel A. Pennington	3372941	Campbell, PA/SARD CAC Fort Screven
Cpl. Raymond Pfetszing	813860	SARD CAC Fort Screven
Pvt. Neil Phillips	2595810	Northton, GA/SARD CAC Fort Screven

Name	Service Number	Home and Unit
Pvt. Willie **Phillips**	2595604	Augusta, GA/SARD CAC Fort Screven
Pvt. Rad C. **Porter**	2902754	Jacksonville, AL/SARD CAC Fort Screven
Paul **Portington**		Moundsville, WV
Pvt. Burr Wise **Powell**	2595518	Tyler, TX/SARD CAC Fort Screven
Sgt. James R. **Powell**	708975	Jacksonville, FL/SARD CAC Fort Screven
W. O. **Prescott**		
Cpl. Joseph B. **Presnell**	720454	Old Fort, NC/SARD CAC Fort Screven
Pvt. Thomas **Preston**	719060	Tullahoma, TN/SARD CAC Fort Screven
Sgt. Sam W. **Pridgen**	470083	Wiggins, MS/SARD CAC Fort Screven
Cpl. David R. **Probasco**	813839	SARD CAC Fort Screven
Pvt. Hamption **Radabaugh**	3372126	SARD CAC Fort Screven
Pvt. Charlie **Railey** [**Bailie? Bailey?**]	2595824	Alapaha, GA/SARD CAC Fort Screven
Pvt. William K. **Ralston**	813682	SARD CAC Fort Screven
Pvt. Gilbert **Randolph**		Sparta, TN/406th Overseas Casual Co.
Pvt. Elisha W. **Rawls**	719062	Crystal River, FL/SARD CAC Fort Screven
Sgt. Ralph Scott **Ray**	719107	Savannah, GA/SARD CAC Fort Screven
Cpl. Willie **Ready**	718852	Augusta , GA/SARD CAC Fort Screven
Pvt. Claude C. **Reddick**	2595687	Millen, GA/SARD CAC Fort Screven
Sgt. Harold D. **Redman** [Name appears on both survivor and casualty lists.]		
Pvt. John Henry **Reese**	2595455	Augusta, GA/SARD CAC Fort Screven
Pvt. Aubrey D. **Renchen**	3241411	Trinity, KY/SARD CAC Fort Screven
Pvt. Patrick **Repalone**	2299706	406th Overseas Casual Co.

Name	Service Number	Home and Unit
Pvt. William L. **Ricks**	2595025	Moultrie, GA/SARD CAC Fort Screven
Pvt. Gale E. **Riggs**	3372187	Parkersburg, WV/SARD CAC Fort Screven
Pvt. Francis B. **Ritchley**	3372093	SARD CAC Fort Screven
Pvt. John P. **Roach** [**Reach?**]	2595559	Macon, GA/SARD CAC Fort Screven
Pvt. Alba Leon **Roberts**	718855	Cedar Springs, GA/SARD CAC Fort Screven
Pvt. Will **Roberts**	2595801	Herndon, GA/SARD CAC Fort Screven
Pvt. Leon **Robinson**	373616	406th Overseas Casual Co.
Pvt. Tillman W. **Robinson**	2595849	Enigma, GA/SARD CAC Fort Screven
Pvt. Cecil M. **Rogers**	2595734	Quitman, GA/SARD CAC Fort Screven
Pvt. Charles H. **Rolston**	3241313	Mount Clinton, VA/SARD CAC Fort Screven
Pvt. Mead **Rose**	1701926	406th Overseas Casual Co.
Sullie **Rourque**		Lafayette, LA
Pvt. Henry O. **Rudd**	2902710	Sylacauga, AL/SARD CAC Fort Screven
Pvt. Ashley Franklin **Rushing**	2595521	Augusta, GA/SARD CAC Fort Screven
A. C. **Savannah**		
Sgt. Emmons C. **Scherbert**	470518	Stevens Point, WI/SARD CAC Fort Screven
Pvt. Joseph F. **Schmitt**	546491	406th Overseas Casual Co.
William H. **Schrenk**		Ellabell, GA
Pvt. James Frank **Scott**	2595689	Woodcliff, GA/SARD CAC Fort Screven
Pvt. Walter B. **Scott**	813746	Henderson, IL/SARD CAC Fort Screven
Pvt. Eugene B. **Sedberry**	29978	Smithland, KY/SARD CAC Fort Screven
Pvt. Coley L. **Sellars**	719072	DeFuniak Springs, FL/SARD CAC Fort Screven
Pvt. Fred L. **Seward**	3239007	SARD CAC Fort Screven
Pvt. Ray M. **Shane**	3372088	SARD CAC Fort Screven
David **Shapiro**	4155600	406th Overseas Casual Co.
Pvt. John H. **Sharpe**	2902580	Brundidge, AL/SARD CAC Fort Screven

Name	Service Number	Home and Unit
Pvt. Donzell **Shavers**	2901416	Phoenix City, AL/SARD CAC Fort Screven
Pvt. Robert T. [F.?] **Shawd**		Lebanon, PA
Pvt. John M. **Sheffield**	2595705	Statesboro, GA/SARD CAC Fort Screven
Pvt. Orlando Watson **Sheppard**	2595693	Halcyondale, GA/SARD CAC Fort Screven
Pvt. Harry C. **Shields**	3370981	SARD CAC Fort Screven
Pvt. William H. **Shrenk** [**Schrenk?**]		Atlanta, GA/SARD CAC Fort Screven
Lewis W. **Shuetz**	3804363	406th Overseas Casual Co.
H. Bowles **Sidman**	24800 [?]	
Pvt. Robert **Simmons**	3239008	Owensboro, KY/SARD CAC Fort Screven
Raymond A. **Simpson**	844815	Pendleton, SC
Pvt. Thomas Jefferson **Sirmons**	2595842	Nashville, GA/SARD CAC Fort Screven
Pvt. Edward J. **Smith**	2413263	406th Overseas Casual Co.
Pvt. Edwin A. **Smith**	2595745	Waynesboro, GA/SARD CAC Fort Screven
Pvt. Ira **Smith**	2900488	Villa Rica, GA/SARD CAC Fort Screven
Pvt. [Lawrence] Larnie **Smith**	814892	Bennettsville, SC/SARD CAC Fort Screven
Pvt. Lonnie L. **Smith**	2595773	Quitman, GA/SARD CAC Fort Screven
Pvt. Paul F. **Smith**	793373	Pensacola, FL/SARD CAC Fort Screven
Sgt. Russell **Smith**	718859	SARD CAC Fort Screven
Sgt. Samuel L. **Smith**		406th Overseas Casual Co.
Pvt. Sanford T. **Smith**	2900428	Haddock, GA/SARD CAC Fort Screven
Pvt. Walter Cornelius **Smith**	793322	Cedartown, GA/SARD CAC Fort Screven
Pvt. Capers W. **Smoak**	2595656	Sylvania, GA/SARD CAC Fort Screven
Pvt. Albert N. **Spaugh**	3238931	Winston-Salem, NC/SARD CAC Fort Screven
Pvt. Maurice **Stafford**	870042	Rhinelander, WI/SARD CAC Fort Screven

Name	Service Number	Home and Unit
Cpl. Marvin J. **Stansell**	719079	Lindale, GA/SARD CAC Fort Screven
Pvt. John E. **Steel**	3372061	SARD CAC Fort Screven
Pvt. Carl O. **Stensvold**	470498	Braham, TX/SARD CAC Fort Screven
Pvt. Amedro **Steo**	3722531	New York, NY/406th Overseas Casual Co.
Pvt. Alonzo [Lonnie] **Steptoe**	2595779	Kite, GA/SARD CAC Fort Screven
Pvt. Colie L. **Stevens**	814895	Chapples, SC/SARD CAC Fort Screven
Pvt. Clifton E. **Stewart**	2595798	Covena, GA/SARD CAC Fort Screven
Pvt. William T. **Stewart**	3368206	Covena, GA/SARD CAC Fort Screven
Pvt. Roland B. **Stout**	3241395	Greensboro, NC/SARD CAC Fort Screven
Cpl. Clarence J. **Strand**	470180	SARD CAC Fort Screven
Perque **Sulmie [Sullie?]**	3005452	
Russell H. **Swadner**	3239979	SARD CAC Fort Screven
Pvt. William H. **Talley**	2995562	Atlanta, GA/SARD CAC Fort Screven
Pvt. Edward **Threadway**	813476	Quitman, GA/SARD CAC Fort Screven
Pvt. Andrew **Thrift**	2595640	Hebardsville, GA/SARD CAC Fort Screven
Pvt. Thomas J. **Tims**	369481	Brooklyn, NY/410th Overseas Casual Co.
Pvt. Lummie **Todd**	714592	Vidalia, GA/SARD CAC Fort Screven
Pvt. Rudolf V. **Torck**	2595528	Charleston, SC/SARD CAC Fort Screven
Pvt. Hiram **Treadway**	2595744	Quitman, GA/SARD CAC Fort Screven
Cpl. Julius **Trimpe**	813865	SARD CAC Fort Screven
Pvt. Elsie O. **Turner**	718864	Greenville, SC/SARD CAC Fort Screven
Pvt. Frank **Tuten**	2595633	Beach, GA/SARD CAC Fort Screven
Pvt. Edwin A. **Unger**	813737	Knoxville, IL/8th Co. Engineers, CAC

Name	Service Number	Home and Unit
Sgt. Wade L. **Usher**	2595943	Sylvania, GA/SARD CAC Fort Screven
Pvt. Charles E. **Vail**		406th Overseas Casual Co.
Pvt. Joel McDonald **Vandiver**	2902771	Atlanta, GA/SARD CAC Fort Screven
Cpl. Charles Stephen **Walden**	720313	Millwood, GA/SARD CAC Fort Screven
Pvt. Maurice L. **Walnau** [**Wallnau?**]	2595598	Macon, GA/SARD CAC Fort Screven
Pvt. William O. **Ward**	814821	Batesburg, SC/SARD CAC Fort Screven
Cpl. William Eugene **Warth**	719601	Savannah, GA/SARD CAC Fort Screven
Pvt. Grover **Waters**	2902765	Munford, AL/SARD CAC Fort Screven
Cpl. Archie Y. **Watts**	2902811	Selma, AL/SARD CAC Fort Screven
Pvt. Shellie Lloyd **Webb**	2595853	Ray City, GA/SARD CAC Fort Screven
Pvt. Aaron [Aron?] Washington **Weeks** [**Meeks?**]	2595755	Waynesboro, GA/SARD CAC Fort Screven
Pvt. Henry Verdell **Wells**	2595496	Augusta, GA/SARD CAC Fort Screven
Pvt. Joe **Wheeler**	2595827	Nashville, GA/SARD CAC Fort Screven
Hearne C. **Whitaker**	2902445	Baldwin, MS/SARD CAC Fort Screven
Pvt. Charles **Whiteaker**		McMinnville, TN/410th Overseas Casual Co.
Pvt. Vern E. **Willey**	1426339	406th Overseas Casual Co.
Pvt. Carl **Williams**	2595566	Augusta, GA/SARD CAC Fort Screven
Pvt. Edward **Williams**	3370985	SARD CAC Fort Screven
George **Williams**		Quitman, GA
Cpl. James W. **Williams**	2595708	Brooklet, GA/SARD CAC Fort Screven
Pvt. Joe **Williams**	2595788	Summit, GA/SARD CAC Fort Screven
Cpl. Lee **Williams**	719091	Seneca, SC/SARD CAC Fort Screven
Cpl. Luther F. **Williams**	2902734	Republic, AL

Name	Service Number	Home and Unit
Pvt. Robert L. **Williams**	2595742 [?]	Quitman, GA
Pvt. Cecil H. **Williamson**	2596065	Sylvania, GA/SARD CAC Fort Screven
Pvt. James Ollie **Wilson**	2595567	Chamblee, GA/SARD CAC Fort Screven
Pvt. John T. **Wilson**	719092	Oneco, FL
Pvt. John W. **Windsor**	1292800	410th Overseas Casual Co.
Pvt. Louis F. **Wise**	429648	Wendell, NC/SARD CAC Fort Screven
Pvt. Grover C. **Wright**	3333015	Streator, IL/406th Overseas Casual Co.
Pvt. Edwin N. **Young**	4158262	Ponchatoula, LA/SARD CAC Fort Screven
Pvt. Milton G. **Zartman**	3372313	Denver, PA/SARD CAC Fort Screven
Pvt. William C. **Zeigler** [**Ziegler?**]	2595855	Sparks, GA/SARD CAC Fort Screven
Pvt. Michael **Zuerlein**	470398	Humphrey, NE

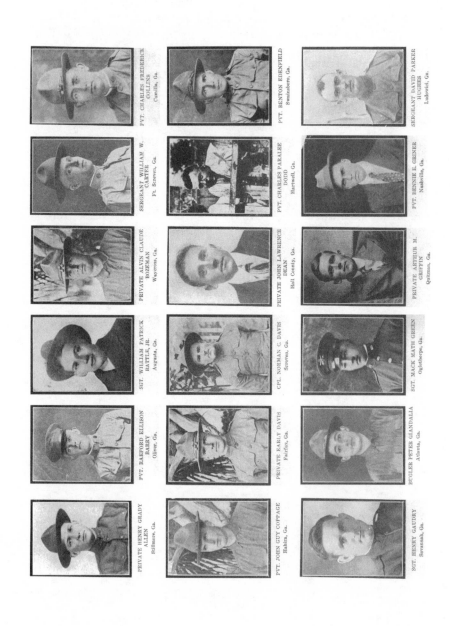

PVT. CHARLES FREDERICK
COLLINS
Camilla, Ga.

PVT. BENTON EDENFIELD
Swainsboro, Ga.

SERGEANT DAVID PARKER
HUGHES
Lodowld, Ga.

SERGEANT WILLIAM W.
CARTER
Ft. Screven, Ga.

PVT. CHARLES PARALEE
DODD
Hartwell, Ga.

PVT. BENNIE E. GRINER
Nashville, Ga.

PRIVATE ALVIN CLAUDE
BOZEMAN
Waycross, Ga.

PRIVATE JOHN LAWRENCE
DEAN
Hall County, Ga.

PRIVATE ARTHUR M.
GRIFFIN
Quitman, Ga.

SGT. WILLIAM PATRICK
RATTLE, JR.
Augusta, Ga.

CPL. NORMAN C. DAVIS
Screven, Ga.

SGT. MACK MATH GREEN
Ogdethorpe, Ga.

PVT. RASFORD ELLISON
BARRY
Oliver, Ga.

PRIVATE EARLY DAVIS
Fairfax, Ga.

BUGLER PETER GIANDALIA
Atlanta, Ga.

PRIVATE HENRY GRADY
ALLEN
Stillmore, Ga.

PVT. JOHN GUY COPPAGE
Habira, Ga.

SGT. HENRY GAUDRY
Savannah, Ga.

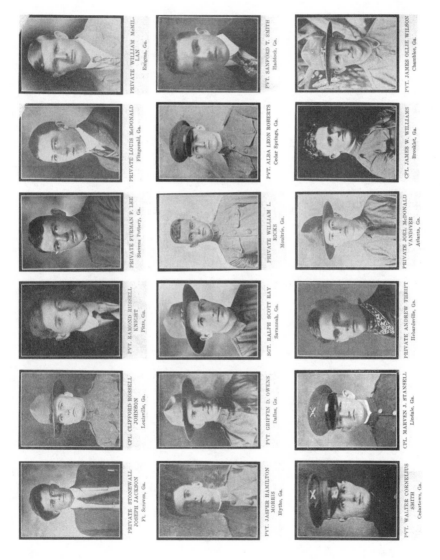

PRIVATE WILLIAM McMILLAN
Enigma, Ga.

PVT. SANFORD T. SMITH
Hadlock, Ga.

PVT. JAMES OLLIE WILSON
Chamblee, Ga.

PRIVATE LOUIS McDONALD
Fitzgerald, Ga.

PVT. ALBA LEON ROBERTS
Cedar Springs, Ga.

CPL. JAMES W. WILLIAMS
Brooklet, Ga.

PRIVATE FURMAN P. LEE
Stevens Pottery, Ga.

PRIVATE WILLIAM L. RICKS
Moultrie, Ga.

PRIVATE JOEL McDONALD VANDIVER
Atlanta, Ga.

PVT. RAMOND RUSSELL KNIGHT
Pitts, Ga.

SGT. RALPH SCOTT RAY
Savannah, Ga.

PRIVATE ANDREW THRIFT
Hohatchville, Ga.

CPL. CLIFFORD ROSSELL JOHNSON
Louisville, Ga.

PVT. GRIFFIN D. OWENS
Dallas, Ga.

CPL. MARVEN J. STANSELL
Lindale, Ga.

PRIVATE STONEWALL JOSEPH JACKSON
Ft. Screven, Ga.

PVT. JASPER HAMILTON MORRIS
Blythe, Ga.

PVT. WALTER CORNELIUS SMITH
Cedartown, Ga.

APPENDIX 2

HMS *Otranto* American Survivors

ABBREVIATIONS

*S*ARD CAC Fort Screven: September Automatic Replacement Draft, Coastal Artillery Corps, Fort Screven, GA

Pvt. Boyd **Abernethy**	718790	Gaffney, SC/SARD CAC Fort Screven
Pvt. Mitch **Adkins**	3242315	Sandy Hook, KY/SARD CAC Fort Screven
Pvt. Charles W. **Allen**		Batt. C, 55th Artillery
Pvt. Raymond **Applebey**	604553	Knoxville, PA/Batt. A, 8th FA
Pvt. Arvid A. **August**	813477	SARD CAC Fort Screven
Cpl. Calenford **Avirett**	813271	Marco, FL/SARD CAC Fort Screven
Pvt. George E. **Ayer**	813478	SARD CAC Fort Screven
Pvt. William R. **Bagby**	2595459	Augusta, GA/SARD CAC Fort Screven
Pvt. Richard L. **Baker** Jr.	793301	Berry, AL/SARD CAC Fort Screven
Pvt. William J. **Balupey** [Balsley?]	3241232	Sekitan, OH/SARD CAC Fort Screven
Pvt. Peter **Bassakas**	3201897	Base Hospital 79
Pvt. George **Batter**	3241326 [3241316?]	Cincinnati, OH/SARD CAC Fort Screven
Pvt. Quint **Baxter**	3005351	SARD CAC Fort Screven

Pvt. Thomas **Bazemore**	2595667	Sylvania, GA/SARD CAC Fort Screven
Pvt. Elvin **Beagle**	3241310	Covington, KY/SARD CAC Fort Screven
Pvt. E. W. **Bell**	366273	Brooklyn, NY/SARD CAC Fort Screven
Pvt. Clyde B. **Benson**	2595460	Augusta, GA/SARD CAC Fort Screven
Pvt. James A. **Bishop**	2595437	Summertown, GA/SARD CAC Fort Screven
Pvt. Tyman M. **Blake**	1271487	Merchantville, NJ/Co. D, 104th Engineers
Pvt. Lawrence **Blau**		New York, NY/5th Div., Amb. Batt. Co. 25
Pvt. Tracy O. **Blue**	719254	Grafton, WV/SARD CAC Fort Screven
Pvt. H. **Boogay**	1223660	Philadelphia, PA/410th Casual Co.
Pvt. Harry **Bornstine**	719000	Goodletsville, TN/SARD CAC Fort Screven
Sgt. Edward J. **Boucher**	743442	Fall River, MA/330th Labor Batt., Quartermaster Corps
Pvt. Julian **Bouks**	2595766	Saint Claire, GA/SARD CAC Fort Screven
Pvt. Oxford Knox **Bourgeois**	2595945	Atlanta, GA/SARD CAC Fort Screven
Pvt. Benjamin E. **Brehm**	2595530	Atlanta, GA/SARD CAC Fort Screven
Pvt. Simeon **Brock**	2902684	SARD CAC Fort Screven
Pvt. Jim M. **Brown**	2595777	Stillmore, GA/SARD CAC Fort Screven
Pvt. John **Brown**	3238879	Normal, KY/SARD CAC Fort Screven
Pvt. Robert Lee **Brown**	2595461	406th Casual Co.
Cpl. Fred H. **Bubert**	813506	Easton, IL/SARD CAC Fort Screven
Pvt. Leo **Bubet**		Irvington, NJ/Co. B, 312th Engineers
Sgt. H. C. **Bucher**	1287220	Washington, DC/406th Casual Co.
Pvt. Eddie H. **Bunton**		Burlington, NC/406th Casual Co.

Cpl. George E. **Bush**	470024	Fond-du-Lac, WI/SARD CAC Fort Screven
Sgt. Thomas B. **Caddell**	718945	SARD CAC Fort Screven
Pvt. Edgar F. **Cadle**	2595653	Augusta, GA
Pvt. George A. **Campbell**	470993	Ozawkie, KS
T. L. **Campbell**		Memphis, TN/YMCA officer
Pvt. Leon G. **Canning**	372953	Lansdale, PA
Pvt. Bert H. **Cannon**	3005366	Merryville, LA/SARD CAC Fort Screven
C. A. **Carpenter** [Name appears on both survivor and casualty lists.]		Waukesha, WI/YMCA officer
Pvt. Jones E. **Carpenter**	2595462	Graymont, GA/SARD CAC Fort Screven
Pvt. James E. **Casey**	3005256	Pine Bluff, AR/SARD CAC Fort Screven
Pvt. William **Champ**	470403	Eldon, IA
Pvt. Hoyt **Christian**		Covena, GA/SARD CAC Fort Screven
Pvt. Armand P. **Christman**	2299349	Worcester, MA/406th Casual Co.
Pvt. Oliver F. **Clark**		Chatham, NJ/Co. B, 348th Infantry
Horace Matthew **Cleary**	2595679	Oliver, GA/SARD CAC Fort Screven
Pvt. John O. **Clements**	3005379	New Orleans, LA/SARD CAC Fort Screven
Pvt. Beckham **Cobb**	2902720	Birmingham, AL
Pvt. Alva J. **Cochran**		Atlanta, GA/SARD CAC Fort Screven
2nd Lt. Bierne [Bernie J.?] **Coffman**, DMA [Name appears on both casualty and survivor lists.]		406th Overseas Casual Co.
William J. R. **Cogney**		SARD CAC Fort Screven
Sgt. Harvey L. **Collins**	718754	Hickman, KY/SARD CAC Fort Screven
Sgt. Erle E. **Colomy**	1850472	410th Casual Co.
Pvt. Joe **Conforti**	1276190	Newark, NJ/82nd Aviation
Pvt. Charles I. **Connett**	813859	San Jose, IL/SARD CAC Fort Screven
Pvt. Vincent C. **Connor**	471010	Springfield, IL/SARD CAC Fort Screven

2nd Lt. Harry M. **Conwell**   Lynbrook, Long Island, NY/
Co. M, 355th Infantry/
commander of 406th and
410th Casual Cos.

Pvt. Clarence **Cook**   3241466   Cincinnati, OH/SARD CAC
Fort Screven

Pvt. McKinley **Cook**   3005507   Bono, AR/SARD CAC Fort
Screven

Pvt. Donald **Cooper**   2655034   Sylvania, GA

Pvt. Edward J. **Cordes**   Mason City, IL/SARD CAC
Fort Screven

Pvt. William B. **Covington**   762155   Columbus, GA/SARD CAC
Fort Screven

Pvt. Aiken P. **Cox**   814808   Greer, SC/SARD CAC Fort
Screven

Pvt. Dana H. **Craig**   719008   Tioga, WV

Pvt. Milton **Crews**   3241318   Wickliffe, KY/SARD CAC
Fort Screven

Pvt. Gustave **Cromey**   393447   Bayonne, NJ/Quartermaster
Corps

Pvt. Ernest **Cunningham**   2902663   Manchester, TN/SARD CAC
Fort Screven

Pvt. Willis R. **Cupps**   2582980   Greensburg, PA/SARD CAC
Fort Screven

Sgt. George W. **Cuvall**   SARD CAC Fort Screven
[Duval?]

Sgt. Amzie J. **Davidson**   718955   St. Cloud, FL/SARD CAC
Fort Screven

Cpl. Melvin F. **Davies**   470528   Omaha, NE/SARD CAC Fort
Screven

Pvt. Ralph E. **Davis**   813846   San Jose, IL/SARD CAC Fort
Screven

William J. **DeHaven**   1033838   Philadelphia, PA/Co. I, 64th
Infantry

Pvt. Henry E. **Delaney**   2595830   Savannah, GA/SARD CAC
Fort Screven

Pvt. James M. **Deloach**   2595833   Halvaira, GA/SARD CAC
Fort Screven

Pvt. Albert F. **DeMoss**   3005162   Eros, LA/SARD CAC Fort
Screven

Cpl. Walter E. **Dennis**   2595613   Hopkinsville, KY/SARD CAC
Fort Screven

Pvt. Anthony **DiNicola**   4241257   Bellville, NJ/Medical Corps

Cpt. Charles A. **Dixon**, MC		Akron, OH/Medical Corps
Cpl. John K. **Doherty**	1987855	Brooklyn, NY/Amb. Co. 336th, 84th Div.
Sgt. Edward J. **Donahue**	3534568	Columbus, OH/Co. H, 336th Infantry
Cpl. William G. **Dutiel**	814475	Laurel, KY/SARD CAC Fort Screven
Sgt. George W. **Duval** [**Cuvall?**]	720441	Enid, OK/SARD CAC Fort Screven
Pvt. Steward **Early**		SARD CAC Fort Screven
Cpl. Ralph C. **Ebner**	719012	Springfield, SC/SARD CAC Fort Screven
Pvt. Sidney Watson **Edenfield**	2595685	Woodcliff, GA/SARD CAC Fort Screven
Pvt. Everett **Eller**		Sparta, TN/410th Casual Co.
Pvt. Frank **Enes**	813546	SARD CAC Fort Screven
Cpl. Arthur E. **Engdahl**	470831	Chicago, IL/SARD CAC Fort Screven
Pvt. Harold F. **English**	3372193	Saginaw, MI/SARD CAC Fort Screven
Pvt. Hubert **Estep**	3241233	Lucasville, OH/SARD CAC Fort Screven
Sgt. Howard C. **Farley**	390516	Bridgeport, CT/491st Truck Co.
Pvt. Charles E. **Farris**	2274472	Takoma, WA/MP, 410th Casual Co.
Sgt. William C. **Fick**		Carlton Hill, NJ/308th Batt. FA 79th Div.
Cpl. Christopher **Finnegan**	2790079	Base Hospital 79
Pvt. Willis **Finnell**	2890227	Lexington, KY/Batt. F, 327th FA
Pvt. Michael J. **Flanagan**	3372826	Bellaire, OH/SARD CAC Fort Screven
Pvt. Henry G. **Flynt**	2595580	Ashburn, GA/SARD CAC Fort Screven
Cpl. John H. **Ford**	470985	Cherokee, IA/SARD CAC Fort Screven
Pvt. John Thomas **Ford**	3005389	McCrory, AR/SARD CAC Fort Screven
Cpl. Rhynard **Forsberg**	471007	Marguette, KS/SARD CAC Fort Screven
Pvt. Joe **Frank**	4162052	SARD CAC Fort Screven

Pvt. James **Frechette**	3200729	New York, NY/MC Base Hospital 79
Pvt. Colder **Freeman**	813123	Abbotsburg, NC/SARD CAC Fort Screven
Pvt. James A. **Fulwood**	2595645	Waresboro, GA/SARD CAC Fort Screven
Pvt. Chancey **Futch**	2595709	Groveland, GA/SARD CAC Fort Screven
Pvt. Earl **Garver**	3239972	Cincinnati, OH/SARD CAC Fort Screven
Cpl. Clarence W. **German**	813562	Williamsfield, IL/SARD CAC Fort Screven
Pvt. Clarence **Gill**		Batt. A, 321st FA
Pvt. William F. **Glass** [Gloss?]	3238992	Baltimore, MD/SARD CAC Fort Screven
Pvt. Robert E. **Godsey**	3363764	Peerless, IN/SARD CAC Fort Screven
Pvt. Pincus **Goldbard**	1901043	New York, NY/Co. C, 326th Infantry
Pvt. Julius **Golden**	2595542	Augusta, GA/SARD CAC Fort Screven
Pvt. 1st Class Edward J. **Gordes**		SARD CAC Fort Screven
Pvt. Dallas G. **Greenler**	3372758	Holgate, OH/SARD CAC Fort Screven
Pvt. John T. **Groseclose**		Fallsville, AR/Co. F., 111th Engineers
Pvt. Dewey A. **Gross**	719019	Stroud, AL/SARD CAC Fort Screven
Pvt. Joseph F. **Gruenthal**	3241410	Raum, IL/SARD CAC Fort Screven
Pvt. Earl W. **Hagerman**	3097091	Findlay, OH/SARD CAC Fort Screven
Sgt. Emory D. **Hall**	719104	Savannah, GA/SARD CAC Fort Screven
Pvt. George **Hallor**		
Pvt. Perry **Handley**		Summit, GA/SARD CAC Fort Screven
Cpl. Lloyd W. **Harmison**	813570	Williamsfield, IL/SARD CAC Fort Screven
Pvt. James A. **Harmon**	718867	Inman, SC/SARD CAC Fort Screven

Pvt. Frank L. **Harris**	3239973	Newport, KY/SARD CAC Fort Screven
Pvt. Joseph W. **Hartig**		Newport, KY/SARD CAC Fort Screven
Pvt. **Haskin**	209268	SARD CAC Fort Screven
Cpt. Fred S. **Heimer**, MC		Hamden, NY/Medical Corps
Albert J. **Heink**	3241467	Cincinnati, OH
Pvt. Joseph T. **Hendrick**	3236081	Southside, NC/SARD CAC Fort Screven
James **Hendrix**	718644	Tampa, FL
Pvt. John H. **Herndon**	2595544	Mayfield, GA/SARD CAC Fort Screven
Pvt. Joseph **Hess**	4157121	Bordenville, LA/SARD CAC Fort Screven
Pvt. Joseph E. **Hewell**	2595584	Bairdstown, GA/SARD CAC Fort Screven
Sgt. Benjamin F. **Hill**	718820	Greenville, SC/SARD CAC Fort Screven
Pvt. Robert A. **Hinegardner**	813866	Havana, IL/SARD CAC Fort Screven
Pvt. Floyd C. **Hoagland**	3372145	Youngstown, OH/SARD CAC Fort Screven
Sgt. Thomas J. **Holmes**	1894355	Brockton, MA/Batt. A, 325th Field Artillery
Pvt. Peter **Horemans**	3372259	St. Lawrence, SD/SARD CAC Fort Screven
Pvt. Pearl B. **Horn**	1262391	SARD CAC Fort Screven
Charles F. **Horrigan** [**Harrigan?**]	3238881	Cincinnati, OH
Robert C. **Horton**	2595439	Savannah, GA
Pvt. William P. **Hoskins**	2902698	Gross, KY
Pvt. Clyde K. **Hughes**	814810	Belton, SC/SARD CAC Fort Screven
Mack O. **Hughes**	2595752	Colerain, NC
Abram C. **Humphries**	2595547	Atlanta, GA
Pvt. Stansell S. **Hutto**		Augusta, GA
Pvt. Aaron **Inglett**	2595477	Augusta, GA/SARD CAC Fort Screven
Cpl. Raymond M. **Ingram**	2595624	Savannah, GA/SARD CAC Fort Screven
James L. **Jackson** Jr.	814792	Iva, SC
Pvt. Jerry **Jackson**	814862	Greenville, SC/SARD CAC Fort Screven

Pvt. Arthur Neil **Jenkins**   Hiltonia, GA/SARD CAC
Fort Screven

Pvt. Frank **Jensen**   888543   Seattle, WA/485th Motor
Truck Co.

Otto **Jobe**   3238969   Gladys, KY
Halus **Johnson**   813599   Bath, IL
Pvt. Harry T. **Johnson**   813598   Galesburg, IL/Co. C, 57th
CAC, 31st Div.

Harry W. **Johnson**   720245
Pvt. Homer L. **Johnson**   406th Casual Co.
Cpl. Percy G. **Johnson**   Galesburg, IL/8th Co., Batt.
D, 54th CAC

William D. **Johnson**   2902767   Huntsville, AL
Sgt. John T. **Jones**   718868   Homerville, GA/SARD CAC
Fort Screven

Pvt. Joseph W. **Kea**   2595774   Adrian, GA/SARD CAC Fort
Screven

Pvt. Comodore **Kelley**   718831   Gaffney, SC/SARD CAC Fort
Screven

Pvt. William E. **Kelley**   2595442   Ridgeland, SC/SARD CAC
Fort Screven

Pvt. Thomas A. **Kelly**   2595479   Augusta, GA/SARD CAC
Fort Screven

Cpl. James **Kerns**   1245765   Philadelphia, PA/406th
Casual Co.

Ralph W. **Kesner**   2595548   Atlanta, GA
Pvt. Harry J. **Kett**   2590540   Brooklyn, NY/Med. Base
Hospital 79

Pvt. Scott **Kinchsley**   SARD CAC Fort Screven
Cpl. Jay E. **King**   2595549   Atlanta, GA/SARD CAC Fort
Screven

Pvt. Kenneth R. **Kingsley**   3368277   Kent, OH/SARD CAC Fort
Screven

Charles A. **Kolda [Golds?]**   470062   Cedar Rapids, IA
Leo **Kowalski**   3375242   Bay City, MI
Sgt. Jess L. **Kramer**   720034   Cleveland, OH/SARD CAC
Fort Screven

Pvt. Daniel L. **Lacy**   3211335   New York, NY/Co. F, 323rd
Infantry

Pvt. Ralph C. **Lambert**   3375236   Saranac, MI/SARD CAC Fort
Screven

Pvt. Arthur **Lang**   718966   Indianapolis, IN/SARD CAC
Fort Screven

Horace Lee **Lariscy**	2595681	Sylvania, GA/SARD CAC Fort Screven
Pvt. Lloyd M. **Lariscy**	2595700	Sylvania, GA/SARD CAC Fort Screven
Pvt. Homer H. **Larsen**	813618	Williamsfield, IL/SARD CAC Fort Screven
Pvt. Martin C. **Larsen**	470725	SARD CAC Fort Screven
Pvt. Rosco **Lawson**	793361	Knoxville, TN/SARD CAC Fort Screven
Pvt. Thomas R. **Lawther**	3372526	Jeannette, PA/SARD CAC Fort Screven
Cpl. Charles F. **Lee**	813310	Estell, SC/SARD CAC Fort Screven
Ernest V. **Lee**	2595940	Ogeechee, GA/SARD CAC Fort Screven
Pvt. John D. **Lee**	2595715	Statesboro, GA
Val **Lee**		SARD CAC Fort Screven
Columbus **Lenard**	2595702	Pembroke, GA
C. C. **Leonard**		Savannah, GA
2nd Lt. Samuel E. **Levy**		Atlanta, GA/SARD CAC Fort Screven/commander of American troops aboard the *Otranto*
Sgt. James R. **Lewis**	841394	Santiago, CA/Co. 54th Amn. Train
Keith H. **Linton**	3372643	Elm Grove, WV
Pvt. William W. **Lockwood**	400844	Brooklyn, NY/14th Band CAC Fort Screven
Pvt. Joseph W. **Loechle**	3240270	Newport, KY/SARD CAC Fort Screven
Pvt. Oscar **Lott**	2595711	SARD CAC Fort Screven
Pvt. John **Love**	2902755	Oliver Springs, TN
Pvt. Joseph M. **Lyons**	3723222	New York, NY/410th Casual Co.
Pvt. Joseph A. **McCance**	813811	Marietta, IL/SARD CAC Fort Screven
Sgt. Charles A. **McDonald**	813640	Galesburg, IL/Batt. D, 54th Regiment, 1st Army Artillery
Pvt. John **McGahey**	813642	Galesburg, IL/SARD CAC Fort Screven
Pvt. John J. **McGinley**	3188513	Brooklyn, NY/Co. F, 156th Infantry

Cpl. Erich L. **McInnis**	719043	Porterdale, GA/SARD CAC Fort Screven
Robert J. **McKinney**	429957	Bakersville, NC
Pvt. David R. **Mack**	2595791	Augusta, SC/SARD CAC Fort Screven
Bugler Lawrence W. **Mallory**	470075	Fall River, WI/SARD CAC Fort Screven
Pvt. Andrew S. **Marsee**	2902688	Warren, KY/SARD CAC Fort Screven
Harville **Marsh**	2595724	Portal, GA
Pvt. James Solomon **Marsh**	2595682	Dover, GA/SARD CAC Fort Screven
Pvt. Merrill E. **Matheny**	3372084	Columbus, OH/SARD CAC Fort Screven
Pvt. James C. **Meaders**	2595553	Atlanta, GA/SARD CAC Fort Screven
Moses **Meadows**	2902706	Alexander City, LA
Wheeler **Mercer**	2595737	Berlin, GA
Pvt. Vito **Mercury**	318850	Brooklyn, NY/31st Co., 8th Batt.
Pvt. David C. **Miller**	719048	Dandridge, TN/SARD CAC Fort Screven
Ira W. **Miller**		Salisburg, NC
Sgt. Julius S. **Miller**	719861	Savannah, GA/SARD CAC Fort Screven
Pvt. Michael A. **Mitchell**	4084344	Scranton, PA/US Engineers
Sgt. Paul T. **Mitchell**	710951	Savannah, GA/SARD CAC Fort Screven
Pvt. Edward V. **Mix**	3372151	Jacksonburg, WV/SARD CAC Fort Screven
Pvt. Jesse E. **Mixon**	2595629	Waycross, GA/SARD CAC Fort Screven
Cpl. George H. **Mobley**	814724	Milledgeville, GA/SARD CAC Fort Screven
Vannie Woodson **Morris**	2595657	Sylvania, GA/SARD CAC Fort Screven
Pvt. Zophar **Morse**	4158239	Robert, LA/SARD CAC Fort Screven
Pvt. Thomas **Moser** [**Moses**]	2902424	Coaling, AL/SARD CAC Fort Screven
Harry S. **Muckle**	3375233	Charleroi, PA
Pvt. Pearl **Napier**	3241324	Oakley, KY/SARD CAC Fort Screven

Pvt. Axel H. **Nelson**	471003	SARD CAC Fort Screven
Pvt. Johnannes L. **Nelson**	813662	Galesburg, IL/SARD CAC Fort Screven
Pvt. Lloyd A. **Ney**	3371489	Pottsville, PA/SARD CAC Fort Screven
Pvt. Thomas W. **O'Dell**	2953353	Patterson, NJ/Batt. A, 335th Infantry
Cpl. Williams C. **O'Shields**	718846	Tuscapau, SC/SARD CAC Fort Screven
Pvt. James I. **O'Steen**	2902736	Kirkland, GA/SARD CAC Fort Screven
Pvt. J. Ernest **Oglesby**	2595677	Sylvania, GA/SARD CAC Fort Screven
Charles E. **Opp**	813666	Havana, IL
Pvt. Anthony **Orbit**	3372104	Gallitzin, PA/SARD CAC Fort Screven
Pvt. Charles R. **Orth**	1061932	410th Casual Co.
Raymond **Owens**	2595670	Ziglar, GA/SARD CAC Fort Screven
2nd Lt. William H. **Papenfoth**		Columbus, OH/SARD CAC Fort Screven
Pvt. William R. **Parrett**	2902827	Monterey, TN/SARD CAC Fort Screven
Pvt. Ernest L. **Patrick**	2595792	Summit, GA/SARD CAC Fort Screven
Pvt. Harless H. **Payne**	3241440	Pilot, VA/SARD CAC Fort Screven
2nd Lt. Frank A. **Perkins**		Augusta, GA/SARD CAC Fort Screven
Victor M. **Perrin**	2595948	Atlanta, GA
Pvt. Emil **Petersen**	813672	SARD CAC Fort Screven
Pvt. Homer A. **Pettis**	2895949	Vandelt, GA/SARD CAC Fort Screven
Pvt. Harvey **Pichnic**	4159847	SARD CAC Fort Screven
Cpl. John **Picosky**	1271572	Newark, NJ/Co. D, 104th Engineers
John **Piening**	3372765	Grand Rapids, MI
Pvt. Joseph M. **Pollock**	2595483	SARD CAC Fort Screven
Pvt. Frank H. **Pool**	3238970	Paris, TN/SARD CAC Fort Screven
Pvt. Jess **Powell**		McMinnville, TN/Co. F, 125th Infantry

Pvt. John **Powers**	2897782	Cincinnati, OH/Batt. F, 325th Field Artillery
Walter F. **Powers**	719059	Macon, GA
Cpl. J. Kerns **Prauns**		
Cpl. Glenn M. **Rankin**	813817	Vermont, IL/SARD CAC Fort Screven
Pvt. Fred S. **Rashid**	813684	Canton, IL/SARD CAC Fort Screven
Sgt. John E. **Rauber**	718882	Savannah, GA
Fred R. **Redd**	2902639	Ensley, AL
Pvt. Andrew J. **Reddy**		New York, NY/Co. I, 306th Infantry
Sgt. Harold D. **Redman** [Name appears on both survivor and casualty lists.]	718760	Fort Lauderdale, FL/SARD CAC Fort Screven
Pvt. Joseph S. **Richards**	718854	SARD CAC Fort Screven
Pvt. William H. **Richards**	3239975	SARD CAC Fort Screven
Pvt. Charlie H. **Riddle**	2595750	Munnerlyn, GA/SARD CAC Fort Screven
Pvt. David R. **Roberts**	3372669	SARD CAC Fort Screven
Pvt. Jessie E. **Rodgers**	3236401	Emmett, TN/SARD CAC Fort Screven
Pvt. Joseph **Roman**	4240258	Philadelphia, PA/SARD CAC Fort Screven
Pvt. Virgil Joseph **Rosier**	2596694	Sylvania, GA/SARD CAC Fort Screven
Pvt. Winnifred **Rudisell**	3239976	Sekitan, OH/SARD CAC Fort Screven
Pvt. Hubert **Salyer**	3238884	Normal, KY/SARD CAC Fort Screven
Harry **Say**	3372132	Knox, PA
Cpl. Harold A. **Schumann**	720283	Silver City, NC/SARD CAC Fort Screven
Pvt. Francis Parker **Scott**	2595684	Sylvania, GA/SARD CAC Fort Screven
Pvt. Kinchsley **Scott**	2595665	Sylvania, GA/SARD CAC Fort Screven
Pvt. Roy J. **Scott**	2902425	Plainville, GA/SARD CAC Fort Screven
Pvt. C. S. **Setty**	718981	410th Casual Co.
Cpl. Milton G. **Sewell**	2902786	Anniston, AL/SARD CAC Fort Screven

Pvt. Robert F. **Shand**	3372671	Lebanon, PA/SARD CAC Fort Screven
Pvt. Samuel G. **Shaver**	3371526	Kalamazoo, MI/SARD CAC Fort Screven
Pvt. Lewis Lonzon **Sheley**	2595688	Sylvania, GA/SARD CAC Fort Screven
Edgar A. P. **Sheppard**	2595560	Augusta, GA
Cpl. Carl **Sheriff**	793362	Gainesville, GA/SARD CAC Fort Screven
Sgt. Harry E. **Shondel**	3344300	Philadelphia, PA/Co. G, 336th Infantry
Pvt. Thomas **Sloane**	368759	Brooklyn, NY/Co. F, 114th Infantry
Pvt. Ben **Smith**	2595522	SARD CAC Fort Screven
Pvt. Conor C. **Smith**	2595950	Atlanta, GA/SARD CAC Fort Screven
John A. **Smith**	3372497	Harbor Springs, MI
Pvt. Lonnie C. **Smith**	3238930	Marshville, NC/SARD CAC Fort Screven
Cpl. Manuel **Smith**	1909542	Taunton, MA/Co. B, 328th Infantry
Cpl. Reasy J. **Smith**	719077	Kilbourne, LA/SARD CAC Fort Screven
Pvt. William E. **Smith**	2595747	Mathews, GA/SARD CAC Fort Screven
Pvt. Charles E. **Smithson**	719078	Bessemer, AL/SARD CAC Fort Screven
Pvt. Harry **Spyke**	3372657	Jenison, MI/SARD CAC Fort Screven
Richmond H. **Stafford**	3236038	Eddyville, KY
Pvt. Walter D. **Stallard**	2595870	Colburn, VA/SARD CAC Fort Screven
Cpl. Robert A. **Starling**		Cascade, VA/SARD CAC Fort Screven
Pvt. Edwin J. **Starr**	813718	Galesburg, IL/60th Regiment CAC
John P. **Steele**	2595596	Hawkinsville, GA
Pvt. Henry A. **Steiner**	3241217	Dayton, OH/SARD CAC Fort Screven
Pvt. Earl Y. **Steward**		Nashville, GA/SARD CAC Fort Screven
Sgt. Glenn P. **Stine**	470535	Omaha, NE/SARD CAC Fort Screven

Pvt. Howard **Strohm**	3371843	Emaus, PA/SARD CAC Fort Screven
2nd Lt. David R. **Sutton**		Glendale, SC/SARD CAC Fort Screven
Pvt. George C. **Tague**	718862	Indianapolis, IN/SARD CAC Fort Screven
Pvt. George S. **Taylor**	720309	SARD CAC Fort Screven
Pvt. H. B. **Taylor**	3238885	Durham, NC
Pvt. Noah E. **Taylor**	2902652	Spruceburg, KY/SARD CAC Fort Screven
Pvt. Thomas J. **Taylor**	2595666	Hiltonia, GA/SARD CAC Fort Screven
Pvt. Alex H. **Telford**		Galesburg, IL/Batt. C, 54th Artillery, CAC
Pvt. John W. **Thompson**	3368119	Montgomery, WV/SARD CAC Fort Screven
Pvt. Almon E. **Tinkelpaugh**	470086	El Reno, OK/SARD CAC Fort Screven
Pvt. Joseph M. **Tollock**		
Walter E. **Tuckmantle**	2960834	Newark, NJ/A Mortar Batt., 87th Div.
Pvt. Joseph **Tullock**	2595488	SARD CAC Fort Screven
Pvt. Eugene **Turro**	3721092	New York, NY
Sgt. Joseph H. **Underwood**	718766	Herrin, IL/SARD CAC Fort Screven
Pvt. Lucian B. **Vance**	2902772	Vance, AL/SARD CAC Fort Screven
Pvt. Earl R. **Verniand**	1139821	410th Casual Co.
Charles C. **Vogt** Jr.	3375262	Allentown, PA
Pvt. Harry **Wagner**	719045	Philadelphia, PA/SARD CAC Fort Screven
Charles Von **Waldner**	2595917	Savannah, GA
Pvt. Joseph A. **Walsh**	3371977	Boston, MA/SARD CAC Fort Screven
Pvt. Henry H. **Warren**	793389	Madison, AL/SARD CAC Fort Screven
Cpl. Paul P. **Warsky**	2301285	Englewood, NJ/Mach. Gun. Co., 49th Infantry
Sgt. Joe E. **Waters**	718762	Hartford, IN/SARD CAC Fort Screven
Pvt. John E. **Wean**	1278382	Newark, NJ/406th Casual Co.
Pvt. James **Weathers**	2595563	Augusta, GA/SARD CAC Fort Screven

Cpl. William J. **Weidgenant**		Chicago, IL/Quartermaster Corps
Fred C. **Weisner**	3238932	Winston-Salem, NC
Pvt. Leholmes Perry **Wells**	2595944	Sylvania, GA/SARD CAC Fort Screven
Pvt. Charles A. **Wetherington**	2595852	Lenox, GA/SARD CAC Fort Screven
Pvt. Howard E. **Wharton**	3372043	Summerfield, OH/SARD CAC Fort Screven
Cpl. Coley B. **White** Jr.	719899	Galesburg, IL/SARD CAC Fort Screven
Pvt. Lonnie W. **White**	2595646	Manor, GA/SARD CAC Fort Screven
Pvt. James **Whitman**		New York, NY/ Quartermaster Corps
Pvt. Buford M. **Wilcoxson**	719089	Loretto, TN/SARD CAC Fort Screven
Pvt. Corbett **Williams**	2595691	Sylvania, GA/SARD CAC Fort Screven
Pvt. Walter **Williams**	3372038	Dexter City, OH/SARD CAC Fort Screven
Pvt. Hugh Virgil **Willis**	2595668	Oliver, GA/SARD CAC Fort Screven
Pvt. Herbert F. **Wilson**	3369467	Shaft, MD/SARD CAC Fort Screven
Cpl. Frank I. **Wise**	813856	Havana, IL/SARD CAC Fort Screven
Pvt. James G. **Wright**	2593835	Adel, GA/SARD CAC Fort Screven
Shoemaker J. **Wood**	429987	Nicholsville, VA
Pvt. Wingfield **Woodward**	2595600	Augusta, GA
Pvt. Anthony **Wulkoski**	3189614	Vater Fleet, NY/52nd Infantry
Edgar F. **Yarborough**	2595524	Augusta, GA
Cpl. Chester G. **Young**	814844	Havana, IL/SARD CAC Fort Screven

APPENDIX 3

Soldiers Reported AWOL from HMS *Otranto* in New York Harbor

Pvt. Arthur **Goodwin**	3719521	406th Casual Co.
Pvt. Charles **Lehman**	395307	410th Casual Co.
Pvt. Frederick **Rabb**	3211939	406th Casual Co.
Pvt. Alfred **Sametzki**	3189960 [?]	406th Casual Co.
Pvt. Frank **Stransky**	2443965 [?]	410th Casual Co.

APPENDIX 4
HMS *Otranto* British Casualties

*T*he author acknowledges permission from Don Kindell for the following list of Otranto's British casualties taken from his copyrighted work,
World War 1, Casualty Lists of the Royal Navy and Dominion Navies, published on the Web at http://www.naval-history.net/xDKCas1918-10Oct.htm.

Information regarding British casualties is offered in the following
order: first name, initial(s), surname; service number; and rank and
part of the service other than Royal Navy (RNR, RNVR, RFR, RMLI,
etc.) and ratings only; also if Dominion or Indian navies or on the books
of another ship/shore establishment.

ABBREVIATIONS

MMR: Mercantile Marine Reserve
RMLI: Royal Marine Light Infantry (World War I)
RNVR: Royal Naval Volunteer Reserve
RNR: Royal Naval Reserve
SS: Special Service (Royal Marines)
(Ch): Chatham (after service number)

Joseph **Acton**	699685	Greaser, MMR
John E. **Aindow**	927413	Trimmer, MMR
John **Audley**	202381	Able Seaman
George **Barnes**	782710	Fireman, MMR
Henry W. **Barrett**	10877	Private, RMLI, (Ch)

William **Barton**	880996	Trimmer, MMR
Thomas **Battersby**	17267	Corporal, RMLI (Ch)
Herbert, **Baxter**	899708	Trimmer, MMR
George **Bell**	339202	Shipwright, MMR
Archibald P. **Bender**	3012	Petty Officer, J (Ch)
Horace W. E. **Bowles**	4800	Signalman, RNVR, Bristol Z
James **Brennan**	1470	Signalman, RNVR, Clyde Z
John R. **Brooker**	7827	Ordinary Seaman, RNVR, London Z
Peter **Brown**		Ty/Engineer Lieutenant, RNR
John W. H. **Burnard**	212592	Able Seaman, (Ch)
Edward C. **Cale**	29204	Ordinary Seaman, J (Ch)
George W. **Campbell**	864415	Trimmer, MMR
Thomas **Campbell**	864144	Greaser, MMR
Thomas **Campbell**	941848	Trimmer, MMR
Frank **Carter**	852746	Trimmer, MMR
Stewart **Christie**	883262	Chief Baker, MMR
William C. **Clare**	934619	Fireman, MMR
James W. **Clarkson**		Ty/Engineer Sub Lieutenant, RNR
George **Cole**	734838	Fireman, MMR
Joseph **Cook**	927245	Assistant Steward, MMR
John **Coombs**	51650	Able Seaman, J
Arthur **Corran**	949773	Cook, MMR
Ernest G. W. **Davidson**		Captain
John **Deas**	741543	Fireman, MMR
Edwin E. **Edmonds**	3266	Able Seaman, SS (Ch)
Carmelo **Falzon**	754524	Greaser, MMR
James **Forsyth**	904115	Trimmer, MMR
John **Fuller**	69782	Able Seaman, J
Charles **Gannon**	928609	Trimmer, MMR
Benjamin C. **Gibbons**		Ty/Midshipman, RNR
George **Gilmour**		Cook, MMR
Thomas **Goodwin**	192409	Able Seaman (RFR B 7523) (Ch)
Alex **Gordon**	843805	Carpenter, MMR
Oswald **Gott**	14561	Leading Seaman, J (Ch)
Henry J. **Greenwood**	2034	Petty Officer, J (Ch)
Arthur **Greer**	933130	Trimmer, MMR
Charles **Hacking**		Ship's Cook, MMR
Oswald P. **Hall**		Ty/Lieutenant, RNR
James **Hanington**	9769	Colour Sergeant, RMLI (Ch)
Thomas H. **Haworth**	2662	Able Seaman, RNVR, Mersey Z

John **Heyes**	9240	Junior Reserve Attendant, M
James P. **Hogan**	831080	Trimmer, MMR
William A. **Hulse**	149859	Chief Petty Officer
George **Hunter**	804692	Fireman, MMR
Norman J. **Johnson**	926561	Plumber, MMR
Benjamin **Kent**		G R Ty/Lieutenant, RNR
Ernest C. **Kett**		Ty/Engineer Lieutenant, RNR
Charles **Knowles**	467024	Storekeeper, MMR
Maurice **Kurinsky**	889297	Trimmer, MMR
Frederick J. **LaHive**	213954	Petty Officer (Ch)
Charles **Laurence**	905077	Assistant Baker, MMR
Daniel W. **Lawson**	341119	Chief Armourer (Ch)
Benjamin **Lewitt**		Surgeon
Arthur **Lund**	928693	Trimmer, MMR
Chris **McKeown**	905251	Trimmer, MMR
George E. **Makinson**	930379	Carpenter's Mate, MMR
Arthur T. **Middlebrook**	3647	Leading Signalman, RNVR, Bristol Z
Thomas **Noone**	20725	Private, RMLI (Ch)
John J. **Nugent**	20772	Private, RMLI (Ch)
Alfred **Osborne**	930380	Carpenter's Mate, MMR
Edward **Padgett**		Ordinary Seaman, MMR
Reginald **Parnham**	896983	2nd Steward, MMR
Fred **Pattimore**	3816	Able Seaman, RNVR, Wales Z
Albert G. **Pattison**	20765	Private, RMLI (Ch)
Leslie A. **Poynter**	896982	A Steward, MMR
William C. **Prescott**	20784	Private, RMLI (Ch)
Harry **Purcell**	928634	Trimmer, MMR
William A. **Reid**	932056	Fireman, MMR
George **Richards**	4343	Petty Officer, J
Charles **Ritson**	681650	Cook, MMR
Robert **Roberts**	897860	Carpenter, MMR
Robert **Robertson**		McC, Junior Engineer, MMR
Charles W. **Rowe**	34795	Painter 2c, M
Denis **Shaughnessy**	859619	Fireman, MMR
Ernest **Shulver**	20623	Private, RMLI (Ch)
William J. **Silvester**	464065	Greaser, MMR
Charles D. **Simmons**		Lieutenant Commander, RNR
William **Sinclair**		Ty/Engineer Commander
Albert E. **Smith**	20846	Private, RMLI (Ch)
James H. **Snow**	20860	Private, RMLI (Ch)
David **Swann**	9443	Senior Reserve Attendant, M

Sidney **Tildsley**	930370	Trimmer, MMR
Thomas D. **Tulley**	820796	Assistant Steward, MMR
Dugald McPhail **Twaddle**	71830	Ordinary Seaman, J
Frank **Watts**	860905	2nd Cook and Baker, MMR
Christopher C. **Williams**	832105	Fireman, MMR
Walter **Williams**	746613	Assistant Cook, MMR
James B. **Wood**		Ty/Engineer Lieutenant, RNR

NOTES

FOREWORD

1. An earlier version of this essay was previously published as "When Islay Came to the Aid of America," in the (London) *Sunday Times*, August 26, 2007, and subsequently reprinted in Bowmore, Islay's *Ileach* newspaper.

CHAPTER 1

1. Neil McCart, "*Otranto* 1909," in *Passenger Ships of the Orient Line* (Wellingborough, Great Britain: Patrick Stephens, 1987), 83.
2. "Orient Line S.S. '*Otranto*'," typed ms. (TMs), 1 p., n.d., Orient Steam Navigation Co. Ltd. Collection, OSN/14/45 [Greenwich, London, England:] Caird Library at the National Maritime Museum.
3. McCart, "*Otranto* 1909," 83.
4. McCart, "*Otranto* 1909," 83.
5. Colin M. Castle, "The *Otranto* Disaster," *Ships Monthly* (October 1984): 30.
6. "The New Orient Liners," *The Shipbuilder* (1909): 27.
7. "*Otranto*-1909," TMs, 1 p., July 1977, Peninsular & Oriental Steam Navigation Company Collection, P&O/65/178 [Greenwich, London, England:] Caird Library at the National Maritime Museum.
8. "Orient Line: *Otranto Orvieto*" [photocopy inscribed "From: L. Dunn, Famous Liners of the Past Belfast Built, p. 120"], 1 p., n.d., in "RMS *Otranto* 1909–1918 II: A Collection of Previously Published Accounts and Data Concerning the Orient and Steam Navigation Company's Passenger Liner R.M.S.

Otranto, 1909–1918 Collected by Alasdair M. Aitken," accession IMT.01.001, *Otranto* Archive W1/4a-w1/4, Museum of Islay Life, Islay, Scotland.

9. McCart, "*Otranto* 1909," 86.

10. Charles Hocking, "*Otranto*," in *Dictionary of Disasters at Sea during the Age of Steam Including Sailing Ships and Ships of War Lost in Action 1924–1962: Volume II, M–Z* (Sussex, England: Lloyd's Register of Shipping, 1969), [n.p.].

11. A. B. Campbell, "The Drama of the *Otranto*," *Yarns of the Seven Seas* (London: Sir Isaac Pitman & Sons, 1944), 82.

12. McCart, "*Otranto* 1909," 86.

13. McCart, "*Otranto* 1909," 86.

14. McCart, "*Otranto* 1909," 83.

15. McCart, "*Otranto* 1909," 83.

16. McCart, "*Otranto* 1909," 85.

17. McCart, "*Otranto* 1909," 85.

18. McCart, "*Otranto* 1909," 85.

19. "Australia's Mail Service: A Description of the T.S.S. *Otranto*, Built for the Orient Steam Navigation Company, by Messrs. Workman, Clark & Co., of Belfast," *Syren and Shipping Illustrated*, July 28, 1909, [n.p.].

20. Angus McNeill, "The Fate of the H.M.S. *Otranto*," TMs, [5 pp.], Peninsular & Oriental Steam Navigation Company Collection, P&O/65/178 [Greenwich, London, England:] Caird Library at the National Maritime Museum.

21. McCart, "*Otranto* 1909," 86.

22. Campbell, "The Drama of the *Otranto*," 82.

23. Stephen Rabson [historian and archivist, Peninsular & Oriental Steam Navigation Company] to R. Neil Scott, e-mail, January 11, 2005.

24. McCart, "*Otranto* 1909," 87.

25. "*Otranto* (MT Records at P.R.O.): 4.8.1914" [n.d.], TMs (photocopy), 3 pp., "RMS *Otranto* 1909–1918 II: A Collection of Previously Published Accounts and Data Concerning the Orient and Steam Navigation Company's Passenger Liner R.M.S. *Otranto*, 1909–1918 Collected by Alasdair M. Aitken," accession IMT.01.001, *Otranto* Archive W1/4a-w1/4, Museum of Islay Life, Islay, Scotland.

26. McNeill, "The Fate of the HMS *Otranto*."

27. Kenneth Poolman, *Armed Merchant Cruisers* (London: Cooper/Secker & Warburg, 1985), 14.

28. Rabson e-mail to Scott.

29. Gerhard Hummelchen, "German Armed Merchant Raiders," in *The European Powers in the First World War: An Encyclopedia*, ed. Spencer C. Tucker (New York: Garland Publishing, 1996), 290.

30. McCart, "*Otranto* 1909," 87.

31. McNeill, "The Fate of the HMS *Otranto*."

32. "Orient Line S.S. '*Otranto*.'"

33. McNeill, "The Fate of the HMS *Otranto*."

34. McCart, "*Otranto* 1909," 87.

35. "*Otranto* I 1909–1918."

36. McCart, "*Otranto* 1909," 88.

37. McCart, "*Otranto* 1909," 88.

38. McCart, "*Otranto* 1909," 88.

39. "Cradock, Sir Christopher George Francis Maurice," in *Biographical Dictionary of World War I*, ed. Holgier H. Herwig and Neil M. Heyman (Westport, CT: Greenwood Press, 1982).

40. Robert K. Massie, *Castles of Steel: Britain, Germany, and the Winning of the Great War at Sea* (New York: Random House, 2003), 208.

41. Massie, *Castles of Steel*, 221.

42. McCart, "*Otranto* 1909," 88.

43. Massie, *Castles of Steel*, 223.

44. Poolman, *Armed Merchant Cruisers*, 31.

45. Massie, *Castles of Steel*, 238.

46. "2 British Ships Survive Battle: Cruiser *Glasgow* Heard Calling Comrades Off Chile," *Washington Post*, November 6, 1914, 1.

47. "2 British Ships Survive Battle."

48. "Eyewitness, in Vivid Pen Picture Engagement Off Coronel, Describes How Gallant British Commander Went Back in Face of Death to Let Others Escape," *Washington Post*, January 17, 1915, R5.

49. McCart, "*Otranto* 1909," 88.

50. "Eyewitness, in Vivid Pen."

51. "*Otranto*: Letter from a Crew Member *Otranto* 11.14.1914 Posted from Montevideo," [n.d.], TMs (photocopy), 1 p., in "RMS *Otranto* 1909–1918 II: A Collection of Previously Published Accounts and Data Concerning the Orient and Steam Navigation Company's Passenger Liner R.M.S. *Otranto*, 1909–1918 Collected by Alasdair M. Aitken," accession IMT.01.001, *Otranto* Archive W1/4a-w1/4, Museum of Islay Life, Islay, Scotland.

52. "Eyewitness, in Vivid Pen."

53. G. M. McCarthy, "The Cruise of H.M.S. *Otranto* during the Great European War," [n.d.], TMs (photocopy), p. 12, in "RMS *Otranto* 1909–1918 II: A Collection of Previously Published Accounts and Data Concerning the Orient and Steam Navigation Company's Passenger Liner R.M.S. *Otranto*, 1909–1918 Collected by Alasdair M. Aitken," accession IMT.01.001, *Otranto* Archive W1/4a-w1/4, Museum of Islay Life, Islay, Scotland.

54. Massie, *Castles of Steel*, 238.

55. Christopher A. Long, "The Battles of Coronel & the Falkland Islands, November & December 1914," Christopher Long Personal & Professional Pages, http://www.christopherlong.co.uk/pub/coronelfalklands.html.

56. "Eyewitness, in Vivid Pen."

57. "*Otranto* I 1909–1918."
58. Long, "The Battles of Coronel & the Falkland Islands."
59. "Eyewitness, in Vivid Pen."
60. Long, "The Battles of Coronel & the Falkland Islands."
61. "2 British Ships Survive Battle."
62. Massie, *Castles of Steel*, 228.
63. Long, "The Battles of Coronel & the Falkland Islands."
64. Massie, *Castles of Steel*, 229.
65. Poolman, *Armed Merchant Cruisers*, 32.
66. Massie, *Castles of Steel*, 236.
67. "Cradock," *Biographical Dictionary*.
68. Long, "The Battles of Coronel & the Falkland Islands."
69. Massie, *Castles of Steel*, 244.
70. McCart, "*Otranto* 1909," 89.
71. McCart, "*Otranto* 1909," 89.
72. Massie, *Castles of Steel*, 257.
73. Massie, *Castles of Steel*, 257.
74. Long, "The Battles of Coronel & the Falkland Islands."
75. Long, "The Battles of Coronel & the Falkland Islands."
76. Long, "The Battles of Coronel & the Falkland Islands."
77. Massie, *Castles of Steel*, 260.
78. Long, "The Battles of Coronel & the Falkland Islands."
79. Long, "The Battles of Coronel & the Falkland Islands."
80. Long, "The Battles of Coronel & the Falkland Islands."
81. "Maximilian Reichsgraf von Spee," in *Biographical Dictionary of World War I*, ed. Holgier H. Herwig and Neil M. Heyman (Westport, CT: Greenwood Press, 1982), 324.
82. Long, "The Battles of Coronel & the Falkland Islands."
83. Massie, *Castles of Steel*, 285.
84. McCart, "*Otranto* 1909," 89.
85. McCart, "*Otranto* 1909," 89.
86. A. B. Campbell, "Armed Merchantmen," in *With the Corners Off: My Adventurous Life on Land and Sea* (London: G. G. Harrap, 1937), 214–17.
87. Campbell, "Armed Merchantmen," 222.
88. Campbell, "Armed Merchantmen," 222.
89. Campbell, "Armed Merchantmen," 222.
90. Campbell, "Armed Merchantmen," 225–26.
91. Campbell, "Armed Merchantmen," 89.
92. "*Otranto* I 1909–1918."
93. Campbell, "Armed Merchantmen," 253.
94. Campbell, "Armed Merchantmen," 259.
95. McCart, "*Otranto* 1909," 89.

96. McCart, "*Otranto* 1909," 89.
97. McCart, "*Otranto* 1909," 90.
98. McCart, "*Otranto* 1909," 90.
99. McNeill, "The Fate of the HMS *Otranto*."

CHAPTER 2

1. Michael Hanlon, "America's Turn from Neutrality to Intervention, 1914–1917," World War I, http://www.WorldWar1.com/tgws/re1001.htm.
2. Hanlon, "America's Turn."
3. John Carver Edwards, "Georgia Guardsmen and the Politics of Survival, 1915–1916," *Georgia Historical Quarterly* 60, no. 4 (winter 1976): 345.
4. Milton L. Ready, "Georgia's Entry into World War I," *Georgia Historical Quarterly* 52, no. 3 (September 1968): 261.
5. Mitchell Yockelson, "They Answered the Call: Military Service in the United States Army during World War I," *Prologue: Quarterly of the National Archives and Records Administration* 30, no. 3 (fall 1998): [n.p.].
6. Todd Womack, *Georgia and the Great War* (Douglas: GA: Southern Heritage Publications, 2002), 12.
7. "AEF Fact Sheet: Manpower, Organization and Casualties," Doughboy Center: The Story of the American Expeditionary Forces, http://www.WorldWar1.com/dbc/facts.htm.
8. Warren Blatt, "World War I Draft Registration Cards," JewishGen, http://jewishgen.org/infofiles/wwidraft.htm.
9. Blatt, "World War I Draft Registration Cards."
10. Blatt, "World War I Draft Registration Cards."
11. Blatt, "World War I Draft Registration Cards."
12. Womack, *Georgia and the Great War*, 43.
13. Blatt, "World War I Draft Registration Cards."
14. Yockelson, "They Answered the Call."
15. "AEF Fact Sheet."
16. Joseph M. Toomey, "Georgians Serving in the United States Army during the World War 1917–18," in *Georgia's Participation in the World War and the History of Georgia American Legion* (Macon, GA: J. W. Burke Co., 1936), 32.
17. "AEF Fact Sheet."
18. "AEF Fact Sheet."
19. Ready, "Georgia's Entry into World War I," 262.
20. "Fighting a War 'Over There,'" in [Screven County History Project], *The History of Screven County, Georgia*, ed. Dixon Hollingsworth (Dallas, TX: Curtis Media Corp., 1989), 74.

21. "Soldiers Are Given a Royal Sendoff," *Bulloch* [GA] *Times*, September 1917, n.p.

22. "Soldiers Are Given a Royal Sendoff."

23. "Soldiers Are Given a Royal Sendoff."

24. "Soldiers Are Given a Royal Sendoff."

25. "Fighting a War," 74.

26. Lonzon Sheley, "The Men of the *Otranto*," in [Screven County History Project], *The History of Screven County, Georgia*, ed. Dixon Hollingsworth (Dallas, TX: Curtis Media Corp., 1989), 76.

27. "Fighting a War."

28. L. P. Wells, "The Men of the *Otranto*," in [Screven County History Project], *The History of Screven County, Georgia*, ed. Dixon Hollingsworth (Dallas, TX: Curtis Media Corp., 1989), 76.

29. James Mack Adams, *A History of Fort Screven Georgia* (Tybee Island, GA: Tybee Island Historical Society, 2002), 1.

30. Joseph M. Toomey, "Fort Screven," in *Georgia's Participation in the World War and the History of Georgia American Legion* (Macon, GA: J. W. Burke Co., 1936), 21.

31. Womack, *Georgia and the Great War*, 15.

32. Toomey, "Fort Screven," 21.

33. Womack, *Georgia and the Great War*, 15.

34. Womack, *Georgia and the Great War*, 43.

35. Womack, *Georgia and the Great War*, 43.

36. Joseph E. Hewell Jr., "Joseph E. Hewell World War I Journal: The Sinking of the HMS *Otranto*," http://www.geocities.ws/josephehewell.

37. Andrew Sparks, "He Survived Shipwreck That Cost 20 Georgians Their Lives," *Atlanta Journal and Constitution*, April 28, 1963, 48.

38. Rick Hollingsworth, "Nightmare in the North Atlantic: Nightmare at Sea Recalled," *Lil' Fish Wrapper* (Sylvania, Georgia), [n.d.], 1.

39. Sparks, "He Survived Shipwreck," 48.

40. "The *Otranto* Story, Off Islay, Island, October 6, 1918—Edgar A. P. Sheperd—Survivor," TMs, [9 pp.], [n.d.], accession # IMT.01.001, *Otranto* Archive W1/4a-w1/4, Museum of Islay Life, Islay, Scotland.

41. Womack, *Georgia and the Great War*, 34.

42. Hewell, "Joseph E. Hewell."

43. *The Blue Print*, Vol. 10 (Atlanta, GA: Student Body, Georgia School of Technology, 1917 [n.d.]).

44. *The Blue Print*.

45. "Department of Mechanical Engineering," *Bulletin of the Georgia School of Technology* 14.11 [Catalog Number 1916–1917], 133.

46. "Department of Mechanical Engineering."

47. Harold F. English, *Sinking of the "H.M.S. Otranto" in Collision with the "H.M.S. Kashmir" Off the Northeast Coast of Ireland, October 6, 1918* (Clinton, IA: Pinney Printing Co., n.d.), 3.

48. Hewell, "Joseph E. Hewell."

49. Lonzon Sheley, "The Story of the *Otranto* Disaster," in [Screven County History Project], *The History of Screven County, Georgia*, ed. Dixon Hollingsworth (Dallas, TX: Curtis Media Corp., 1989), 75.

50. English, *Sinking of the "H.M.S. Otranto,"* 3.

51. "The *Otranto* Story."

52. "The *Otranto* Story."

53. Sheley, "The Men of the *Otranto*," 75.

54. English, *Sinking of the "H.M.S. Otranto,"* 3.

55. Hewell, "Joseph E. Hewell."

56. English, *Sinking of the "H.M.S. Otranto,"* 4.

57. Sheley, "The Story of the *Otranto*."

58. Benedict Crowell and Robert Forrest Wilson, *The Road to France: The Transportation of Troops and Military Supplies, 1917–1918* (New Haven, CT: Yale University Press, 1921), 1:173.

59. "Camp Merritt, New Jersey," Bergen County Historical Society, http://www.bergencountyhistory.org/Pages/campmerrittphamplet.html.

60. Michael L. Cooper, "Sailing for France," in *Hell Fighters: African American Soldiers in World War I* (Dutton, NY: Lodestar Books, 1997), 18.

61. "Camp Merritt, New Jersey."

62. English, *Sinking of the "H.M.S. Otranto,"* 4.

63. Cooper, "Sailing for France," 18.

64. Hewell, "Joseph E. Hewell."

65. English, *Sinking of the "H.M.S. Otranto,"* 4.

66. "Camp Merritt, New Jersey."

67. Cooper, "Sailing for France," 18.

68. Sheley, "The Story of the *Otranto*."

69. Crowell and Wilson, *The Road to France*, 1:178.

70. Crowell and Wilson, *The Road to France*, 1:188.

71. English, *Sinking of the "H.M.S. Otranto,"* 4.

72. English, *Sinking of the "H.M.S. Otranto,"* 4.

73. Sheley, "The Story of the *Otranto*."

74. English, *Sinking of the "H.M.S. Otranto,"* 5.

75. Crowell and Wilson, *The Road to France*, 1:170.

76. Crowell and Wilson, *The Road to France*, 1:173.

77. "Camp Merritt, New Jersey."

78. Crowell and Wilson, *The Road to France*, 1:207.

79. English, *Sinking of the "H.M.S. Otranto,"* 5.

80. Sheley, "The Story of the *Otranto.*"

81. Angus McNeill, "The Fate of the H.M.S. *Otranto*," TMs, [5 pp.], Peninsular & Oriental Steam Navigation Company Collection, P&O/65/178 [Greenwich, London, England]: Caird Library of the National Maritime Museum.

82. Hewell, "Joseph E. Hewell."

83. Crowell and Wilson, *The Road to France*, 1:170.

84. Crowell and Wilson, *The Road to France*, 1:202.

85. McNeill, "The Fate of the HMS *Otranto.*"

CHAPTER 3

1. Harold F. English, *Sinking of the "H.M.S. Otranto" in Collision with the "H.M.S. Kashmir" Off the Northeast Coast of Ireland, October 6, 1918* (Clinton, IA: Pinney Printing Co., n.d.), 8.

2. Paul Frederickson, "The *Otranto*: The AEF's Great Sea Tragedy," *New York Times Magazine*, October 2, 1938, 9.

3. Angus McNeill, "The Fate of the H.M.S. *Otranto*," TMs, [5 pp.], Peninsular & Oriental Steam Navigation Company Collection, P&O/65/178 [Greenwich, London, England]: Caird Library of the National Maritime Museum.

4. Frederickson, "The *Otranto*," 9.

5. A. B. Campbell, "Armed Merchantmen," in *With the Corners Off: My Adventurous Life on Land and Sea* (London: G. G. Harrap, 1937), 230.

6. McNeill, "The Fate of the HMS *Otranto.*"

7. Benedict Crowell and Robert Forrest Wilson, *The Road to France: The Transportation of Troops and Military Supplies, 1917–1918* (New Haven, CT: Yale University Press, 1921), 1:555.

8. Joseph E. Hewell Jr., "Joseph E. Hewell World War I Journal: The Sinking of the HMS *Otranto*," http://www.geocities.com/josephhewell.

9. McNeill, "The Fate of the HMS *Otranto.*"

10. McNeill, "The Fate of the HMS *Otranto.*"

11. Correspondence, "Convoy Sailings, Chief of Naval Operations to Naval District Commandants," August 20, 1918, RG 165, Records of the War Department General and Special Staffs. "Correspondence of the Military Intelligence Division (MID)" #2355-A-40, 1, Box 1322, 370/72/17/06. National Archives at College Park, College Park, Maryland.

12. Crowell and Wilson, *The Road to France*, 2:463.

13. B. B. Brown, "Troopships," published for National War Work Council of the Young Men's Christian Association, 1918. Reprinted at "Troopships, Battleships, Subs, Cruisers, Destroyers: A History of How the United States Navy Moved the Army to the War in Europe during World War I," Remembering

the Sounds of My Grandfather's Footsteps, http://freepages.military.rootsweb. com/~cacunithistories/ships_histories.html.

14. Neil McCart, "*Otranto* 1909," in *Passenger Ships of the Orient Line* (Wellingborough, Great Britain: Patrick Stephens, 1987), 90.

15. Campbell, "Armed Merchantmen," 212.

16. English, *Sinking of the "H.M.S. Otranto,"* 6.

17. Brown, "Troopships."

18. English, *Sinking of the "H.M.S. Otranto,"* 6.

19. English, *Sinking of the "H.M.S. Otranto,"* 6.

20. English, *Sinking of the "H.M.S. Otranto,"* 6.

21. Rick Hollingsworth, "Nightmare in the North Atlantic: Nightmare at Sea Recalled," *Lil' Fish Wrapper* (Sylvania, Georgia), [n.d.], 1.

22. Brown, "Troopships."

23. English, *Sinking of the "H.M.S. Otranto,"* 6.

24. English, *Sinking of the "H.M.S. Otranto,"* 6.

25. Patricia C. Taylor, "The 1918–19 Influenza Epidemic: The Social Impact in Rural Georgia" (master's thesis, California State University, Dominguez Hills, 1989), 3.

26. English, *Sinking of the "H.M.S. Otranto,"* 7.

27. Lonzon Sheley, "The Men of the *Otranto*," in [Screven County History Project], *The History of Screven County, Georgia*, ed. Dixon Hollingsworth (Dallas, TX: Curtis Media Corp., 1989), 75.

28. English, *Sinking of the "H.M.S. Otranto,"* 7.

29. English, *Sinking of the "H.M.S. Otranto,"* 7.

30. Joseph M. Toomey, "His Majesty's Ship *Otranto*," in *Georgia's Participation in the World War and the History of Georgia American Legion* (Macon, GA: J. W. Burke Co., 1936), 53.

31. English, *Sinking of the "H.M.S. Otranto,"* 3.

32. Campbell, "Armed Merchantmen," 260.

33. Campbell, "Armed Merchantmen," 260.

34. English, *Sinking of the "H.M.S. Otranto,"* 1.

35. English, *Sinking of the "H.M.S. Otranto,"* 1.

36. English, *Sinking of the "H.M.S. Otranto,"* 1.

37. English, *Sinking of the "H.M.S. Otranto,"* 1.

38. English, *Sinking of the "H.M.S. Otranto,"* 1.

39. English, *Sinking of the "H.M.S. Otranto,"* 2.

40. "*Kashmir*," in *P&O: A Fleet History* (Kendal, England: World Ship Society, 1988), 179.

41. "*Kashmir–1915*," press release, Peninsular & Oriental Steam Navigation Co., P&O Information and Public Relations Department, [1 p.], P&O/65/178 [Greenwich, London, England:] Caird Library of the National Maritime Museum.

42. ["JKNC"], *"Kashmir–1915,"* P&O/65/178 [Greenwich, London, England:] Caird Library of the National Maritime Museum.

43. ["JKNC"], *"Kashmir–1915."*

44. ["JKNC"], *"Kashmir–1915."*

45. *"Kashmir,"* in *P&O: A Fleet History,* 179.

46. *"Kashmir–1915,"* press release.

47. ["JKNC"], *"Kashmir–1915."*

48. *"Kashmir–1915,"* press release.

49. *"Kashmir"* [one-page article, source unknown], P&O/65/178 [Greenwich, London, England:] Caird Library of the National Maritime Museum.

50. *"Kashmir–1915,"* press release.

51. *"Kashmir"* [one-page article, source unknown].

52. *"Kashmir"* [one-page article, source unknown].

53. English, *Sinking of the "H.M.S. Otranto,"* 2.

54. English, *Sinking of the "H.M.S. Otranto,"* 2.

55. English, *Sinking of the "H.M.S. Otranto,"* 2.

56. Michael L. Cooper, "African American Soldiers," in *Hell Fighters: African American Soldiers in World War I* (Dutton, NY: Lodestar Books, 1997), 6.

57. Mitchell Yockelson, "They Answered the Call: Military Service in the United States Army during World War I," *Prologue: Quarterly of the National Archives and Records Administration* 30, no. 3 (fall 1998): 228–34.

58. Christopher C. Meyers, "'Killing Them by the Wholesale': A Lynching Rampage in South Georgia," *Georgia Historical Quarterly* 90, no. 2 (summer 2006): 217.

59. Meyers, "'Killing Them by the Wholesale,'" 215.

60. Todd Womack, *Georgia and the Great War* (Douglas: GA: Southern Heritage Publications, 2002), 35.

61. *The Blue Print,* Vol. 10 (Atlanta, GA: Student Body, Georgia School of Technology, 1917), [n.p.].

62. Womack, *Georgia and the Great War,* 35–36.

63. Womack, *Georgia and the Great War,* 36.

64. Yockelson, "They Answered the Call," 228–34.

65. Michael L. Cooper, "The Great War," in *Hell Fighters: African American Soldiers in World War I* (Dutton, NY: Lodestar Books, 1997), 2.

66. Michael L. Cooper, "Laborers in Uniform," in *Hell Fighters: African American Soldiers in World War I* (Dutton, NY: Lodestar Books, 1997), 26.

67. Correspondence, "War Department, O.Q.M.G., Washington, D.C. June 8, 1921 to the Adjutant General of the Army," RG 165, Records of the War Department General and Special Staffs. "Correspondence of the Military Intelligence Division (MID)" #2355-A-40, 1, Box 1322, 370/72/17/06. National Archives at College Park, College Park, Maryland.

68. [Response of September 18, 1935] Lt. Cdr. J. U. Lademan, Jr. to F. J. Reynolds, *Collier's* [*Magazine*], September 25, 1935, RG 45 U.S. Navy Subject, 1910–27 SD "S.S. Kashmir," National Archives at College Park, College Park, Maryland.

69. English, *Sinking of the "H.M.S. Otranto,"* 3.

70. English, *Sinking of the "H.M.S. Otranto,"* 3.

71. Crowell and Wilson, *The Road to France*, 2:471.

72. Crowell and Wilson, *The Road to France*, 2:469.

73. Crowell and Wilson, *The Road to France*, 2:469–70.

74. Hollingsworth, "Nightmare in the North Atlantic," 1.

75. Correspondence, "War Department, O.Q.M.G."

76. A. B. Campbell, "The End of the H.M.S. *Otranto*," in *With the Corners Off: My Adventurous Life on Land and Sea* (London: G. G. Harrap, 1937), 263.

77. "SS Adriatic: Mediterranean Cruise by the United States and Royal Mail," Immigrant Ships Transcribers Guild, http://immigrantships.net/v2/1900v2/adriatic19300309.html.

78. Campbell, "The End of the H.M.S. *Otranto*," 263.

79. Crowell and Wilson, *The Road to France*, 2:474.

80. McCart, "*Otranto* 1909," 90.

81. Crowell and Wilson, *The Road to France*, 2:474.

82. Frederickson, "The *Otranto*," 9.

83. Hollingsworth, "Nightmare in the North Atlantic," 1.

84. English, *Sinking of the "H.M.S. Otranto,"* 7.

85. Crowell and Wilson, *The Road to France*, 2:473.

86. Crowell and Wilson, *The Road to France*, 2:473.

87. Crowell and Wilson, *The Road to France*, 2:475.

88. Crowell and Wilson, *The Road to France*, 2:474.

89. Crowell and Wilson, *The Road to France*, 2:560–61.

90. English, *Sinking of the "H.M.S. Otranto,"* 8.

91. McCart, "*Otranto* 1909," 90.

92. McCart, "*Otranto* 1909," 90.

93. "Navy Department, Historical Section Room 3635," February 3, 1925, RG 45 U.S. Navy Subject, 1910–27 SD "S.S. *Kashmir*," National Archives at College Park, College Park, Maryland.

94. "*Otranto* Saga, 1914–18," *Sea Breezes* 7 (January–June 1949), 176.

95. Crowell and Wilson, *The Road to France*, 2:474.

96. Hewell, "Joseph E. Hewell."

97. Ira Wolfert, "The Drama of a North Atlantic Crossing," *Reader's Digest*, December 1956, 30.

98. English, *Sinking of the "H.M.S. Otranto,"* 8.

99. Crowell and Wilson, *The Road to France*, 2:474.

100. McNeill, "The Fate of the HMS *Otranto*."

101. English, *Sinking of the "H.M.S. Otranto*," 8.

102. Bernard Fitzsimons, "U-Boats: The Tide Turns," *Warships & Sea Battles of World War I* (New York: Beekman House, 1973), 145.

103. Wolfert, "The Drama of a North Atlantic Crossing," 30.

104. English, *Sinking of the "H.M.S. Otranto*," 8.

105. Crowell and Wilson, *The Road to France*, 2:483.

106. Crowell and Wilson, *The Road to France*, 2:485.

107. Crowell and Wilson, *The Road to France*, 2:481.

108. Crowell and Wilson, *The Road to France*, 2:461.

109. Brown, "Troopships."

110. Brown, "Troopships."

111. Womack, *Georgia and the Great War*, 44.

CHAPTER 4

1. Angus McNeill, "The Fate of the H.M.S. *Otranto*," TMs, [5 pp.], Peninsular & Oriental Steam Navigation Company Collection, P&O/65/178 [Greenwich, London, England]: Caird Library of the National Maritime Museum.

2. Neil McCart, "*Otranto* 1909," in *Passenger Ships of the Orient Line* (Wellingborough, Great Britain: Patrick Stephens, 1987), 91.

3. Harold F. English, *Sinking of the "H.M.S. Otranto" in Collision with the "H.M.S. Kashmir" Off the Northeast Coast of Ireland, October 6, 1918* (Clinton, IA: Pinney Printing Co., n.d.), 8.

4. Lonzon Sheley, "The Men of the *Otranto*," in [Screven County History Project], *The History of Screven County, Georgia*, ed. Dixon Hollingsworth (Dallas, TX: Curtis Media Corp., 1989), 75.

5. English, *Sinking of the "H.M.S. Otranto*," 9.

6. English, *Sinking of the "H.M.S. Otranto*," 9.

7. English, *Sinking of the "H.M.S. Otranto*," 9.

8. "*Otranto* Saga, 1914–18," *Sea Breezes* 7 (January–June 1949), 176.

9. McCart, "*Otranto* 1909," 91.

10. Rick Hollingsworth, "Nightmare in the North Atlantic: Nightmare at Sea Recalled," *Lil' Fish Wrapper* (Sylvania, Georgia), n.d., 1.

11. Paul Frederickson, "The *Otranto*: The AEF's Great Sea Tragedy," *New York Times Magazine*, October 2, 1938, 9.

12. Marcel Choyer, "Le double naufrage des marins de Croisine en 1918," http://72.14.207.104/search?q=cache:d4szzTi-DfAJ:cancagen.free.fr/Documents/croisine.htm+croisine+1.

13. "*Otranto* Saga, 1914–18," 176.

14. "*Otranto* Saga, 1914–18," 176.

15. A. B. Campbell, "The End of the H.M.S. *Otranto*," in *With the Corners Off: My Adventurous Life on Land and Sea* (London: G. G. Harrap, 1937), 264.

16. "*Otranto* Saga, 1914–18," 176.

17. "*Otranto* Saga, 1914–18," 176.

18. Campbell, "The End of the H.M.S. *Otranto*," 264.

19. English, *Sinking of the "H.M.S. Otranto,"* 10.

20. Lonzon Sheley, "The Story of the *Otranto* Disaster," in [Screven County History Project], *The History of Screven County, Georgia*, ed. Dixon Hollingsworth (Dallas, TX: Curtis Media Corp., 1989), 75.

21. Frederickson, "The *Otranto*," 9.

22. Frederickson, "The *Otranto*," 9, 19.

23. McCart, "*Otranto* 1909," 91.

24. English, *Sinking of the "H.M.S. Otranto,"* 10.

25. English, *Sinking of the "H.M.S. Otranto,"* 10.

26. Campbell, "The End of the H.M.S. *Otranto*," 265.

27. English, *Sinking of the "H.M.S. Otranto,"* 11.

28. Sheley, "The Story of the *Otranto*," 75.

29. Campbell, "The End of the H.M.S. *Otranto*," 265.

30. Frederickson, "The *Otranto*," 9.

31. Hollingsworth, "Nightmare in the North Atlantic," 1.

32. Sheley, "The Story of the *Otranto*," 75.

33. Stephanie True Peters, "What Is Influenza?," in *Epidemic! The 1918 Influenza Pandemic* (New York: Benchmark Books, 2005), 7.

34. Peters, "What Is Influenza?," 7.

35. Peters, "What Is Influenza?," 11.

36. Peters, "What Is Influenza?," 8.

37. Peters, "What Is Influenza?," 8.

38. John M. Barry, *The Great Influenza: The Epic Story of the Deadliest Plague in History* (New York: Viking, 2004), 4.

39. Peters, "What Is Influenza?," 1.

40. Peters, "What Is Influenza?," 2.

41. Peters, "What Is Influenza?," 3.

42. Stephanie True Peters, "The Second Wave," in *Epidemic! The 1918 Influenza Pandemic* (New York: Benchmark Books, 2005), 24.

43. Peters, "The Second Wave," 25.

44. Peters, "The Second Wave," 25–26.

45. Barry, *The Great Influenza*, 2.

46. Peters, "The Second Wave," 27.

47. Peters, "The Second Wave," 30–31.

48. Peters, "The Second Wave," 27.

49. Peters, "The Second Wave," 27.

50. Barry, *The Great Influenza*, 5.

51. Hollingsworth, "Nightmare in the North Atlantic," 1.

52. English, *Sinking of the "H.M.S. Otranto,"* 9.

53. English, *Sinking of the "H.M.S. Otranto,"* 9.

54. "Smith, Lonnie L.," [2 folders], in "Smith, Leslie-Smith, Looney," Box 4564 [NM81/E-1942 NHFY 2000]. Records of the Office of the Quartermaster General, Cemeterial Division 1915–19, Record Group 92, File 293. National Archives at College Park, College Park, Maryland.

55. English, *Sinking of the "H.M.S. Otranto,"* 11.

56. Campbell, "The End of the H.M.S. *Otranto*," 266.

57. "Smith, Lonnie L."

58. "Smith, Lonnie L."

59. "Smith, Lonnie L."

60. McCart, "*Otranto* 1909," 91.

61. Thomas Gamble, "Charles Von Waldner Tells a Vivid Story of the *Otranto*," *Savannah Morning News*, October 7, 1938, 16.

62. Frederickson, "The *Otranto*," 9.

63. Anonymous, ["Troop Storekeeper of the *Kashmir*"]; "The Sinking of the *Otranto* [1909]," [3 pp.], OSN/14/45 [Greenwich, London, England:] Caird Library of the National Maritime Museum, 2.

64. English, *Sinking of the "H.M.S. Otranto,"* 12.

65. [2nd Lt.] R. E. Condon, "[Report:] Loss of the Troopship *Otranto*," TMs, [5 pp.], October 21, 1918. Box 407, Misc. File Box 1 [Doc. 1–150], 1. National Archives at College Park, College Park, Maryland.

66. Benedict Crowell and Robert Forrest Wilson, *The Road to France: The Transportation of Troops and Military Supplies, 1917–1918* (New Haven, CT: Yale University Press, 1921), 1:441.

67. "Twenty-five Hundred Flu Cases in Savannah," *Atlanta Constitution*, October 18, 1918, 5.

68. English, *Sinking of the "H.M.S. Otranto,"* 12.

69. English, *Sinking of the "H.M.S. Otranto,"* 12.

70. Campbell, "The End of the H.M.S. *Otranto*," 266.

CHAPTER 5

1. Neil McCart, "*Otranto* 1909," in *Passenger Ships of the Orient Line* (Wellingborough, Great Britain: Patrick Stephens, 1987), 91.

2. Angus McNeill, "The Fate of the H.M.S. *Otranto*," TMs, [5 pp.], Peninsular & Oriental Steam Navigation Company Collection, P&O/65/178 [Greenwich, London, England]: Caird Library of the National Maritime Museum, 3.

3. David Roberts, "*Otranto* Survivor Tells of Scenes as Vessel Goes to the Bottom," TMs. Copied from the *Lorain Times Herald*, [2 pp.], November 4,

1918, accession #1MT.01.001, *Otranto* Archive W1/4a-w1/4, Museum of Islay Life, Islay, Scotland.

    4. A. B. Campbell, "The End of the H.M.S. *Otranto*," in *With the Corners Off: My Adventurous Life on Land and Sea* (London: G. G. Harrap, 1937), 266.

    5. Campbell, "The End of the H.M.S. *Otranto*," 266.

    6. Thomas Gamble, "Charles Von Waldner Tells a Vivid Story of the *Otranto*," *Savannah Morning News*, October 7, 1938, 16.

    7. Lonzon Sheley, "The Men of the *Otranto*," in [Screven County History Project], *The History of Screven County, Georgia*, ed. Dixon Hollingsworth (Dallas, TX: Curtis Media Corp., 1989), 76.

    8. Paul Frederickson, "The *Otranto*: The AEF's Great Sea Tragedy," *New York Times Magazine*, October 2, 1938, 9.

    9. Frederickson, "The *Otranto*," 9.

    10. Frederickson, "The *Otranto*," 9.

    11. "*Otranto* Saga, 1914–18," *Sea Breezes* 7 (January–June 1949), 177.

    12. "*Otranto* Saga, 1914–18," 177.

    13. McCart, "*Otranto* 1909," 91.

    14. Harold F. English, *Sinking of the "H.M.S. Otranto" in Collision with the "H.M.S. Kashmir" Off the Northeast Coast of Ireland, October 6, 1918* (Clinton, IA: Pinney Printing Co., n.d.), 12.

    15. English, *Sinking of the "H.M.S. Otranto,"* 13.

    16. English, *Sinking of the "H.M.S. Otranto,"* 13.

    17. McNeill, "The Fate of the HMS *Otranto*," 3.

    18. English, *Sinking of the "H.M.S. Otranto,"* 13.

    19. English, *Sinking of the "H.M.S. Otranto,"* 13.

    20. English, *Sinking of the "H.M.S. Otranto,"* 13.

    21. English, *Sinking of the "H.M.S. Otranto,"* 13.

    22. English, *Sinking of the "H.M.S. Otranto,"* 13.

    23. Gamble, "Charles Von Waldner," 16.

    24. Frederickson, "The *Otranto*," 9.

    25. English, *Sinking of the "H.M.S. Otranto,"* 13.

    26. Frederickson, "The *Otranto*," 9.

    27. Frederickson, "The *Otranto*," 19.

    28. Frederickson, "The *Otranto*," 9.

    29. Campbell, "The End of the H.M.S. *Otranto*," 267.

    30. McNeill, "The Fate of the HMS *Otranto*," 3.

    31. Frederickson, "The *Otranto*," 19.

    32. English, *Sinking of the "H.M.S. Otranto,"* 14.

    33. Campbell, "The End of the H.M.S. *Otranto*," 268.

    34. English, *Sinking of the "H.M.S. Otranto,"* 14.

    35. Frederickson, "The *Otranto*," 19.

    36. McNeill, "The Fate of the HMS *Otranto*," 3.

37. English, *Sinking of the "H.M.S. Otranto,"* 15.

38. Anonymous, "*Otranto* I 1909–1918," TMs, [1 p.], OSN/14/45 [Greenwich, London, England]: Caird Library of the National Maritime Museum.

39. Anonymous, "*Otranto* I 1909–1918."

40. English, *Sinking of the "H.M.S. Otranto,"* 15.

41. Frederickson, "The *Otranto*," 19.

42. Campbell, "The End of the H.M.S. *Otranto*," 268.

43. "*Otranto* Saga, 1914–18," 177.

44. Frederickson, "The *Otranto*," 19.

45. English, *Sinking of the "H.M.S. Otranto,"* 15.

46. Anonymous, ["Troop Storekeeper of the *Kashmir*"]; "The Sinking of the *Otranto* [1909]," [3 pp.], OSN/14/45 [Greenwich, London, England:] Caird Library of the National Maritime Museum, 2.

47. Anonymous, ["Troop Storekeeper of the *Kashmir*"], 2.

48. Anonymous, ["Troop Storekeeper of the *Kashmir*"], 2.

49. English, *Sinking of the "H.M.S. Otranto,"* 15.

50. Anonymous, ["Troop Storekeeper of the *Kashmir*"], 2–3.

51. English, *Sinking of the "H.M.S. Otranto,"* 15.

52. English, *Sinking of the "H.M.S. Otranto,"* 15.

53. McNeill, "The Fate of the HMS *Otranto*," 3.

54. Rick Hollingsworth, "Nightmare in the North Atlantic: Nightmare at Sea Recalled," *Lil' Fish Wrapper* (Sylvania, Georgia), n.d., 1.

55. McNeill, "The Fate of the HMS *Otranto*," 3.

56. Lonzon Sheley, "The Story of the *Otranto* Disaster," in [Screven County History Project], *The History of Screven County, Georgia*, ed. Dixon Hollingsworth (Dallas, TX: Curtis Media Corp., 1989), 76.

57. Joseph E. Hewell Jr., "Joseph E. Hewell World War I Journal: The Sinking of the HMS *Otranto*," http://www.geocities.com/josephhewell.

58. Frederickson, "The *Otranto*," 19.

59. "*Otranto* Saga, 1914–18," 177.

60. Frederickson, "The *Otranto*," 19.

61. Hewell, "Joseph E. Hewell."

62. Hewell, "Joseph E. Hewell."

63. Hewell, "Joseph E. Hewell."

64. Sheley, "The Story of the *Otranto* Disaster," 75–76.

65. Campbell, "The End of the H.M.S. *Otranto*," 268.

66. Frederickson, "The *Otranto*," 19.

67. Frederickson, "The *Otranto*," 19.

68. Campbell, "The End of the H.M.S. *Otranto*," 268.

69. English, *Sinking of the "H.M.S. Otranto,"* 16.

70. Kevin Lollar, "Preservation Pioneer Crunched Numbers, Saved Beaches," *Florida Times-Union* (Jacksonville), July 29, 2002, 10S.

71. Campbell, "The End of the H.M.S. *Otranto*," 268.

72. Campbell, "The End of the H.M.S. *Otranto*," 268.

73. English, *Sinking of the "H.M.S. Otranto,"* 16.

74. Campbell, "The End of the H.M.S. *Otranto*," 268.

75. McNeill, "The Fate of the HMS *Otranto*," 3.

76. McNeill, "The Fate of the HMS *Otranto*," 268–69.

77. English, *Sinking of the "H.M.S. Otranto,"* 16.

78. McNeill, "The Fate of the HMS *Otranto*," 3–4.

79. Frederickson, "The *Otranto*," 19.

80. McNeill, "The Fate of the HMS *Otranto*," 3.

81. Andrew Sparks, "He Survived Shipwreck That Cost 20 Georgians Their Lives," *Atlanta Journal and Constitution*, April 28, 1963, 48.

82. Gamble, "Charles Von Waldner," 16.

83. English, *Sinking of the "H.M.S. Otranto,"* 17.

84. Campbell, "The End of the H.M.S. *Otranto*," 269.

85. Gamble, "Charles Von Waldner," 16.

86. Frederickson, "The *Otranto*," 19.

87. Campbell, "The End of the H.M.S. *Otranto*," 270.

88. [Memoir by Pvt. Edgar A. P. Sheperd], TMs, [15 p.], accession # IMT.01.001, *Otranto* Archive W1/4a-w1/4, Museum of Islay Life, Islay, Scotland, 13.

CHAPTER 6

1. Harold F. English, *Sinking of the "H.M.S. Otranto" in Collision with the "H.M.S. Kashmir" Off the Northeast Coast of Ireland, October 6, 1918* (Clinton, IA: Pinney Printing Co., n.d.), 13.

2. "Destroyers before 1918," Battleships-Cruisers.co.uk, http://www.battleships-cruisers.co.uk/destroyers_before_1900.htm.

3. "Destroyers before 1918."

4. English, *Sinking of the "H.M.S. Otranto,"* 13.

5. English, *Sinking of the "H.M.S. Otranto,"* 13.

6. English, *Sinking of the "H.M.S. Otranto,"* 13.

7. English, *Sinking of the "H.M.S. Otranto,"* 17–18.

8. Lonzon Sheley, "The Story of the *Otranto* Disaster," in [Screven County History Project], *The History of Screven County Georgia*, ed. Dixon Hollingsworth (Dallas, TX: Curtis Media Corp., 1989), 76.

9. Paul Fredericksen, "Otranto: The A.E.F.'s Great Sea Tragedy." *New York Times Magazine*, October 2, 1938, 19.

10. Thomas Gamble, "Charles Von Waldner Tells a Vivid Story of the *Otranto*," *Savannah Morning News*, October 7, 1938, 16.

11. Fredericksen, "Otranto: The A.E.F.'s Great Sea Tragedy," 19.

12. English, *Sinking of the "H.M.S. Otranto,"* 19.

13. Harville Marsh, "My Experience on the Troopship *Otranto*," papers of the American Legion Auxiliary, Dexter Allen Unit, Post 90, 1917–1934, Archives, Zach S. Henderson Library, Georgia Southern University, Statesboro, Georgia.

14. Fredericksen, "Otranto: The A.E.F.'s Great Sea Tragedy," 19.

15. Joseph E. Hewell Jr., "Joseph E. Hewell World War I Journal: The Sinking of the HMS *Otranto*," http://www.geocities.com/josephehewell.

16. "Gallant Rescue Work: An American Survivor's [T. L. Campbell] Account," [London] *Times*, October 12, 1918, 8.

17. English, *Sinking of the "H.M.S. Otranto,"* 19.

18. Fredericksen, "Otranto: The A.E.F.'s Great Sea Tragedy," 19.

19. Rick Hollingsworth, "Nightmare in the North Atlantic: Nightmare at Sea Recalled," *Lil' Fish Wrapper* (Sylvania, Georgia), n.d., 1.

20. Hollingsworth, "Nightmare in the North Atlantic," 1.

21. English, *Sinking of the "H.M.S. Otranto,"* 19.

22. Sheley, "The Story of the *Otranto*," 76.

23. Angus McNeill, "The Fate of the H.M.S. *Otranto*," TMs, [5 pp.], Peninsular & Oriental Steam Navigation Company Collection, P&O/65/178 [Greenwich, London, England]: Caird Library of the National Maritime Museum, 4.

24. Hewell, "Joseph E. Hewell."

25. Fredericksen, "Otranto: The A.E.F.'s Great Sea Tragedy," 19.

26. "372 U.S. Soldiers Lost as Result of Sinking of Transport," *Atlanta Constitution*, October 12, 1918, 1.

27. Marsh, "My Experience."

28. English, *Sinking of the "H.M.S. Otranto,"* 19.

29. Sheley, "The Story of the *Otranto*," 76.

30. English, *Sinking of the "H.M.S. Otranto,"* 20.

31. A. B. Campbell, "The End of the H.M.S. *Otranto*," in *With the Corners Off: My Adventurous Life on Land and Sea* (London: G. G. Harrap, 1937), 271.

32. Fredericksen, "Otranto: The A.E.F.'s Great Sea Tragedy," 19.

33. English, *Sinking of the "H.M.S. Otranto,"* 20.

34. Sheley, "The Story of the *Otranto*," 76.

35. English, *Sinking of the "H.M.S. Otranto,"* 20.

36. English, *Sinking of the "H.M.S. Otranto,"* 20.

37. English, *Sinking of the "H.M.S. Otranto,"* 21.

38. Sheley, "The Story of the *Otranto*," 76.

39. "372 U.S. Soldiers Lost," 1.

40. "HMS *Otranto*," http://freepages.military.rootsweb.com/~cacunit histories/HMS%20Otranto.html.

41. "HMS *Otranto*."

42. Hollingsworth, "Nightmare in the North Atlantic," 2F.

43. McNeill, "The Fate of the HMS *Otranto*," 4.

44. Andrew Sparks, "He Survived Shipwreck That Cost 20 Georgians Their Lives," *Atlanta-Journal Constitution Magazine*, April 28, 1963, 8–9, 48–49.

45. Hewell, "Joseph E. Hewell."

46. Correspondence, "Report of Investigation Concerning Conduct of the Military Personnel On Board H. M. Transport *Otranto*," October 18, 1918, RG 120, Records of the American Expeditionary Forces—World War I. Base Section 3, HQ Correspondence 1917–19, Box 14 Relative *Tuscania* to Relative *Otranto* E-2471 HMFY 1999, Box 15 Relative *Otranto* to Relative *Otranto* E-2471 HMFY 1999. National Archives at College Park, College Park, Maryland.

47. McNeill, "The Fate of the HMS *Otranto*," 4.

48. "Another Ocean Tragedy: Belfast-Built Liner's Fate, 431 Lives Lost—Naval Heroism," [newspaper clipping, source unknown], [1 p.], accession # IMT.01.001, *Otranto* Archive W1/4a-w1/4, Museum of Islay Life, Islay, Scotland.

49. Fredericksen, "Otranto: The A.E.F.'s Great Sea Tragedy," 19.

50. "HMS *Otranto*."

51. Hollingsworth, "Nightmare in the North Atlantic," 1.

52. English, *Sinking of the "H.M.S. Otranto,"* 21.

53. Marsh, "My Experience."

54. "372 U.S. Soldiers Lost," 1.

55. English, *Sinking of the "H.M.S. Otranto,"* 21.

56. English, *Sinking of the "H.M.S. Otranto,"* 21.

57. McNeill, "The Fate of the HMS *Otranto*," 4.

58. Campbell, "The End of the H.M.S. *Otranto*," 272.

59. Lonzon Sheley, "The Story of the *Otranto* Disaster," in *The History of Screven County Georgia: Screven County History Project*, edited by Dixon Hollingsworth (Dallas, TX: Curtis Media Corp., 1989), 76.

60. English, *Sinking of the "H.M.S. Otranto,"* 22.

61. Fredericksen, "Otranto: The A.E.F.'s Great Sea Tragedy," 19.

62. English, *Sinking of the "H.M.S. Otranto,"* 22.

63. English, *Sinking of the "H.M.S. Otranto,"* 22.

64. Gamble, "Charles Von Waldner," 16.

65. English, *Sinking of the "H.M.S. Otranto,"* 22.

66. English, *Sinking of the "H.M.S. Otranto,"* 22.

67. English, *Sinking of the "H.M.S. Otranto,"* 22.

68. Hollingsworth, "Nightmare in the North Atlantic," 2F.

69. William H. Whitten, "*Otranto* Survivors Recall Disaster," *Savannah Morning News*, October 7, 1968, 4B, 8B.

70. Fredericksen, "Otranto: The A.E.F.'s Great Sea Tragedy," 19.

71. English, *Sinking of the "H.M.S. Otranto,"* 23.

72. English, *Sinking of the "H.M.S. Otranto,"* 23.
73. English, *Sinking of the "H.M.S. Otranto,"* 23.
74. English, *Sinking of the "H.M.S. Otranto,"* 23.
75. English, *Sinking of the "H.M.S. Otranto,"* 23.
76. Hollingsworth, "Nightmare in the North Atlantic," 2F.
77. Campbell, "The End of the H.M.S. *Otranto*," 273.
78. English, *Sinking of the "H.M.S. Otranto,"* 23.
79. English, *Sinking of the "H.M.S. Otranto,"* 24.
80. Hollingsworth, "Nightmare in the North Atlantic," 2F.
81. Hewell, "Joseph E. Hewell."
82. Campbell, "The End of the H.M.S. *Otranto*," 273.
83. English, *Sinking of the "H.M.S. Otranto,"* 24.
84. Fredericksen, "Otranto: The A.E.F.'s Great Sea Tragedy," 19.
85. "*Otranto* Death List Put at 527," *Washington Post*, October 16, 1918, 2.
86. Hollingsworth, "Nightmare in the North Atlantic," 2F.
87. English, *Sinking of the "H.M.S. Otranto,"* 24.
88. Sheley, "The Story of the Otranto Disaster," 76
89. [Memoir by Pvt. Edgar A. P. Sheperd], TMs, [15 p.], accession # IMT.01.001, *Otranto* Archive W1/4a-w1/4, Museum of Islay Life, Islay, Scotland, 16.
90. "R. M. S. *Leinster* Story" (supplied by Greenwich, London, England, National Maritime Museum), Dún Laoghaire Online, http://www.dun-laoghaire.com/mvleinster.html.
91. Whitten, "*Otranto* Survivors Recall Disaster."
92. English, *Sinking of the "H.M.S. Otranto,"* 24.
93. Hewell, "Joseph E. Hewell."

CHAPTER 7

1. Angus McNeill, "The Fate of the H.M.S. *Otranto*," TMs, [5 pp.], Peninsular & Oriental Steam Navigation Company Collection, P&O/65/178 [Greenwich, London, England]: Caird Library of the National Maritime Museum, 4.
2. A. B. Campbell, "The End of the H.M.S. *Otranto*," in *With the Corners Off: My Adventurous Life on Land and Sea* (London: G. G. Harrap, 1937), 269.
3. Campbell, "The End of the H.M.S. *Otranto*," 270.
4. McNeill, "The Fate of the HMS *Otranto*," 5.
5. Neil McCart, "*Otranto* 1909," in *Passenger Ships of the Orient Line* (Wellingborough, Great Britain: Patrick Stephens, 1987), 93.
6. "Getting Bodies from Wreckage," *Atlanta Constitution*, October 16, 1918, 7.
7. "Getting Bodies from Wreckage."

8. McNeill, "The Fate of the HMS *Otranto*," 5.

9. Harold F. English, *Sinking of the "H.M.S. Otranto" in Collision with the "H.M.S. Kashmir" Off the Northeast Coast of Ireland, October 6, 1918* (Clinton, IA: Pinney Printing Co., n.d.), 25.

10. T. J. Beck, "The *Otranto* Heroes," *Sylvania* [Georgia] *Telephone*, November 8, 1918, 1.

11. Paul Frederickson, "The *Otranto*: The AEF's Great Sea Tragedy," *New York Times Magazine*, October 2, 1938, 19.

12. "Many of Survivors Landed in Ireland," *Atlanta Constitution*, October 13, 1918, 3.

13. Frederickson, "The *Otranto*," 19.

14. Frederickson, "The *Otranto*," 19.

15. "Getting Bodies from Wreckage," 7.

16. David Roberts, "*Otranto* Survivor Tells of Scenes as Vessel Goes to the Bottom," TMs. Copied from the *Lorain Times Herald*, [2 pp.], November 4, 1918, accession #1MT.01.001, *Otranto* Archive W1/4a-w1/4, Museum of Islay Life, Islay, Scotland.

17. English, *Sinking of the "H.M.S. Otranto,"* 25–26.

18. [Typewritten "Report as to the Nature of the Services Rendered by the Inhabitants of Islay"] [handwritten version is dated November 22, 1918], [4 pp.], accession # IMT.01.001, *Otranto* Archive W1/4al, Museum of Islay Life, Islay, Scotland, 1.

19. McNeill, "The Fate of the HMS *Otranto*," 5.

20. English, *Sinking of the "H.M.S. Otranto,"* 25.

21. [Typewritten "Report as to the Nature"], 3.

22. English, *Sinking of the "H.M.S. Otranto,"* 27.

23. [Typewritten "Report as to the Nature"], 3.

24. English, *Sinking of the "H.M.S. Otranto,"* 27.

25. English, *Sinking of the "H.M.S. Otranto,"* 27.

26. "Recovering Corpses from *Otranto* Wreck," *Atlanta Constitution*, October 15, 1918, 11.

27. "Getting Bodies from Wreckage," 7.

28. "Searching for *Otranto*'s Dead: Many Killed by Timbers, Regarded as a Miracle That Anyone Survived," *Savannah Morning News*, October 16, 1918, 1.

29. English, *Sinking of the "H.M.S. Otranto,"* 27.

30. Leo Zimmerman [historian, National *Tuscania* Survivors Association, Milwaukee, Wisconsin], "H.M.S. *Tuscania* Sunk by U-Boat # 77, North Channel, between Scotland and Ireland, February 5, 1918," TMs, 16 pp. Mariner's Museum Research Library and Archives, Newport News, Virginia.

31. Great War Society, "The Sinking of the *Tuscania*," World War I, http://www.worldwar1.com/dbc/tuscania.htm.

32. Frederickson, "The *Otranto*," 19.

33. "Personal Effects Saved," *Atlanta Constitution*, October 13, 1918, 3.

34. English, *Sinking of the "H.M.S. Otranto,"* 27.

35. English, *Sinking of the "H.M.S. Otranto,"* 28.

36. "American Survivors of the *Otranto* Who Reached Shore Alive," TMs, [1 p.], [n.d.], accession # IMT.01.001, *Otranto* Archive W1/4a-w1/4, Museum of Islay Life, Islay, Scotland.

37. [2nd Lt.] R. E. Condon, "[Report:] Loss of the Troopship *Otranto*," TMs, [5 pp.], October 21, 1918. Box 407, Misc. File Box 1 [Doc. 1–150], 1. National Archives at College Park, College Park, Maryland, 2.

38. Condon, "[Report:] Loss of the Troopship *Otranto*."

39. Condon, "[Report:] Loss of the Troopship *Otranto*."

40. Condon, "[Report:] Loss of the Troopship *Otranto*," 3.

41. Condon, "[Report:] Loss of the Troopship *Otranto*," 3.

42. English, *Sinking of the "H.M.S. Otranto,"* 28.

43. "Searching for *Otranto*'s Dead."

44. "First Pictures of the *Otranto* Disaster," *Atlanta Constitution*, November 27, 1918, 1.

45. "Getting Bodies from Wreckage," 7.

46. "Buried in Wide Grave," *Atlanta Constitution*, October 13, 1918, 3.

47. "Buried in Wide Grave," 3.

48. Condon, "[Report:] Loss of the Troopship *Otranto*," 3.

49. "Buried in Wide Grave," 3.

50. "Recovering Corpses from *Otranto* Wreck," *Atlanta Constitution*, October 15, 1918, 11.

51. "One U.S. Officer Lost on *Otranto*," *Atlanta Constitution*, October 16, 1918, 7.

52. Condon, "[Report:] Loss of the Troopship *Otranto*," 3.

53. Thomas Gamble, "Charles Von Waldner Tells a Vivid Story of the *Otranto*," *Savannah Morning News*, October 7, 1938, 16.

54. "Getting Bodies from Wreckage," 7.

55. "Personal Effects Saved," 3.

56. "Personal Effects Saved," 3.

57. "Receipt of Property Found on the Body of Captain Davidson. Argyllsire Constabulary," handwritten ms., [1 p.], November 2, 1918, accession # IMT.01.001, *Otranto* Archive W1/4a-w1/4, Islay, Scotland: Museum of Islay Life.

58. Condon, "[Report:] Loss of the Troopship *Otranto*," 3.

59. "American Anthem Sung at Funeral of *Otranto* Victims," *Atlanta Constitution*, November 17, 1918, B10.

60. "Buried in Wide Grave," 3.

61. English, *Sinking of the "H.M.S. Otranto,"* 28.

62. "American Anthem Sung at Funeral."

63. English, *Sinking of the "H.M.S. Otranto,"* 28.
64. English, *Sinking of the "H.M.S. Otranto,"* 28.
65. "American Anthem Sung at Funeral."
66. "American Anthem Sung at Funeral."
67. English, *Sinking of the "H.M.S. Otranto,"* 28.
68. "American Anthem Sung at Funeral."
69. "American Anthem Sung at Funeral."
70. "American Anthem Sung at Funeral."
71. "American Anthem Sung at Funeral."
72. Condon, "[Report:] Loss of the Troopship *Otranto*," 4.
73. Condon, "[Report:] Loss of the Troopship *Otranto*," 4.
74. Condon, "[Report:] Loss of the Troopship *Otranto*," 4.
75. English, *Sinking of the "H.M.S. Otranto,"* 29.
76. Frederickson, "The *Otranto*," 19.
77. "*Otranto* Death List Put at 527," *Washington Post*, October 16, 1918, 2.
78. "Naval War Notes: Three Hundred and Sixty-four Americans Lost on *Otranto*," [U.S. Naval Institute] *Proceedings* (November 1918): 2671.
79. "Naval War Notes," 2671.
80. Andrew Sparks, "He Survived Shipwreck That Cost 20 Georgians Their Lives," *Atlanta Journal and Constitution*, April 28, 1963, 48.
81. Lt. Cdr. J. U. Lademan Jr. to Mr. F. J. Reynolds [*Collier's Magazine*], September 25, 1935, RG 45 U.S. Navy Subject, 1910–27 SD "S.S. *Kashmir*," National Archives at College Park, College Park, Maryland.
82. R. H. Puffer [Captain, ACD, Personnel Adjutant] Report, "Survivors, Identified Dead and Unaccounted for," RG 45 U.S. Navy Subject, 1910–27 SD "S.S. *Kashmir*," National Archives at College Park, College Park, Maryland.
83. Puffer, "Survivors."

CHAPTER 8

1. "Other Augustans Are Reported Saved," *Atlanta Constitution*, October 14, 1918, 3.
2. Dixon Hollingsworth, "1918: The *Otranto* Disaster," *Screven County through the Years* (Sylvania, GA: Partridge Pond Press, n.d.), 12. Hollingsworth identifies twenty who died from Screven County: Raiford Ellison Barry, Brooks Beasley, George Harrison Bragg, Daniel E. Brown, Martin Luther Bryan, Pearl Crews, Henry Jerome Freeman, Harlan P. Griner, Marion Hankinson, William A. Hunter, Stonewall Jackson, John Leslie Kelly, Clyde Lee, Claude C. Reddick, James F. Scott (brother of Robert H. Scott of Bulloch County), Orlando Watson Sheppard, Capers W. Smoak, Wade L. Usher, James W. Williams, and Cecil H. Williamson.

3. Sheley Lonzon, "The Story of the *Otranto* Disaster," in [Screven County History Project], *The History of Screven County Georgia*, ed. Dixon Hollingsworth (Dallas, TX: Curtis Media Corp., 1989), 76.

4. B. B. Brown, "Troopships," published for National War Work Council of the Young Men's Christian Association, 1918. Reprinted in "Troopships, Battleships, Subs, Cruisers, Destroyers: A History of How the United States Navy Moved the Army to the War in Europe during World War I," Remembering the Sounds of My Grandfather's Footsteps, http://freepages.military.rootsweb.com/~cacunithistories/ships_histories.html.

5. "British Transport Torpedoed with 2,179 Americans Aboard," *Bulloch Times and Statesboro News*, February 7, 1918, 1.

6. "Over 360 Soldiers Lost on *Otranto*," *Atlanta Constitution*, October 13, 1918, 3.

7. "List of *Otranto*'s Dead," *Savannah Morning News*, October 20, 1918, 8.

8. "The *Otranto* a Total Wreck: Over Three Hundred American Soldiers Perish in Disaster," *Savannah Morning News*, October 13, 1918, 1.

9. "Anxiety over *Otranto* List of Saved and Lost Still Stirs Augusta," *Atlanta Constitution*, October 20, 1918, B5.

10. L. P. Wells, "The Men of the *Otranto*," in [Screven County History Project], *The History of Screven County, Georgia*, ed. Dixon Hollingsworth (Dallas: TX: Curtis Media Corp., 1989), 76. The survivors from Screven County, Georgia, included Thomas Bazemore, Horace Matthew Cleary, Sidney Watson Edenfield, Arthur Neil Jenkins, Lloyd Lariscy, Horace Lee Lariscy, Ernest Lee, Val Lee, James Solomon Marsh, Vannie Woodson Morris, Ernest Oglesby, Raymond Patsey Owens, Virgil Joseph Rosier, Kinchley Scott, Francis Parker Scott, Lewis Lonzon Sheley, Thomas J. Taylor, Leholmes Perry Wells, Corbett Williams, and Hugh Virgil Willis.

11. "Fred Johnson Arrives Safely 'Overseas,'" *Atlanta Constitution*, October 27, 1918, A4.

12. "Adel Men Lost When *Otranto* Went Down," *Savannah Morning News*, October 28, 1918, 8.

13. "Georgia Hit Hard by *Otranto*'s Loss," *Atlanta Constitution*, October 28, 1918, 1.

14. "List of Dead on *Otranto*," *Savannah Morning News*, October 28, 1918, 1.

15. "Two Macon Men Lost," *Atlanta Constitution*, October 28, 1918, 5.

16. "Survivors of the *Otranto*: Partial List Received from Bureau in Washington," *Savannah Morning News*, November 4, 1918, 6.

17. "Sergeant G. H. Kennedy Not on Board *Otranto*," *Atlanta Constitution*, November 5, 1918, 10.

18. "Anxiety over *Otranto* List."

19. "Anxiety over *Otranto* List," B5.

20. "Anxiety over *Otranto* List," B5.

21. "Augusta Mourns the Loss of 12 Young Men on *Otranto*," *Atlanta Constitution*, October 29, 1918, 11.

22. "Augusta Mourns," 11.

23. "The *Ticonderoga* (1918)," Wikipedia, http://en.wikipedia.org/wiki/USS_Ticonderoga_%281918%29.

24. "Two More Georgians Lost with *Otranto*," *Atlanta Constitution*, October 29, 1918, 4.

25. "Seventh Savannah *Otranto* Victim," *Atlanta Constitution*, October 31, 1918, 12.

26. Thomas Gamble, "Charles Von Waldner Tells a Vivid Story of the *Otranto*," *Savannah Morning News*, October 7, 1938, 16.

27. "Another *Otranto* Victim," *Atlanta Constitution*, November 19, 1918, 13.

28. "Additional Georgians Lost on the *Otranto*," *Atlanta Constitution*, November 15, 1918, 2.

29. "Additional Georgians Lost," 2.

30. "Another Georgia Boy Lost with *Otranto*," *Atlanta Constitution*, November 23, 1918, 10.

31. "48 Georgia Boys Added to Roll of *Otranto* Lost: Names of 100 More Victims Made Public," *Atlanta Constitution*, November 25, 1918, 1.

32. "Waynesboro Mother Seeks Information of Her Son," *Bulloch Times and Statesboro News*, November 21, 1918, 1.

33. "Berrien County Paid Big Toll on the *Otranto*," *Atlanta Constitution*, November 28, 1918, 9.

34. "Berrien County," 9.

35. Gamble, "Charles Von Waldner," 16.

36. "48 Georgia Boys Added," 1.

37. "Four More Brooks Boys Lost When *Otranto* Sunk," *Atlanta Constitution*, November 30, 1918, 7.

38. Rick Hollingsworth, "Nightmare in the North Atlantic: Nightmare at Sea Recalled," *Lil' Fish Wrapper* (Sylvania, Georgia), n.d., 2F.

39. Andrew Sparks, "He Survived Shipwreck That Cost 120 Georgians Their Lives," *Atlanta-Journal Constitution Magazine*, April 28, 1963, 49.

40. Sparks, "He Survived Shipwreck," 49.

41. Sparks, "He Survived Shipwreck," 49.

42. Hollingsworth, "Nightmare in the North Atlantic," 2F.

43. Sparks, "He Survived Shipwreck," 49.

44. "News of Alexandria," *Washington Post*, January 9, 1919, 3.

45. "Paul Portington's Body Buried," *Washington Post*, June 9, 1919, 3.

46. "Fighting a War 'Over There,'" in [Screven County History Project], *The History of Screven County, Georgia*, ed. Dixon Hollingsworth (Dallas, TX Curtis Media Corp., 1989), 74.

47. "Made to Publicly Kiss Flag: Marched through Streets," *Savannah Morning News*, November 13, 1918, 16.

48. "Executed by Rumor," *Savannah Morning News*, October 27, 1918, 6.

49. "Executed by Rumor," 6.

50. Todd Womack, *Georgia and the Great War* (Douglas, GA: Southern Heritage Publications, 2002), 50.

51. "City Unites in Welcoming Her Boys Home: Joyous Greeting Given Returned Soldiers, Sailors and Marines," *Savannah Morning News*, March 5, 1919, 1.

52. "City Unites in Welcoming."

53. "Another *Otranto* Survivor in City: C. C. Leonard Recalls Wartime Tragedy," *Savannah Morning News*, October 8, 1938, 14.

54. "City Unites in Welcoming," 1.

55. "City Unites in Welcoming," 1.

56. Caddie M. Scott, "James Frank Scott," papers of the American Legion Auxiliary, Dexter Allen Unit, Post 90, 1917–1934, Archives, Zach S. Henderson Library, Georgia Southern University, Statesboro, Georgia.

57. "City Unites in Welcoming," 1.

58. "Then and Now: In Line with the Suggestion," *American Legion Monthly* 7, no. 4 (October 1929): 39.

59. "Then and Now," 39.

60. Hollingsworth, "Nightmare in the North Atlantic," 2F.

CHAPTER 9

1. Harold F. English, *Sinking of the "H.M.S. Otranto" in Collision with the "H.M.S. Kashmir" Off the Northeast Coast of Ireland, October 6, 1918* (Clinton, IA: Pinney Printing Co., n.d.), 3.

2. English, *Sinking of the "H.M.S. Otranto,"* 3.

3. English, *Sinking of the "H.M.S. Otranto,"* 3.

4. "British Commander Lauded," *Washington Post*, November 3, 1918, ED-6.

5. Letter from Adm. William S. Sims, commander U.S. Naval Forces in European waters, to the secretary of the [British] admiralty, October 22, 1918, RG 45 U.S. Navy Area File: Europe, October 6, 1916–. National Archives at College Park, Maryland.

6. "U.S. Army Individual Decorations, Chapter 3, Army Regulation 600-8-22 (Military Awards): [Sec.] 3-8, Distinguished Service Medal," February 25, 1995, 3-8. Distinguished Service Medal.

7. "Naval Intelligence: U.S.A. Medal for British Officer," n.d., RG 45 U.S. Navy Area File: Europe, October 6, 1916–. National Archives at College Park, Maryland.

8. "Distinguished Service Order (DSO)," Wikipedia, http://en.wikipedia.org/wiki/Distinguished_Service_Order.

9. "London Gazette," First World War, http://www.firstworldwar.com/atoz/londongazette.htm.

10. "Prenton Officer's Bravery: D.S.O. for Saving 600 Americans," n.d., RG 45 U.S. Navy Area File: Europe October 6, 1916–. National Archives at College Park, Maryland.

11. "Getting Bodies from Wreckage," *Atlanta Constitution*, October 16, 1918, 7.

12. "A. J. Cochran Escapes When *Otranto* Sinks," *Atlanta Constitution*, December 17, 1918, 4.

13. "A. J. Cochran Escapes," 4.

14. "Lost on the *Otranto*," *Atlanta Constitution*, November 28, 1918, 12.

15. "Two Young Georgian's, Survivors of *Otranto*, Arrive at McPherson," *Atlanta Constitution*, December 28, 1918, 7.

16. "489 Bodies to Be Returned: Scotch Islanders Beg to Keep U.S. Dead Lost in Collision," *Washington Post*, June 26, 1920, 6.

17. "489 Bodies to Be Returned," 6.

18. Letter from chief, Graves Registration Service, QMC, to Minnie McDonald, Box 516, Richton, Miss., n.d., RG 92 Records of the Office of the Quartermaster General. Cemeterial Division. "Correspondence, Reports, etc. . . . 1915–1939, McDonald, Ronald–McDonald, John," Box 3215 NM-81/ E-1942. NWCH HMFY 2000 File 293. McDonald, Tom. National Archives at College Park, Maryland.

19. Marcel Choyer, "Le double naufrage des marins de Croisine en 1918," http://72.14.207.104/search?q=cache:d4szzTi-DfAJ:cancagen.free.fr/Documents/croisine.htm+croisine+1.

20. Choyer, "Le double naufrage."

21. Constance Potter, "World War I Gold Star Mothers Pilgrimages, Part I," *Prologue* 31, no. 2 (summer 1999). http://www.archives.gov/publications/prologue/1999/summer/gold-star-mothers-1.html.

22. Potter, "World War I Gold Star Mothers Pilgrimages."

23. Letter to Mrs. Elizabeth Edenfield of March 11, 1932, RG 92 Records of the Office of the Quartermaster General, "Correspondence, Reports, Telegrams, Applications and Other Papers Relating to the Burials of Service Personnel ('Burial Case Files'), 1915–19," Edelson, Samuel M.–Edgar, Matthew. Box No. 1476. NM-81/E-1942/HN 1998. National Archives at College Park, Maryland.

24. Potter, "World War I Gold Star Mothers Pilgrimages."

25. Alison Davis Wood, "Gold Star Mothers: Pilgrimage of Remembrance," press info for WILL-TV's *Gold Star Mothers: Pilgrimage of Remembrance*.

26. "Then and Now," *American Legion Weekly* 7, no. 10 (March 6, 1925): n.p.

27. "Then and Now," *American Legion Weekly* 7, no. 10 (March 6, 1925): n.p.

28. "Then and Now," *American Legion Weekly* 7, no. 10 (March 6, 1925): n.p.

29. Clair Price, "The Navy's Share in Winning the War," *Atlanta Constitution*, January 26, 1919, 23.

30. Paul Frederickson, "The *Otranto*: The AEF's Great Sea Tragedy," *New York Times Magazine*, October 2, 1938, 19.

31. "$30,826 for Monument: Red Cross to Erect Obelisk to U.S. Dead at Island of Islay," *Washington Post*, February 4, 1919, 6.

32. "Islay Place Names in Kildalton" (photocopied page, source unknown). [1 p.], accession # IMT.01.001, *Otranto* Archive W1/4a-w1/4, Museum of Islay Life, Islay, Scotland.

33. "Then and Now," *American Legion Monthly* 8, no. 5 (May 1930): 31.

34. Todd Womack, *Georgia and the Great War* (Douglas, GA: Southern Heritage Publications, 2002), 52.

35. Womack, *Georgia and the Great War*, 52.

36. Womack, *Georgia and the Great War*, 96.

37. Womack, *Georgia and the Great War*, 53.

38. "Then and Now," *American Legion Monthly* 8, no. 5 (May 1930): 31.

39. "Ships of the Sea Maritime Museum" (brochure) (Savannah GA: Ships of the Sea Museum, n.d.).

40. "Military Honors for Macon Man Killed in War," *Atlanta Constitution*, August 16, 1920, 3.

41. "*Otranto* Victims Buried," *Atlanta Constitution*, September 1, 1920, 2.

42. "Children Plant Tree for *Otranto* Victim," *Atlanta Constitution*, November 13, 1920, 6.

43. "To Hold Services for Heroes of War," *Atlanta Constitution*, June 24, 1922, 6.

44. English, *Sinking of the "H.M.S. Otranto,"* A5.

45. "Then and Now: In Line with the Suggestion," *American Legion Monthly* 7, no. 4 (October 1929): 30.

46. "Then and Now," *American Legion Monthly* 7, no. 4 (October 1929): 30. Harold English died in Saginaw on July 3, 1973, at the age of seventy-four, and any materials that he may have collected as historian of the National Otranto-Kashmir Association have, apparently, disappeared over time.

CHAPTER 10

1. Peter Hart, foreword to Richard Abbott's *Police Casualties in Ireland, 1919–1922* (Dublin: Mercier Press, 2000), 10.

2. Richard Abbott, *Police Casualties in Ireland, 1919–1922* (Dublin: Mercier Press, 2000), 195–96.

3. Abbott, *Police Casualties*, 195–96.

4. Abbott, *Police Casualties*, 195–96.

5. Harold F. English, *Sinking of the "H.M.S. Otranto" in Collision with the "H.M.S. Kashmir" Off the Northeast Coast of Ireland, October 6, 1918* (Clinton, IA: Pinney Printing Co., n.d.), 24.

6. "*Otranto* Survivors Plan Organization," *Atlanta Constitution*, July 31, 1919, 9.

7. "*Otranto* Chapter Formed in Atlanta," *Atlanta Constitution*, May 27, 1920, 16.

8. "*Otranto* Survivors Will Meet Tonight to Organize Club," *Atlanta Constitution*, May 26, 1920, 8.

9. "*Otranto* Chapter Formed in Atlanta," 16.

10. Letter from A. H. Telford, secretary of the National Otranto-Kashmir Association, dated October 15, 1942, to members, TMs, 5 pp., from "Correspondence—Cornell University Archives—Guy Grantham Papers."

11. Letter from A. H. Telford.

12. Letter from A. H. Telford.

13. Letter from A. H. Telford.

14. Letter from A. H. Telford.

15. Dorothy G. Boyer, "*Otranto* Survivors Plan Reunion Fifty Years after World War I Tragedy," *Sylvania* [Georgia] *Telephone*, July 26, 1968, 1.

16. "*Otranto* Reunion Draws Survivor Group for 50th Anniversary Celebration," *Sylvania* [Georgia] *Telephone*, October 4, 1968, n.p.

17. "The *Otranto* Survivors," *Sylvania* [Georgia] *Telephone*, October 11, 1968, 2.

18. "*Otranto* Survivors' Reunion Scheduled for Sylvania on October 5 and 6," *Sylvania* [Georgia] *Telephone*, October 11, 1968, n.p.

19. Andrew Sparks, "He Survived Shipwreck That Cost 120 Georgians Their Lives," *Atlanta-Journal Constitution Magazine*, April 28, 1963, 48.

20. L. P. Wells, "The Men of the *Otranto*," in [Screven County History Project], *The History of Screven County, Georgia*, ed. Dixon Hollingsworth (Dallas: TX: Curtis Media Corp., 1989), 76.

21. De Weese Martin, "*Otranto* Survivors Reunited," in *Spirit of a People: Celebrating 200 Years of Bulloch County History: 1796–1996*, 229.

22. William H. Whitten, "Reunion to Recall *Otranto* Tragedy," *Savannah Morning News*, September 9, 1968, 6B, 10B.

23. Dorothy G. Boyer, "*Otranto* Survivors Relive Experiences during 50th Anniversary Reunion Here," *Sylvania* [Georgia] *Telephone*, October 11, 1968, n.p.

24. "*Otranto* Reunion Attracts Visitors from Out of State," *Sylvania* [Georgia] *Telephone*, September 27, 1968, n.p.

25. Boyer, "*Otranto* Survivors Relive," n.p.

26. Boyer, "*Otranto* Survivors Relive," n.p.
27. William H. Whitten, "*Otranto* Survivors Recall Disaster," *Savannah Morning News*, October 7, 1968, 4B, 8B.
28. Boyer, "*Otranto* Survivors Relive," n.p.
29. Boyer, "*Otranto* Survivors Relive," n.p.
30. Boyer, "*Otranto* Survivors Relive," n.p.
31. Boyer, "*Otranto* Survivors Relive," n.p.
32. Martin, "*Otranto* Survivors Reunited," 229.
33. Keith Jessop, *Goldfinder: The True Story of One Man's Discovery of the Ocean's Richest Secrets* (London: Simon & Schuster, 1998).
34. Jessop, *Goldfinder*, 70–71.
35. Jessop, *Goldfinder*, 72, 74.
36. Jessop, *Goldfinder*, 78.
37. Jessop, *Goldfinder*, 82.
38. Jessop, *Goldfinder*, 93.
39. Charles F. Morris, *Origins, Orient and Oriana* (Brighton, Sussex, England: Teredo Books, 1980), 158.
40. "Today's Fleet," in *Ships of the Orient Line*, ed. Colin Stewart (London: Adlard Coles, Ltd., n.d.), 49.
41. "British and Japanese Steamers in Collision," *Washington Post*, August 12, 1928, M1.
42. "853 Flee New Liner as Flames Destroy It," *Washington Post*, May 17, 1932, 1.
43. "Today's Fleet," 50.
44. "Today's Fleet," 50.
45. Duncan Haws, *Merchant Fleets in Profile* (Cambridge, UK: Patrick Stephens, 1978), 144.
46. Anonymous, ["Troop Storekeeper of the *Kashmir*"]; "The Sinking of the *Otranto* [1909]," [3 pp.], OSN/14/45 [Greenwich, London, England:] Caird Library at the National Maritime Museum, 4.
47. Anonymous, ["Troop Storekeeper of the *Kashmir*"].
48. Anonymous, ["Troop Storekeeper of the *Kashmir*"].
49. "*Kashmir*" [one-page article, source unknown], P&O/65/178. [Greenwich, London, England:] Caird Library at the National Maritime Museum.
50. "*Kashmir*" [one-page article, source unknown].
51. "*Kashmir–1915*," press release, Peninsular & Oriental Steam Navigation Co., P&O Information and Public Relations Department, [1 p.], P&O/65/178. [Greenwich, London, England:] Caird Library of the National Maritime Museum.
52. "*Kashmir–1915*," press release.
53. "*Kashmir–1915*," press release.
54. "*Kashmir–1915*," press release.

55. "Flags and Flowers Placed on Graves of *Otranto* Dead," *Atlanta Constitution*, February 9, 1919, A11.

56. "Flags and Flowers."

57. "Flags and Flowers."

58. "Flags and Flowers."

59. World War I Draft Registration Cards, Screven County, Georgia, "Donald Cooper," National Archives at Morrow, GA.

60. Brandon Haddock, "France Honors WWI Veteran," *Augusta Chronicle*, September 6, 2000, http://chronicle.augusta.com/stories/2000/09/06/met_294996.shtml.

61. Donald Cooper, "Cooper Transcript," transcript of Donald Cooper describing his childhood and service in the U.S. Army as told to Dr. Mark Newell and R. Neil Scott in the U.S. Veterans Hospital in Augusta Georgia, 2001.

62. Morris News Service, "Hometown Pays Tribute to Veteran," *Augusta Chronicle*, June 4, 1999, http://chronicle.augusta.com/stories/1999/06/04/met_262911.shtml.

63. Haddock, "France Honors WWI Veteran."

64. "Obituaries: Mr. Donald Cooper," *Augusta Chronicle*, June 21, 2001, http://chronicle.augusta.com/stories/2001/06/21/obi_314364.shtml.

INDEX

Italicized page numbers locate tables and photographs.

ABOUT THE AUTHOR

R. Neil Scott was a professor and user services librarian in the James E. Walker Library at Middle Tennessee State University until his death in 2012. He held degrees from the University of South Florida (BA in English), Florida State University (MLS in library and information science), and Stetson University (MBA in management).

Over his thirty-five year career, Scott worked as a technical writer (Unisys Corporation), public services librarian (William Carey College), head of reference services (Stetson University), management consultant (KPMG Peat Marwick), associate director for library operations and information services (Georgia College & State University), and director of libraries (Beacon University).

He was included in *Who's Who in America*. His previously published books include *Flannery O'Connor: An Annotated Reference Guide to Criticism* (2002), selected by the American Library Association's *Choice* magazine as a 2002 "Outstanding Academic Title"; coauthored with Val Nye (College of Santa Fe), *Postmarked Milledgeville: A Guide to Flannery O'Connor's Correspondence in Libraries and Archives* (2003); and with Irwin Streight, PhD (Royal Military College), *Flannery O'Connor: The Contemporary Reviews* (2009). He was awarded grants from the National Endowment for the Humanities and had more than twenty-five scholarly articles and numerous presentations to his credit.

Professor Scott lived with his wife, Sheila, just south of Nashville in beautiful Murfreesboro, Tennessee, and had three adult children, Stephanie, Sherry, and David, and four exceptionally handsome grandsons, Taylor, Eli, Dawson, and Cole.

9/12

DISCARD